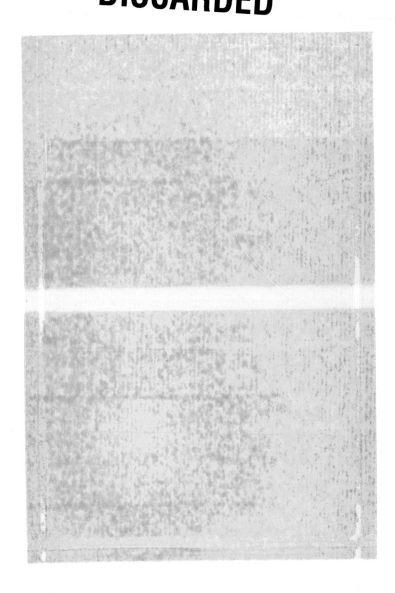

ENGLISH RECUSANT LITERATURE
1558–1640

Selected and Edited by
D. M. ROGERS

Volume 174

JOHN MARTIAL
A Treatyse of the Crosse
1564

MARTIN DE PADILLA
Y MANRIQUE
Consideringe the Obligation . . .
[1597?]

JOHN MARTIAL

A Treatyse of the Crosse

1564

1791780

The Scolar Press

1974

ISBN o 85967 147 x

Published and Printed in Great Britain by
The Scolar Press Limited, 20 Main Street,
Menston, Yorkshire, England

NOTE

The following works are reproduced (original size), with permission:

1) John Martial, *A treatyse of the crosse*, 1564, from a copy in Lincoln Cathedral Library, by permission of the Dean and Chapter.

References: Allison and Rogers 524; STC 17496.

2) Martin de Padilla y Manrique, *Consideringe the obligation* . . ., [1597?], from the unique copy in the Public Record Office, by permission of the Controller of Her Majesty's Stationery Office.

References: Allison and Rogers 593; STC 19842.

A TREATYSE

OF THE CROSSE GA-
THRED OVT OF THE

Scriptures, Councelles, and
auncient Fathers of the primitiue church, by Iohn Martiall
Bachiler of Lavve and
Studient in Di-
uinitie.

*Multi enim ambulant quos sæpe dicebam vobis (nunc au-
tem flens dico) inimicos crucis Christi quorum finis interitus.
&c. Philip. 3.*

For many vvalke of vvhome I haue often told youe,
(and novve tell yovve vveping) that they are enemies
of the crosse of Christ, vvhose end is damnation.

Imprinted at Antwerp by Iohn Latius,
at the signe of the Rape, with Pri-
uilege, Anno. 1 5 6 4.

REgiæ Maieſtatis Priuilegio per
miſſum eſt Ioanni Martiali in
Legibus Baccalaureo & ſacræ
Theologiæ candidato, vti per aliquem
Typographum admiſſorum impunè ei
liceat imprimi curare, & per omnes
ſuæ ditionis Regiones diſtrahere, Li-
bum inſcriptum, A treatiſe of the
croſſe &c. & omnibus alijs inhibitũ,
ne eundem abſque eiuſdem Ioannis
conſenſu imprimant, vel alibi impreſ-
ſum diſtrahant, ſub pœna in Priuile-
go contenta. Datum Bruxellæ. 6.
Octob.Anno.1564.

Subſig.

Facuwez.

TO THE MOST

GRATIOVS AND CLE-
MENT PRINCESSE, ELI-
zabeth by the grace of God Queene of
England, Fraunce and Ireland, youer louing and faithful fubiect Iohn Martial wifheth al heauenly grace, and
peace from god, with long raigne and much fœlicitie, to
his honour, and weale
of yowre Maie-
fties fubiectes.

T hath euer bene (moft
gratious Souerayne) the
wounte of moft men
that committ any mat-
ter to the vewe and fight
of the worlde, to recom
méd the fame to fome noble Perfonna-
ge, ether ftudious in the arte of which
they write, ether wel affectioned to the
matter vppon which they difcourfe:
whofe viual practiffe I thought it expe-
A 2   dient

dient for me to follo in dedicating this litle treatife of mine. And knowing youre Maiefty to be one of the nobleft perfonnages that liueth this day in Europe, in al princely prowes and giftes of nature æqual with the chief, and inferiour to none, and fo wel affectioned to the croffe (which is the matter that I haue taken in hand to treate) that youre Maieftie haue alwayes kept it reuerently in youre chappel, notwithftanding many meanes haue bene made to the contrary, by the priuy fuggeftiōs, and open fermons of fuch, as without order of lawe, or authoritie geuen by expreffe commaundemēt frō youre Maieftie (as it is thought) haue in al churches, chappells, oratories, high wayes, and other places of youre moft noble reaulme throwen downe the figne of the croffe, and image of oure fauiour Chrift, and in moft defpiteful māner abufed it, and in common affembles haue caulled it an Idol, and kepers of the fame idolatours, I haue aduentroufly præfumed to recommend and
dedica-

dedicate this litle treatife of the croſſe
to youre Maieſtie: where by ſufficient
authoritié out of the old auncient fathers it is declared , that euer ſithens
Chriſt ſuffred death vppon the croſſe,
and ſanctified that holy wood with the
water and bloud that fel from his precious body rent vppon the croſſe, Chri-
ſté men haue had the ſigne of the crof-
ſe, in churches, chappels, oratories , priuate houſes, high wayes, and other places mete for the ſame: and that the holy
fathers of the primitiue church woorſhipped and reuerenced the ſigne of the
croſſe , and counſelled others to do the
ſame : and that there can be no feare nor
miſtruſt of idolatrie in Chriſten men
hauing and woorſhipping the croſſe:
with many other ſpecial matters, which
I omit to repete here , vppon hope that
youre grace at ſome vacaunt time , and
oportune leiſure wil take a vewe of the
whole. Which if it may happely ſtand
with youre Maieſties pleaſure I hope
the varietie of the hiſtory and treuth of

A 3   the

the cause fhal both eafe that tedious pay
ne, aud alfo geue youre Maieftie eftlone
occafion to fe , whether their meaning
(who haue blafphemoufly railed ageinft
it , and bereathed youre faithful fubiectes of the fwete fight of it) be fyncere
and correfpondent to the fathers of the
primitiue church(as they pretend) . For
my parte , I haue fulfilled that dewtie
which Sifinnius (conferring for his M.
Socrat.lib.
9.cap.19.
Trip.
Agelius B . of the Nouatianes with Ne-
ctarius for the appeafing of the Arrianes herefy and counfeling that the emperour Theodofius fhuld be moued to
afke the Arrian bifhoppes whether they
wolde admit the old auncient fathers of
the churche who florifhed before that
diuifion or fchifme fproung vp amongeft thé, or refufe them as men that knewe not Chriftianite nor Chrift)faied ap
partaineth to euery Chrifté man in that
cafe:that is to fay:I haue fheued the bokes of the old fathers, by whofe teftimo-
nies the churche his opinion and doctrine of the croffe is auouched and con
firmed;

firmed, I haue repeted their sentences as
they be, in effect word for worde:I haue
coted the boke and chapiter : if the ene- *Pilip.3.*
mies of te crosse wil not admit the authoritie of such holy fathers , then may
we thinke of them as the good emperour Theodosius did of the enemies of
Christe his diuinitie , and trust that for
redresse of such greate outrage,youer
Maiesty wil in some parte do with
these,as he did with them:which
almightie god,(in whose hande the hartes of princes be)
graunte to his honour
and glory,Amen.Frō
Antwerpe . 12 .
Octobris.
1564.

Youer louing subiect and
trewe beedes man.

Iohn Martial.

A 4

S an ambitious prince in-
flamed with the infatia-
ble defire of Soueraynte
and rule, intending vppō
light difpleafure to inuade the countries next ad-
ioining to his, vfeth al fubtil deuifes, po
licie and counfel that mans wit can in-
uent to the better achiuing of his determinate purpofe, as corruption with mony, promeffe of honour, fauour, auhtori
tie, and high aduauncemēt, to the gouer-
ners of the cities, lieutenantes of the countries, capitaines of the caftells, if they
wil betray, and yeld to him, the cities,
countries, and caftells, which they rule,
kepe, and gouerne, at the apointemēt of
their So[u]erayne and lord, commination
of loffe of office, landes, goodes, and liff,
or perpetual ignominie in feruitude,
captiuitie and thrauldome, if they make
refiftaunce and abyde the doureful lot,
and

and dolful end of war, Or if this ſerueth
not, he aſſembleth his nobilitie, caulleth
his capitaines together, prepareth his ar-
mies, equippeth his ſhippes, and after ſuf
ficiēt prouiſion made by water and lād,
entreth in by ſome way or other, and
waſteth his countries, ſpoyleth his ſubiectes, battreth downe his caſtels, and
ſacketh his cities: Euen ſo, the cruel tyraunt and mighty Prince of the worlde
Satan, deſirous to enlarge his Kingdome, which is the Kingdome of darknes,
vppon the diſpleaſure which he conceued ageinſt almighty god for his faulle from the high throne of angels in heauen, hath euer ſithens ſought meanes
to inuade the kingdome of god: (I meane his militaunt churche here in earth)
and neuer ceaſſed to vſe his deceit, craft,
ſubtil deuiſes, and priuy practiſſes by cor-
ruptiō with mony, promeſſe of honour,
worldely wealth, and ſuch liek, to furder
his attempt : and letted not to ǵeue the
aduenture vppon Chriſt him ſelff king
of kinges and lord offal lordes, ſaying
when·

when he had brought him to an high
mountaine, and shewed him the king-
domes of the worlde and glory of the sa
me, *Hæc omnia tibi dabo si cadens adoraue-*
ris me. Al thes thinges I wil geue the, if
thowe wilt faull downe and worshhip
me. And afterward when his head was
brised with the womans seade, and his
pouer discomfited, and he hym selff
brought forthe in triūphe and open shewe by the victorie that oure sauiour
Christ had ouer him by his death vppō
the crosse,taking away as S.Paule saieth,
Quod aduersus nos erat chyrographum decre-
*ti:*the obligation and bond of the lawe
which was ageinst vs, which was cōtra-
ry vnto vs,fastening it vppon his crosse,
he continued his old malice, and practised the lieke by his dere frend Symon
the socerer, with Christes Apostel S.
Peter, and offred him mony for the giftes and graces of the holy ghost, to the
end he might induce him to breake his
masters commaundement, who had saied to him and the rest of the Apostells
Gratis

Mat. 4.
Luc. 4.

Coloß.2.

Actorū.8.

Gratis accepistis, gratis date: youe haue rece- *Math.10.*
ued frely with out peny or peny worth,
geue it as frely ageine , and so bring him
out of fauour with god , discredit hym
with the people, hinder the preaching of
the ghospel, and let the couersion of the
iewes to the faith of Christ . Sone after
he attempted S. Andrewe by his faith-
ful frend Aegeas proconsul in Achaia, *Abdias.li-*
presuading him with faire wordes to *bro.3.*
forsake the faith and doctrine which he
preached , and set his minde vppon the
worshipping of idoles.

In which attemptes of his , although
he could not preuayle, Christ oure sauiour vaunting him with thes wordes of
controlment, *Vade Satana,* Away Satan, *Math. 4.*
and S. Peter despising hym and his mo-
ny, saying. *Pecunia tua sit tecum in perditio-* *Acto.8.*
nem, Thy mony be with the into perdi-
tion , and S. Andrewe vtterly contem-
ning his fayre wordes, saying, I am he O
Proconsul that preacheth the worde of
treuth, and oure lord Iesus that men going from idols made with handes may
                                        beginne

beginne to knowe the trewe god, by
whome al thinges ar made, yet left he
not there, but in like manner assaied
other of Christes stoute and valiaunt
capitaines, as the forthy Martirs by the
Basil. de
40.Mart. general of the field, S.Basile by Valences
lieuetenaunt, Symeon archbishop of *Se-*
Lib.6.c. *leucia* by Sapores kinge of *Persia*, and di-
2.Trip. uerse by Iulian the apostata, who as Eu-
Lib.10. sebius writeth, *Non vi neque tormentis, sed*
cap.32. *præmijs catholicos est aggressus,* assaulted the
catholickes not with violence and tor-
mētes, but with rewardes: which mighty and greate tētatiō coming to naught,
1.Cor.10. (Christ assisting them and al his faithful
souldiers with singular grace, and suf-
fring none to be tempted aboue his
strenght, but with tentation much ad-
uantaging the parson that is tempted)
this ambitious prince and cruel aduersa-
rie off oures vsed another way to winne
vnto him Christes faithful subiectes,
and fel from corruption to cōmination,
from gentil wordes to terrible threates,
from promesse of honour to horrible
terrour:

terrour: and for high dignitie he threatned perpetual ignominie,for richeſſe,po
uertie,for wealth,penury,for abundaunce,beggery, for quietneſſe miſery , for
lightſome houſes,darke doungells , for
fayre māſions, ſtinking priſons,for ſof-
te beddes,hard bordes , for warme clo-
thes , cold yrons , for ſecuritie , vilanie,
for liff,death:Al which as he maliciouſly
threatned,ſo moſt cruelly he performed
by the aſſiſtaunce and help of the princes and tyrauntes of that time,with ſuch
immanitie as mans wit , with the diuels help culd deuiſe,and practiſſe:as eue
ry man may ſee that wil reade the eccle-
ſiaſtical hiſtoires : but when not with
ſtāding al this,the faith of Chriſt incre-
aſed,and the faithful beleuers multipli-
ed,and were made more conſtant by per
ſecutiō,thē he thought it beſt for him to
make open war : wherefore in greate fury and rage he ſummoned many diettes,
caulled his nobilitie to gether,ſent for
his frendes, and made diuerſe congregations, and aſſemblees for that purpoſe,
                                    as at

as at Ariminũ, at Conſtátinople, at Antioche, at Syrmium, at Philippolis, at Se-
leucia, at Nyce in Thracia, by Arrius and
his confederateurs, and fought harde
ageinſt Chriſtes diuinitie: but when the
victorie fel not on their ſide, for malice
to mankinde, and ſorowe for ſo greate a
foyle, he thought it moſt gaynful for
him to come in with a newe battaill, and
therefore in thes later dayes, he caulled
his faithful frédes to gether, at Wittemberg, at Smalcald, at Suymford, by frier
Luther and his abbetteurs, in Berna by
Swinglius, at Geneua by Caluin, at Chal
lon in Burgundy by a numbre of miniſters who concluded to banniſh thre
vermynes (as they caulled them) out of
that ſtate, the church of Rome, the nobilitie of the countrie, the ordre of iuſtice in the kinges courtes of parliament,
in Scotland by Knokes, in England by
Latymer and Crámer, and diuerſe renegate friers, Apoſtatat mounkes, and maried prieſtes, and with al the force thes
fleaſhly friers, and lewde libertines culd
make

make, aſſaied to inuade the catholicke
church, to ſpoile her of her armour, to
rob her of her threaſure, to take away
her ſwete victualls, to beate downe her
caſtels, monaſteries, and houſes of religion, take away her ornamentes, deface
her churches, throwe downe the image
of oure ſauiour Ieſus Chriſt, and ſigne
of his holy croſſe. And in many places
they haue done ſo in deede in moſt lamentable wiſe.

But as in al ages Chriſt for the defence of his deare ſpouſe the church, did
rayſe vp diuerſe faithful capitaines to re-
ſiſt the furious attemptes of ſuch faithleſſe furies : So hath he done in theſe
oure dayes, and geuen them harte, courage, wit, policie, learning, and ſtrenght
to withſtad al the force of his enemies.
And euery man according to the meaſu-
re of his talent hath pleyed his parte má-
fully, and ſtovvtely defended the catholike churche ageinſt her enemies. Amó-
geſt whome albeit I am not woorthy to
be adnumbred for a pore, baſe, and com-
                                    mon

mon fouldier, nether for harte, courage, wit, policie, learning, ne ftrenght, yet becaufe I am apointed by the grace of my fauiour Chrift, to follo his campe, and beare his armes and recognifaunce in my forhead, I thought it my devvtie to fight vnder his banner, and for the defenfe of his dere fpoufe the churche to labour to the vtter moft of my pouer.

Wherefore good readers , feing the church hath bene fo pitifully defaced by Satã and his minifters, and the croffe of Chrift caft out of churches, chappelles, and oratories, beaten downe by high wayes, and otherwife miferably abufed, I haue fet foorth: this litle treatife of the croffe, gathred out of the fcriptures, coũcelles, and auncient fathers of the churche, and diuided it in to ten articles, where-

1. of the firft declareth the fignifications of this woord. *Crux*, Croffe.

2. The fecond that the croffe off Chrift was præfigured in the lawe of nature: forefheuen by the figures of Moyfes his lawe: denounced by the prophetes: and
shewed

fhewed from heauen in the tyme of grace.

The third that euery church , chap-   3.
pel , and oratorie erected to the honour
and feruice of god , fhuld haue the figne
of the croffe.

The fourthe that the figne of the   4.
croffe , is vfed in al facramentes of the
church: and no facrament made and per
fited rightly and in his dewe order with
out it.

The fifte that the Apoftles and fa-   5.
thers of the primitiue churche bleffed
them felues with the figne of the croffe,
and counfelled al Chriften men to do
the fame : and that in thofe dayes the
croffe was fet vp in euery place mete and
conuenient for it.

The fixt that diuerfe holy men and   6.
women got litle pieces of the holy croffe , and inclofed them in gold , or filuer
and ether left them in churches to be
worfhipped, or hâged them aboute their
neckes,therby to be the better warded.

The feuéth that a croffe was borne at   7.
                    B   the

the singing , or saying of the litanie
which we commonly caul procefsion .

8.   The eight that many straunge and
wonderful miracles were done by the signe of the croffe.

9.   The ninhte what commoditie euery
Chriften man hath or may haue by the
signe of the croffe.

10.   The tenth that the adoration and
worfhipping of the croffe is allowed by
the olde auncient fathers.

Which articles when yowe haue read
ouer, and perufed wel, iudge whether the
figne of the croffe is to be taken awaye
from the fight of Chriften men : and
whether the fubtil policie of the deuil in
taking it away vnder pretence of idolatrie, tendeth not to bring vs to paga-
nifme, and vtter forgetting of Chrifte
his pafsion . And with al interprete I befeke youe this my doing in fuch fenfe as
I meane: that is to profit al, and harte none : Yf any thinke my wordes in many
places bitter, and taunting rype, let them
vnderftande, I founde them, or fuch lieke
in the

in the scriptures and holy fathers applied
to such persons : and that I vse them as
the surgeon doth his launce Kniff in fe-
stered sores , and the phisition his sharpe
byting medicines, in olde growen desea-
ses:hoping that the lieke effect wil follo
in the one as in the other , if the malady
be not by longe continuaunce incurable
and past recouery.

For the matter it selff consider what
is written, not who is the writer : Contemne not my youthe. It is often sene
that a younge man abandoning the sin-
gularities of his owne head , and with
mature deliberation consulting with his
elders , and geuing no other aduertise-
ment than he lerneth of them much ad-
uantageth al that follo his counsel. I acknowledg my yeres are younge : but my
counsel is old: my experience simple: but
my medicine is soueraine . They are lerned out of the most grauest fathers, and
best Phisitions of Christe his churche:
wherefore if taylers coming from the
shopp; smithes from the forge , tapsters
                    B   2   from

from the tauerne, oftlers from the ftable, botemen from the whirry, cokes frō
the kichin, weuers from the lome,
fchollers from the fchole, proteftantes
from Geneua, and lepping ftreit to the
pulpet, deferue credit, although they
fpeake nothing but the imaginations of
their owne heades, and leane to their
owne wifdome, (for they leane to their

Jn.3. Pro- owne wifdome faieth S. Hierome who
uerb. prefer the thinges which they muft fay
or do, before the decrees of the auncient
fathers) I truft although I come from
humanitie to lawe, and from lawe to diuinitie, yet I fhall deferue credit amongeft youe, feing I auouche nothing of
the imagination of my owne head, but
alleage fcripture, auncient doctour, or
councell, for al pointes of doctrine vt-
tred in this treatife, and fo cite the chapiter and cotethe place : that eche mā may
confer, and fee from what fountaiue
I fet this fwete water, that I offer yowe
to drinke: which although I caul water,
yet let it nothing lothe youe to taft of it.
The

The verdure of it is more fweter than
hony,and more pleafaunter than
al kinde of wine , euer more
flowing into euerlafting-
liffe , which god
graunte vs al.
Amen.

THE NAMES OF THE
AVTHOVRS ALLEAGED
in this treatife with a trewe note of the time when
they lyued.

A.

Abdias anno Domini	50
Athanafius	379
Ambrofius	380
Auguftinus	430
Albertus mag.	1260

B.

Bafilius.	380.
Beda.	720.

C.

Clemens papa.	80.

B 3   *Cy-*

H.

I.

L.

M.

N.

O.

P.

B 4   R.

OF THE SIG-
NIFICATIONS OF
this worde, *Crux*
Crosse.

Ecause this worde *Crux*, crosse, which I nowe intend to treate of, hath diuerse significations in the scripture, and in diuerse places is diuersely take, I though it good to follo the coūsell of the wise Philosopher Atristotel, and at the beginning of this treatise briefely declare the significations of it, that the readers hearing often times in this discourse this woorde Crosse, may better vnderstande to which it is to be referred,

ferred. This woord Croſſe then in the
ſcripture ſignifieth foure thinges . The
1. firſt according to the Greke woorde
κρὄειψ.i *ferire & affligere*,to ſtreke and to af
flicte (of which after the opinion of ſome it is deryued)is perſecution and affli
ction: or according to the nature of the
latine verbe *cruciare* , to troble, to vexe
and torment,tribulatiō, vexation and al
kynde of tormentes:of which ſignifica-
tion Chriſt ſpeaketh many times in the
Math.10. ghoſpell ſaying *Si quis vult venire poſt me*
Luke 9.
Mar.8. *abneget ſemetipſum,& tollat crucem ſuam,&*
ſequatur me,yf any man will follo me,let
him deny him ſelf,and take vp his croſ-
2. ſe,and follo me. The ſecōd is the paſsiō
of Chriſt,in which ſenſe S. Paule often
1.Cor.1. times vſeth it ſaying, *Verbum crucis pereū*
tibus quidem ſtultitia eſt , ijs autem qui ſalui
*fiunt (id eſt,nobis)Dei virtus eſt.*The woorde of the croſſe to them that periſhe is
foliſhneſſe,to them that be ſaued, (that
is to vs) it is the vertue of god: And in
his epiſtle to the Galathians he ſaieth:
Gal.6. *Abſit mihi gloriari niſi in cruce Domini no-*
ſtri

ſtri Ieſu Chriſti: God forbed that I ſhuld
brag or glorie but in the croſſe of oure
lorde Ieſus Chriſte. The thyrde is the   3.
materiall croſſe which the iewes made
Chriſt and Symõ of Cyrene carry to the
mounte of Caluarie: vppon which they
faſtened oure ſauiour Chriſt, ſtreached
his armes, nailed his handes, pearced his
feete: and opened his ſide: which kinde of gibbet they had in the old lawe
to putt men to death: but it was ſo vyle,
ſo haynous, and ſo abhominable, that it
was deteſted of man, and curſed of god
him ſelf: for curſed is euery one that
hangeth vppon the tree, ſayeth the lawe. Of which kinde of tormẽt S. Chri- *Deu.21.*
ſoſtome writing, and aſking what ſigne
of death that was, ſaieth. *Signũ erat mor-* *Demõſtra.*
tis maledictæ, mortis omnium defamatiſſimæ: *con.gẽtiles.*
hoc enim ſolum mortis genus maledictioni ob-
noxium fuit: It was a ſigne of a curſed and
moſt ſhameful death. For that only kinde of death was ſubiect to maledictiõ:
as for example what ſhal I ſay: he that
was faſtened to the gibbet, and hanged
vppon

vppon the gallo tree, did not only fuffer that, as as greuous punifhement , to
the which he was adiudged , but alfo as
a certain curfe : for curfed is euery one
that hangeth vppon the gallo tree : But
after that it pleafed god , when the ful-
neffe of tyme was come, to fuffer his fo
nne to be incarnate of the virgin Mary,
and redeme vs as S.Paule faieth , *De ma-*
G.ala.3. *ledicto legis factus pro nobis maledictum* , *etc.*
from the curfe of the lawe , being made
a curfe for vs: that the bleffing of Abraham might come vppon the gentills in
Chrift Iefu , that we might receue the
promeffe of the holy ghoft by fayth,
Crux, that accurfed and abhominable
figne of extreme punifhment and moft
fhameful death, (as ait foloeth in Chrifoftome) became more bright and honorable than any princes crowne . For
the head is not fo adorned with the
princely and royal crowne , as it is with
the croffe : which is more highly to be
eftemed than all rich apparell , and precious attire . And the very fame which
al men

al men abhorred before, the figure of
that they moſt earneſtly ſeeke. And certes it is founde euery where, amongeſt
princes, amongeſt ſubiectes, amongeſt
women, amongeſt men, amongeſt virgins, amongeſt matrons, amongeſt ſeruantes, amongeſt free men, al men ofté-
times ſigne and bleſſe them ſelues with
the ſame, making it in the nobleſt parte
of the body : for it is dayly figured and
drawen out in oure forheades, as in a
piller : It ſhineth and ſheweth ful bright
in the holy table, in cóſecration of prie- A croſſe
ſtes, in the body of Chriſt in the myſti- in the ho-
cal ſuppers: This croſſe we may ſe to be The croſ-
had in reuerence euery where in houſes, ſe had in
in markettes, in wilderneſſe, in high wa and ho-
yes, in mountaines, in hills, in vallies, in nour eue-
ſea, in ſhippes, in cotages, in beddes, in
cotes, in armour, in chambres, in tauer-
nes in ſiluer and golden plate, in pictures vppon waulles, in brute bodies euil
affected, in bodies poſſeſſed with deuils,
in warres, in peace, in day, in night, in
companies of delicate, in orders of reli-
giouſ:

gious:al men fo gredely take vnto them
this maruelous and goodly gift.

This is a maruelous grace,none bluf-
feth,none is afhamed,yea caulling to remembraunce,and thinking howe it was
fometymes a figne off moft accurfed
death: but al are more adorned with it,
than with ouches of pearle, or chaynes
of golde . And it is not only not fhun-
ned,but defired and loued : euery man is
defirous of it,and hoful for it:It fhineth
euery where , it is fet here and there in
waulles of houfes , in high turrettes , in
bokes,in cities, in villages , in places in-
habited,and others where no man dwel
leth : And a litle after , the fame father
Chrifoftome faieth , *Hoc mortis Symbolum multæ benedictionis argumentum factum
eft, & omnigenæ fecuritatis murus, tempeftiua
diaboli plaga, dæmonū franum , chamus contrarium virtutū, &c.* This figne of death
was made a token of much bleffing,
and a waull of al kinde of fecuritie, a
dewe and timely plage for the deuil , a
bridel for wicked iprites , a bitt for contrary

*(margin: The crof-
fe fet in
vvaulles.)*

trary pouers: This toke away death, this
broke the brafen gates of hel, this ouer-
threwe the diuels toure, cut of the ſtrin
ges of death, deliured al the worlde ſub-
iecte before to damnation, and put a-
way the plage ſent of god for the corrupt nature of man. So much force and
ſtrenght had this ſigne of curſed death
which euery mã did ſhunne, euery man
deſired to eſcape, and accõpted moſt vi-
lanous and ſhameful, after the death of
Chriſt crucified. And thus much Chriſoſtome : before whome certé hundred
yeres: Martialis one of the, 72 . diſciples
ſent out by Chriſt to preach wrote of
the croſſe in this ſorte: *Crux domini ar-* *Epiſt.ad Burdega.*
matura veſtra inuicta contra Satanam, galea
cuſtodiens caput, lorica protegens pectus, cly-
peus tela maligni repellens, gladius iniquita-
tem & angelicas inſidias peruerſæ poteſtatis ſi-
bi appropinquare nullo medo ſinens : The
croſſe of oure lorde is youre inuincible
armour ageinſt Satan : an helmet war-
ding the head, a cote of fence defending
the breaſt, a targat beating back the dartes of

tes of the deuil, a sworde not suffring
iniquitie and ghostely assaultes of per-
uerse pouer to approche nere vnto yowe. Damascenus in other age writeth

Lib. 4. c.
12. Ortho-
dox. fi.

thus: *Hæc nobis signum datum est super frō-*
tem, quemadmodum Israeli circumcisio : per
ipsam fideles ab infidelibus distamus & discer-
nimur. Ipsa est scutum, & arma & tropheum
aduersus diabolum : Ipsa signaculmm est vt
non tangat nos exterminator. etc. This crosse is geuen vs as a signe vppon oure forheades, lieke as circuncision was to the
Israelites: by this we Christen men differ and are discerned from infidels. This
is oure shielde, oure weapon, oure banner and victorie ageinst the deuil. This
is oure marke that the destroyer touch
vs not. This is the lifting vp of them
that faule, the suer stay off them that
stand, the staff of the weake, the rod of
the sheapard, the hande leading of con-
uerses, the perfection of them that profit, the health of body and soule, the put
ting away of al euil, the cause of al good
nesse, the destruction of sinne, the tre of
resure-

refurrection, the wood of liff. By thes
authorities euery man that is not afhamed of the croffe of Chrift , may not
only fee that the holy figne of the croffe was fet vp in al places,had in honour
and reuerence of al men , but alfo note
that it is a fnafle,bit, and brydle for the
deuil,a buckler,targat,and fhield ageinft
wicked fprites,a plage,murryn , and deftruction of fynne, a protection , faulf-
gard,and guide to man,an abandoning
of al euil, and occafion of al goodneffe.

Nowe if fuch as haue throuen downe the figne of the croffe euery where , and in defpite haue hewed it,
hackt it , and burnte it , and in reproche of good Ghriften men reuerently honoring the fame , haue caulled it
an idol, wil fay that al this is to be vn-
derftanded of Chriftes death : and that
the effectes reherfed before, are to be referred to the merites of Chriftes paffio
only, we knowe and acknowledg as
wel as they, that Chriftes death is oure
liff, and the merites of his paffion oure
                    C   iufti-

iuſtification, and that by his death heauen is opened, Satan conquered, the earth bleſſed, ſynne ſubdued, hel gates ſhut vp, al wicked ſprites put to flight, their pouer diſcõfited, their fyery dartes extinguiſhed, and al euil abãdoned, and vertue purchaſed: Marry as notwith ſtãding the merites of Chriſte his paſſion, all that will be the children off god, and coheirs with Chriſt, muſt haue their ſinnes waſhed away with water in the holy ſacrament of baptiſme : (for vnleſſe a mã be borne againe of water and the holy ghoſt he can not enter into the kingdome of god) and after lauful age, and yeres of diſcretion, muſt be made partakers of his precious body and bloud : (for vnleſſe ye eate the fleaſh of the ſonne of man and drinke his bloud, ye ſhall haue no liff in yowe) and beſides muſt kepe the cõmaundementes: (as it is written, *Si vis ad vitam ingredi ſerua mandata,* iff thowe wilt enter into liff, kepe the commaundementes) and iff by frayltie they ſynne, and faull from the fauour of god

Ioan.3.

Ioan.6.

Matth.19.

god, they muſt be recōciled by penaunce ,and haue the merites off Chriſtes
paſsion applied vnto them by thes ſacra
mentes,as external ſignes of a holy thin
ge , ſignes off inuiſible grace , ſignes off
greate efficacy and force,which contei-
ne grace them ſelues,and be the cauſe of
it, and worke the effect oft that which
they ſignifie:Euen ſo albeit Chriſt hath
ſubdued ſinne , conquered the worlde,
diſcōfited the deuil,ranſacked hel,brokē
the braſen gates , and ouerthrowen all
their pouer by his death vppō the croſſe,yet we who haue to fight,not ageinſt
fleaſh and bloud as S.Paule ſaieth,but a- *Ephe.6.*
geinſt princes and pouers,ageinſt the lor
des of the worlde,rulers of this darknes,
ageinſt the wicked ſprites in the ayre:
we I ſay,muſt vſe ageinſt ſuch tentatiōs,
and violent aſſaultes , beſides oure faith
in Chriſte his paſſion , the outward ſigne off the Croſſe alſo , ſo dreadful to all
wicked ſprites , that as holy Athanaſius
writeth, *Dæmones crucem videntes ſæpe tre-* ‌‌*De quæſt:*
munt ,fugiunt ,euaneſcunt & perſecutionem *quæſt.39.*

C 2   *patiun-*

The deuilles tremble at the sight of the crosse. *patiuntur* , that is: The deuils feing the croſſe, oftentimes tremble, fle away, vaniſhe out of fight, and are miſerably tormented: And in the liff off S. Anthony declaring howe the deuils hauing a deadly hatred to Chriſten men, and eſpecially to religious perſons, endeuour to ouercome their mindes with wicked thoughtes, and not preuailíg that waie, aſſaie to make them afraied, taking vnto them ſome tymes the ſhape off ſerpétes, ſome tymes of beaſtes, and ſome tymes of men and ſuch lieke: he ſaieth, *Omnia ad primum crucis ſignum euaneſcunt*: all vaniſheth away at the fyrſt ſigne off the croſſe. Wherefore in the ſame place declaring howe wicked ſprites coming in the night to religious men, fayne them ſelues angells of god, commend their ſtudy, and maruel at their continuaunce, he geueth them counſel to ma-

houſes bleſtvvith the ſigne of the croſſe. ke the ſigne of the croſſe, ſaying: *Quum videritis, tam vos quam domos veſtras crucis armate ſignaculo, & confeſtim ſoluentur in nihilum: &c.* When yowe ſe the wicked ſprites

fprites, arme both youre felues and youre houfes with the figne off the croffe,
and incontinēt all fhal be diffolued, and
brought to naught: for they feare the
banner in which oure fauiour Chrift
fpoyling the pouers of the aier, brought
them foorth in open fhewe:

Whereunto S. Chrifoftome agreeth
expoūding that faying of S. Paule, *precio*
redempti eftis, &c. yowe are redemed with
a greate price, do not become the fer-
uauntes of mē: *Confidera precium quod pro*
te folutum eft, & nullius hominis feruus eris:
Precium autem crucem hic appellauit, quam
non fimpliciter digito in corpore, fed magna
profecto fide in mente prius formare oportet.
Nam fi hoc modo eam faciei tuæ imprefferis
nullus fceleftorum dæmonum quum haftam
videat qua lætale vulnus accæpit congredi te-
cum audebit: Confider the price that was
paied for the, and thowe wilt be no mās
feruaunte: The price he caulled the croffe: which thowe muft not with thy finger only print in they forhead, but firft
of al with greate faith in thy minde. For

C 3 if

Ho. 55. in 56. Math.
1. Cor. 6.

The crof-
fe muft
firft be prī
ted in the
minde by
faith, and
aftervvar
de in the
forhead
by the
hand.

if thowe printe it in thy face after this
maner, none of al the wicked fprites whē
thy fee the fpeare with which they rece
ued a deadly wounde, wil dare to encoū-
ter with the: for if we be fhakē with great
horrour and feare when we do but only
fee the places where fuch as ar condemned to die be put to execution, what fuf
freth the deuil thinkeft thowe, if he fee
the hold that fword with which Chrift
diffolued al his pouer, and with a greate
ftroke cut of the dragōs head? Therefor
be not thowe afhamed of fo greate a thre
fure, left when Chrift fhal come in maiefty, he be afhamed of the. *Hæc crux non
terribles fed defpicabiles hominibus dæmones
effæcit*, This croffe hath made deuils not
only terrible, but contemptible to men:
And thus much Chrifoftome there: by
whome we may lerne that euery man
beleuing in Chrift, and printing firft
the merites of his paffion in his mynde,
and afterward the outwarde figne off
the croffe in his body, is fuerly garded
from al affaultes of the deuil, And that
by this

by this croſſe al wicked ſprites attēpting
man craftely,threatning terribly,aſſaul-
ting furiouſly,and fyghting fearcely,are
put to flight and ſet at naught .Here
might be brought out of this auncient
father diuerſe other places wel expreſ-
ſing the vertues and effectes of this holy
ſigne: but becauſe my intēt is not to tro
ble the readers with many allegatiōs out
of one authour,eſpecially ſeing there be
ſo many holy,vertuous, and lerned fathers of greate antiquitie with one conſent aud accord auouching the ſame , I
will refer al that are deſirous to ſee mo
re out of Chriſoſtome,to his homilie de
cruce & latrone,to his.55 . homilie in Ma-
theũ. and reporte what I finde in other.

Origenes in the expoſition of S.Pau ᴸⁱᵇ·⁶·
les Epiſtle to the Romaynes,ſaieth:*Tā-
ta eſt vis crucis vt ſi ante oculos ponatur,& in
mente fideliter retineatur , ita vt ipſam mortem Chriſti intentis oculis mentis aſpiciat,
nulla concupiſcentia,nulla libido,nulla ſupera
re poſſit inuidia , &c*. that is to ſay . The
pouer of the croſſe is ſo great , that if it
C 4 be ſet

be set before a mans eies, and kept faith-
fully in his minde, so that he looke with
stedfast eies of the minde vppon the
very death of Christ, no concupiscen-
ce, no sensualite, no enuy is hable to
ouercome him, but streitwayes at the
præsence of the crosse, all the force of
the fleash, and pouer of sinne is discō-
Cassiodor. fited and ouerthrowen. Cassiodorus in
his treatise vppon the fourthe psalme
saieth. *Sicut nūmus imperatoris portat ima-*
ginē, ita & fidelibus signa cælestis imperatoris
imprimuntur: hoc munimine diabolus multi-
formis expellitur, & fraudulenta machinatio
ne non præualet superare tentatum, quem ha-
buit primi hominis persuasione captiuū. Crux
est enim humilium inuicta tuitio, superborum
deiectio, victoria Christi, perditio diaboli, in-
fernorum destructio, cælestium confirmatio,
mors infidelium, iustorū vita: that is to saye,
Lieke as the coyne beareth the image of
the emperour, euen so are the signes off
the heauenly prince printed vppon the
faithfull. By this garde and defence the
wily and subtill deuil is expulsed and
driuen

driue away, and hath no pouer to ouercome by his deceytful circumuention
the man that he attempted, whome by
the perfuafion of the firft mã he had in
captiuitie and thrauldome: for the croffe is the inuincible defence of the humble, the ouer throwe off the proude, the
victorie off Chrift, the vndoing off the
deuil, the deftruction of hel, the confirmation of heauenly thinges, the death
of infidels, the liff of the iufte. But here An obie-
peraduéture oure aduerfaries taking oc- ction.
cafiõ of certaine woordes of thefe auncient fathers, wil faie. It is not the bare
figne of the croffe that woorketh thes
great benefittes to man, but faith in the
merites of Chrift his pafsion: for anfwer Anfvver.
we faye, that nothing can auayle, and
profit man, vnleffe he hath a ftedfaft
faith in Chrift, and faithful belieff in
the merites of his pafsion. for as S.Pau-
le faieth. *Accedentem ad Deum oportet cre* Heb.11.
dere: he that cometh to god muft beleue: and. *Sine fide impofsibile eft placere Deo.*
without faith it is not pofsible to pleafe
god.

god.But lieke as faith is the victory that
conquereth the worlde,the meane that
maketh oure foules meete habitations
for the holy ghoft,the way that leadeth
to heauen,Marry not euery fimple,bare,
and naked faith , but fuch as S.Paule faieth worketh by charitie: Euen fo faye
we that faith worketh to man the a fore faied effectes,expelleth deuils,putteth
out their fiery dartes,and defendeth mã
from al their fury and affaultes : Marry
not euery faith , but fuch as is ftedfaft,
conftant,and ftronge,ioyned with charitie, builded vppon hope , ftrenghtned
with prayer, augmented with fafting,
and afsifted by the figne off the holy
croffe:for there is one fort off deuils
which is neuer caft out , but in praying
and fafting: and as that deuil was then
caft out with praying and fafting: So as
Lactantius writeth nowe. *Sectatores Chri-*
fti fpiritus inquinatos de hominibus & nomi-
ne magiftri fui & figno pafsionis excludunt.
The folloers off Chrift do caft wicked
fprites out of men both with the name

Math.7.

Li.4.c.27
de vera fa-
pi.

of their mafter,and figne of the paffion.
And S. Auguftine faieth: we haue receued the remedy of faith ageinft the poy
fon of the old ferpét: *Vt fi quando voluerit* De Sym.ad
aduerfarius diabolus denuo infidiari, nouerit Cathecu
lib.2.cap.
redéptus cũ fimboli facraméto,et crucis vexillo 1.
ei debere occurri:that if oure aduerfarie the
deuil wil at any time ly in wayte againe,
the man that is redemed may knowe,
that he ought to mete with him with a
ftedfaft faith,and figne of the croffe.By
which auctorities we lerne that the figne of the croffe muft côcurrewith faith
and faith with the figne off the croffe:
And they iointly concurring,haue driué
out of mé,not one only fprite,but whole
legiõs of deuils,and made thé defpicable
to mã,and man inuincible to them,in al
affaultes,fkyrmifhes,and cõflictes: but a
naked,fole and only faith had neuer that
force nor at any time wrought by his ow
ne ónly might,that by a Chriftiã,which
the bare figne of the croffe did by an A-
poftata or rather an vnfaithful pagan.
   Iulian the renegate feeking aftrono-
                                                mers

mers, nygromauncers, and coniurers to
lerne whether he fhulde be emperour or
no, founde a fkilful man in that fcience
who promefed to declare vnto him, al
that he defired : And to do this the better he brought him in to a téple off idoles, and led him into a fecret place and
caulled vp the deuilles. *Quibus folemniter*

Theodo. li.
6.cap.1.
Trip.

apparentibus terrore compellitur Iulianus in
fronte fua crucis formare fignaculum : Tunc
dæmones trophæi dominici figuram refpiciētes
& fuæ recordati deuictionis repente difparue-
rūt. That is to fay: The deuilles apearing
folemnely Iulian for feare was compelled to make the figne off the croffe in
his forhead. Then the diuelles looking
backe, and feing the figure off oure lor-
lordes banner , and remembring their
faulle and ouerthrowe , fodaynly vanifhed out off fight . The fame ftorie
Gregory Nazianzene recordeth in thefe
woordes. At the appearing and fodayne

Priori ora-
tio . contra
Iulia.

fyght of the deuelies . A*d crucem con-*
fugit, & ob timorem fignatur,adiutoréque fa-
cit quem perfequebatur: præualuit fignaculum
fuperan-

superantur dæmones, soluuntur timores, respi rat malum , animatur rursus : iterum impe- tus, denuoque signaculū, compescuntur dæmo- nes: he ranne for refuge to the crosse, and for feare was signed with the crosse, and made him his helper whome he did per- sequute: the signe off the crosse præuay- led, the diuelles were ouercomed , feare dissolued, troble ceassed , he toke harte and courage againe , the deuilles made towardes him againe, he made the signe off the crosse agayne , the diuelles were quayled. Iudge by this experiment good readers whether the signe of the cros- se hath not the might, force, and pouer as is a fore saied. This Iuliā had no faith, for he forsooke his Christianitie , and became an Apostata, that is a renegate, a traytour, a forsaker of his faith and pro- fessiō: he had no loue to god, for he perse quuted his some Iesus Christ: he had no hope in Christ. for he practised with cō iurers, and consulted with diuelles , and yet by the only bare signe of the crosse made in his forhead in the greate agoni- es and

es and terrours which he had at the sight
of the deuils he escaped daunger and put
the wicked sprites to flight, A nother ex
Lib.3.dia-
logo.cap.
7. perimēt not much vnlieke this S. Grego
ry sheweth of a iewe, who had no trust,
cōfidēce, hope, nor faith in the passiō of
christ: but yet he prouided alwaies to ha
ue him self armed with the signe off the
crosse. This iewe being cōpelled of ne-
cessitie went into the temple of Apollo,
and toke vp his lodging there that night:
As he laye there, a greate cōpany of wicked sprites came in to the tēple . And he
that was chief and superintendent ouer
thē, cōmaunded the rest to search who
it was that præsumed tu lye in the tēple.
They going vnto him, and looking nar-
rowly rounde about hī, and espying that
he was signed with the crosse, with dis-
dayne aud indignatiō, saied: *Vah vah, vas*
vacuū sed signatū: Quibus hoc renuntiantibus
cuncta illa malignorū spituū turba disparuit:
tuishe, tuishe, here is a voyde and empty
vessel, but signed with the crosse: which
tidinges whē the wicked sprites brought·
back

back to the superintendēt, al the whole
cōpany of thē vanished owt of sight: for
they cā not abyde the signe of the crosse, nor cōtinewe in place where any mā
is that hath the signe off the crosse, nor
hurte thē that haue it, as witnesseth *La-*
ctantius, speaking of the power and force
of the crosse: his wordes be thes . *Quum*
dijs suis immolāt, si assistat aliquis signatā frō
te gerens, sacra nullo modo litāt nec respōsa po- Lib.4.cap.
test cōsultus reddere vates:neq; accedere ad eos 27.de vera
possunt in quibus cœlestē notam viderint,neq; sapient.
ijs nocere quos signum immortale munierit.
When they do sacrifice to their idolls, if
there stand any mā by, that hath his forhead signed wth the crosse, they offer vp
no sacrifice, nether their ridlereader is ha
ble to geue any ansver:nether cā theyco
me to thē in whome they see the heauē-
ly marke nether hurte thēwhome the im
mortal signe doth warde. But what is
this heauenly note and immortal signe?
forsothe the crosse of christ:so cauled of
his effect, becaufe by cōtinuall meditatiō
of heauenly thinges,and the lif to come
                                        it ma-

it maketh men heaueuly and immortall:
And this is the fourthe signification off
this woord crosse, of the which métion
is made in Esaie by god him selff saying.
Exaltabo ad populos signum meum. I will
set owt on high my signe to the people
which signe saieth S. Hierome there, is
vndoutydly *vexillū crucis*: the banner or
signe of the crosse: and Hieremy saieth
Leuate signū in Syō: lift vp a signe in Syon, that is saieth S. Hierome: *Leuate signū
crucis in summitate ecclesiæ*. Lift vpp a signe
af the crosse in the topp of the churche.
Of this signe of god Ezechiel also ipea-
keth in his ninthe chapiter, and S. Mathewe, and S. Iohn in his Apocalipse say
ing that the locustes which came owt
of the smoke of the pitt, had commaun
dement to hurte nothing, *Nisi tantum
homines, qui non habent signum Dei in frontibus suis*: But only those men who had
not the signe off god in their forheades.
By which places of scripture yowe vnderstand I trust (good readers) that there
be two kindes of signes of the crosse, the
one

49.

4.

9.
24.
7.

one made of some earthely matter to be
set vp in churches, and left in the sight of
the people, the other expressed or made
with mans hande in the ayre in forme
and lieknes of the other: and imprinted
in mens forheades, breastes, and other
partes off the body, and vsed as furder
occasion requireth. Off which two signes in this treatise I minde to discourse.
And by the way lest some enemye off
the crosse shuld misconter my meaning
in this behalf, I geue youe to vnderstande, that in al this treatise I attribute nothing to the signe of the crosse with out
speciall relation to the merites of Christes passion, but saye (as in parte I sayed
before) that as it is god that geueth victorie in bataill, health in sicknes, increa-
asse in matrymony, fruict in the fielde,
but by the helpe of me as external meanes, So it is Christe that worketh in the
vertue and merites of his passion, al the
effectes which shal be, or may be metio-
ned, but by the holy signe of his crosse,
as an external meane, which we must

D   vse

vſe in al oure neceſſities , as the phiſiciõ
doth his medicines in ſicknes , and leue the reſt to god.

THAT THE
CROSSE OF CHRI-
STE VVAS PRAEFIGV-
red in the lawe of nature, foreſhe-
wen by the figures of Moyſes
his lawe, denounced by
the prophetes , and
ſhewed frõ hea-
uen in the ti-
me of gra-
ce.

2.

I N the lawe off nature,
Moyſes, and the prophe
tes, the croſſe of Chriſt
is in ſo many figures
præfigured and foreſhe-
wen vnto vs , that yff I
ſhulde repete them here as they are ſet
foorthe at large by the aunciét fathers,
this

this worke wolde paffe the compaffe off
a litle treatife, and growe to a large volume: which thinge I minded not euen
from the beginning. Wherefor I wil note vnto yowe, as nigh as I can, thofe only which do moft liuely expreffe the ho
ly croffe, and figne of faluation : and refer al that are defirours to fee more, to
the authours them felues : and becaufe
the labour to feeke them fhal not be gre
ate, I will cote the boke and chapiter off
euery one that fhalbe alleaged. Firft after
god had created man and blowen into
his face the breath of lyff, he planted for
him a paradife of pleafure : and placed *Ge.2.*
him there: and brought foorth owt off
the earth al kinde of trees, pleafaunt to
to fee, and fweete to eate : *Lignum etiam*
vitæ in medio paradifi: and the tree of lyffe
alfo in the mydeft of paradife: This tree *Lib.4.cap.*
of lyffe fignifieth faieth Damafcene the *12.de or-*
croffe of Chrift : his wordes be thes *thod.fide.*
Hanc præciofam crucem præfigurauit vitæ
lignum, quod in paradifo plantatum eft a deo.
The tree of lyff, which was planted off

god

god in paradife, præfigured this precious
croffe. For feying death came in by the
tree, it was conuenient that lyffe and refurrection fhulde be geuen againe by a
tree. And Cafsiodorus declareth the fame, faying. Oure fauiour Chrift is well
compared to a fruictful tree, for the crof
fe which he toke for the faluation off
man: *Quæ merito lignum vitæ dicitur: quo-
niam ibi Dominus Chriftus qui eft vita no-
ftra fufpenfus eft*, which is worthely cau̅l
led the tree off lyffe, becaufe oure lord
Chrift who is oure lyff, was hanged-
there: To this *Cyrillus* biffhop of *Alexa̅-
dria* agreeth faying. The holy croffe
brought vs vp to heauen who were caft
downe to the bottomeleffe pitt off hell.
For this is the tree of lyf which the fcri
pture faieth was planted in the mydeft
of paradyfe: becaufe from that tree the
lyuely and healthfull medicine came
to vs.

Afterward when god fawe the maly
ce of men multiplie vppon earth, and
their cogitations and thoughts to be
bent

In pfalm.1.

Li.8.c.17.
in Euang.
Ioannis.

bent and inclined to naughtynesse , he
repented that euer he made man , and
being moued inwardly wyth sorowe of
harte, he saied, I will destroy man whome I haue created from the face off the
earth, and al liuing thinges creeping vppō earth, or fleing in the ayre. And therefore he commaunded Noe to make
an arke , as it is set foorth in Genesis: 6.
This arke of Noe prefigured the crosse
off Christ. For as by the arke , Noe and
his familie were preserued from temporal drowning, so by the crosse of Christ
al faithful men are preserued from spiritual drowning in sinne: as Cyrillus speaking of the figure of the crosse sayeth.
Hæc est arca Noe per quam saluamur à di- *Lib.8.cap.*
luuio inundantis aquæ vitiorum & incolumes *17.in E-*
seruamur . This is the arke of Noe , by *uāg. Ioan.*
which we are saued from the flud off
the water off sinne ouerflowing vs, and
are kept salff owt off daunger .

Abraham hearing that *Sodoma* was
inuaded and sacked, and his brother Lot
spoyled and caried away as a captiff, and

D   3   pri-

pryſoner, put thre hundred and eightene of his beſt men in armes , and went
foorth lieke a valiaunt capitayne in battaill araye , and pourſued his enemies.
The ſtanderd or enſigne that he vſed in
that ſkirmiſh (as it may be gathred out
of S.Ambroſe)préfigured the croſſe. For

*Lib.1.de ſi
de ad Gra-
tia, in pro-
lo.* ſaieth he: Abraham brought thre hundred and eightene mén of war to the
batailll, and had the victorie ouer his e-
nemies. *Signeque dominicæ crucis & nominis quinque regum victriciumque turmarum
ſubacto robore , & vltus eſt proximum , & filium meruit & triumphum.* And with the
ſigne of oure lordes croſſe and holy na-

*Abraham
had the
ſigne of
the croſſe
in his ban
ner.* me diſcomfiting the power of fiue enſig
nes that had gotten the victory , he bothe reuenged his neyghbour and deſerued a ſonne, and a greate triumphe . Yf
Abraham in thoſe dayes ouercame his
enemies wyth the ſigne off oure lordes
croſſe, then he had the ſigne of the crof-
ſe:and in a figure declared that with the
ſigne of the croſſe al oure enemies ſhulde be diſcomfited and ouer throwen. A-
gaine

gaine Abraham commaunded by god to
offer vp his sonne Isaac toke his axe and
cutt wood for the sacrifice, and leyed it *Ge.22.*
vppō his sonne Isaac: This wood signified and presigured the crosse of Christ:
and Isaac, oure sauiour hym selff, that *Cyril.lib.*
shuld beare that crosse. *8.cap.17.*
in Euang.
Ioannis.

Againe when Iosephes two sonnes
Manasses and Ephraim were brought
to Iacob to be blessed, Manasses the elder was set at his right hand, and Ephra- *Ge.48.*
im at his left. Thē Iacob leyed his right
hande vppon Ephraims head, and his
left vppon Manasses, and so chaunging
his hādes blessed thē both: This chaunging off Iacob handes, and putting the
one ouer the other presigured the crosse
saieth Damascene. And becaufe Iacob *Lib.4.ca.*
did not this of any ouersight, but of a *12.de or-*
set and determinate purpose, it may wel *tho.fid.*
be gathred, that he sawe in spirite the
forme off the crosse, by whych Christ
taking away al accurses and maledictiōs,
gaue vs his children, elected and caulled
to be the sonnes of god, æternall bene-
D 4 diction

diction, increase of grace, and abundance of mercy.

Moyses whē god appeared vnto him in the mounte and sent him to Pharao for the delyueraunce of his people Israel, had a rod in his hande, by which god declared his omnipotency, might, and power, and afflicted the Aegiptians. This rod saieth Origen with which Aegypt was subdued and Pharao conquered, is the crosse of Christ by which the worlde is ouercomed and the prince of the ayre conquered, and with all his principalitie brought forth in triumphe and open shewe. Agayne when the childrē of Israel were delyured owt off Aegipt, and passed on their way toward the land of promesse, Amalec waged battaill ageinst them, and with all his power endeuored to stay their iourny. where vppon Moyses commaunded his valiaunt and faithfull capitaine Iosue to muster his men, and prepare to the fielde. And he him selff with Aron and Hur went vpp to the hill, and held vp his

⸗ 7.Ex.

Exo.17.

his handes and prayed:and as long as he
held vp his handes, Iſrael ouercame:
and euē at that præſent ſaieth S. Auguſtine Moyſes with holding vp his handes did præfigure the croſſe : his
woordes be theſe. *Nobiſcum eſt Moyſes* *D'.5.hæ-*
ille magnus amicus Dei, qui vt hoſtem vince- *reſ. ad*
ret præliantem,manus ad cœlum extendit,iam *Quod vult*
*tūc figurā crucis Chriſti oſtendēs.*With vs is *Deū.ca.2.*
that Moyſes the great frend off god,
who to the end he might ouerthrowe
his enemies warring ageynſt him, held
vpp his handes to heauen, euen then
foreſhewing the figure ofChriſtes croſſe,And for more euident declaration of
this he ſaieth.Moyſes held vpp his han-
des a croſſe:his woordes be theſe. *Hoſtes* *Lib.10.*
*obuij filijs Iſraël,tranſitumque prohibentes,& * *cap.8.de*
præliantes,or ante Moyſe, manibuſque eius in *ciuita.Dei.*
crucis figuran extenſis , nullo Hebræorum
*cadente,proſtrati ſunt .*The enemies me-
ting the children of Iſrael,and denying
them free paſſage,and ſkirmiſhing with
them, whiles Moyſes prayed and held
vp his haudes a croſſe, were deſtroyed
                              without

without bloudſhead or death of any o-
ne Iſraelite. And as then Amalec lefting
the childrē of Iſrael to paſſe were ouercomed by Moyſes: So ſaieth S. Auguſtine. *Ille ſuperbiſſimus ſpiritus ad ima medi-*
ator, ad ſumma intercluſor, aperte ſæuiens , &
ad terram promiſſionis tranſitum negans, per
crucem domini quæ Moyſi manibus præfigu-
rata eſt ſuperatur. That moſt proude ſprite, mediatour to bring men to hel, and
ſhutter of the doore betwene vs and heauen, raging openly, and with greate re-
ſiſtaunce deniyng vs paſſage to the land
of promeſſe, is diſcomfited and ouerthro
wen by the croſſe of oure lorde which
was præfigured by the handes o ff Moyſes. But by Moyſes handes the ſigne off
the croſſe was præfigured *ergo* by the
ſigne of the croſſe deuils ar ouercomed.

Agayne when Moyſes had brought
the children of Iſrael through the read
ſea, they paſſed into the deſert and wilderneſſe caulled Hur, and wandred there thre dayes, and thre nightes without
water: and at the lenght came to Marah
but

but they culd not drinke of the water,
it was so bitter. Then Moyses hearing
howe they murmured, prayed to god *Exod.15.*
for water, and god shewed him a piece of wood, which when he had cast
into the water,it was very swete and plea
saunte to drinke. This wood saieth Cy *Lib.8.cap.*
rillus,is the crosse of Chrift: his woor- *17.in E-*
des be thes.*Ipsa itidem lignū eft quod fluuio* *uāg. Ioan.*
Marah immiffum amaritudinem aquæ in
*dulcedinē vertit.*In lieke manner the crofse is the wood which sometymes put
in to the flud Marah turned the bitter-
nesse of the water in to sweteneffe. The
same saieth S. Auguftime. *Per lignum* *Lib.2.cap.*
quod oftendit Dominus Moyfi quum populus *57. quæft.*
Ifraël veniffet in Marah, & dulces fecit a- *fuper Exo.*
quas,præfigurauit gloriam & gratiam crucis.
Oure lord by the wood which he shewed to Moyses and made the water
swete, when the people of Ifrael came
to Marah.præfigured the glory and gra- The crof-
ce of the crosse. fe denoun
ced by the
 Nowe that this figne was alfo de- prophe-
nounced vnto vs by the prophetes, it tes.
                                     wel

wel apeareth by diuerſe of them : but to
avoyde tædiouſneſſe I wil repete but
two or three: God being offended with
the abhomination of the iewes deſcri-
8. bed in Ezechiel appeared vnto him and
ſaied that he would haue no pittie nor
compaſsion vppon them when they cri
ed and caulled vnto him . Wheuppon
9. he ſpoke to Ezechiel and ſaied . The
viſitation off this citie draueth nygh,
and euery one hath a veſſel of deſtructi-
on in his hande : But becauſe god wold
not deſtroye the good with the bad , he
ſaied vnto hym *Tranſi per mediam ciuita-*
tem in medio Hieruſalem,& ſigna Tau ſuper
frontes virorum gementium,&c. Paſſe thorough the mideſt of the citie, in the mideſt of Hieruſalem and make the ſigne
Tau vppon their forheades who lamēt
and moorne for the abhominations
which are done in the mideſt of it. And
to other he ſaied, paſſe ye thorough the
citie and follo him deſtroye old and
yoūge, mayde and wife, litle and greate,
but vppō whome youe ſe the ſigne Tau:
kill

kill him not. This lettre Tau: faieth Ter *Lib. 3. ad-*tullian is a kinde of croſſe which god by *uerſus Mar-*his prophete did foreſhewe and ſayed *cio.*ſhuld be in oure for heades in the trewe and catholick Hieruſalem which is the churche. S . Hierome alſo expounding that place off Ezechiel ſaieth. In the old auncient letters of the Hebrewes which the Samaritanes vſe at this præſent, the laſt lettre T. hath the liekneſſe and forme of a croſſe which is ſigned with ofté impreſſion off the hande in Chriſten mens forheades. Hieremy crieth . *Leuate* 4. *ſignum in Syon:* Lift vpp a ſigne in Syon: that is ſaieth S. Hierome (as it is ſaied be fore) *Leuate ſignum crucis in ſummitate ecclesiæ:* Lift vp a ſigne of the croſſe in the topp of the church. Eſaie declaring howe the rote of Ieſſe ſhuld come and ſaue the loſte people of Iſrael ſaieth : *Leuabit* 11. *ſignũ in nationes &c.* He ſhal lift vp a ſigne into al nations, and aſſemble to gether frõ the foure coaſtes of the earth the pil grims of Iſrael , and the diſperſed of Iuda: that is as S. Hierome ſaieth : *Leuabit ſignum*

signum crucis in vniuersas nationes. He shall
lyft vpp the signe of the crosse into al
nations , and gather together owt off
the iewes synagoges the people of Israel, that the Apostells might fulfill that
commaundement off Christes Go-
ye to the loste sheape of Israel . Agayne
by his saied prophete he saieth: Behold
I will lift vp my hand to al nations, and
sett vp my signe on high to all people.
That signe saieth S. Hierome is vndoutydly the signe of the crosse, which god
also signified in the same prophete and
put as S. Hierome there declareth in oure forheades, that we may frely and frāc-
kely saie. *Signatum est super nos lumen vultus tui domine* . O lorde the light of thy
countynanuce is signed and sealed vppon vs . Thus brieffely yowe see good
readers howe the signe of the crosse was
præfigured in the lawe of nature , and
expressed vnto vs by the figures of the
lawe of Moyses, and denounced by the
prophetes: yff any man is desiours to see
more touching this matter he may reade

Math. 10.

49.

66.

Psalm. 4.

de Iuſtine Martir *dialogo cum Tripho.ad-uerſus Iudæos.*Tertullian.*Lib.aduerſus Iudæos & Marcio.* Cyprian *tract de Sina & Syon.*Cyrill Alexand.*Lib 8.c.17.in Euāg. Io.* Damaſcene. *Lib.4.c.12.de ortho. fide.* there ſhall he finde al moſt liuely ex-preſſed.

Nowe it foloeth that I declare, that this ſigne of the croſſe was ſhewed frō heauen in the time off grace. And here to paſſe ouer all hiſtories euen from the houre that oure ſauiour Chriſt ho-nored and ſanctified the croſſe with his precious body, vntill the time of Con-ſtantine the greate, I vnderſtand by Eu-ſebius, Sozomenus, and others, that he conducting and leading his armie a-geynſt Maxentius, being very penſiff and careful what ſucceſſe he ſhulde ha-ue in that battail, and lifting vp his eies to heauen, and by prayer ſeking help from thence, ſawe in the element to-wardes the eaſt, the ſigne of the croſſe, ſhyning as bright as fier: and angells ſtanding by him and ſaying. *O Conſtanti-*

ne in

Lib. 9. ca. 9.hiſto.ec-cleſiaſt. li.1.cap.4. Trip.

ne *in hoc vince* : O Conﬆantine in this
ouercome. And the next night oure ſauiour Chriﬆ ſhewing him the ſame ſigne which he ſawe before, commaunded him to make a ſigne in forme and
proportion lieke vnto that wich apeared vnto hym in the element, and vſe
that as a ſure defence ageynﬆ all the aſſaultes, and conﬂictes off his enemies:
he did ſo. And being nowe ſecure, and
certayne off the victorie, he made the
ſigne off the croſſe in his forhead, painted it in his ﬂagges and enſignes, and
ſhaped his greate banuer Labarum after
the forme off oure lordes croſſe, and
decked it with gold, pearle, and precious ﬆones, and beſides cauſed that ﬁg
ne to be carried rounde aboute his army, by certem off his moﬆe valiaunt
ſouldiers as a ſaulfgard and protection
ageynﬆ his enemies. And ſo he diſcom-
ﬁted Maxentius, and deliured the citie
off Rome from miſerable ſeruitude and
intolerable tyrannie.

Afterward when he came in ſolem-
ne tri-

ne triumphe to Rome he gaue all the honour aud prayſe to god, and in the pillar which bothe the Senate and citie gaue him, and erected in honour of that victorie, he cauſed the ſigne of oure lordes croſſe to be painted at his rigt hande with this inſcription: *Hoc ſalutari ſigno vero virtutis argumento ciuitatē noſtram a iugo Tyranni ereptā liberaui* : by this healthful ſigne a trewe token of vertue, I haue deliured oure citie from the yoke of the tyraunt and made it free. Againe the ſame ſigne was ſhewed vnto him when he triumphed ouer the Bizantiās, and at another time when he ſubdued the Scythians beyonde the riuer Iſter. And in all conflictes, ſkyrmiſhes and battailles afterward he had good ſucceſſe, as lõg as he ſerued god, and honored his croſſe. And as oure cronicles recorde, euen ſo had we in all conflictes ageinſt oure enemies the French and others, as long as we ſerued god trewly, and with horrible blaſphemie contemned not his croſſe: But ſithens trewe religion, and

E ſin-

fincere woorfhipping of god crept a litle and a litle out of mens hartes, and in
lieu of them, libertie, cōtempt of religiō,
herefie, and other abhomination came
in , and fouldiers without feare of god
vfed terrible fwearing , and in fteade off
the croffe commonly vfed to be fett in
their cotes, got feathers on their heades,
and fcarffes about their neckes, all went
backward: fea and lande , fyer and water
heauen and earth, god and man fought
ageinft vs. Which thing to be certayne,
and trewe, euery man that is not yet infatuated may fee, by oure two laft voya-
ges to Lyth and Newe haué. But to oure
purpofe: when Gallus created emperour
by Conftantine, was fent to Antioche,
to be as lieutenant in the eaft , the figne of oure fauiour apeared vnto hym in
the eaft faieth *Socrates* as he was coming
to Antioche: for a piller was fene in the
element , in lickneffe of a croffe to the
greate woundering off all that beheld
it.

Lib. 5. cap.
50. Trip.

    At Hierufalem in the feaft of Pente-
coft

coſt in the raigne of Conſtantius, apeared ſaieth *Cyrillus* archbiſſhop of Hieruſalem, in the element, *Mortis deuictæ tro-*
phæu, beata inqua crux, The banner or in-
ſigne of death conquered. I meane the
bleſſed croſſe: and it was ſaieth he, no
fantaſticall ſight, but a trewe viſion.
For all the whole citie did ſee it, and
woundred at it, and for feare went to
the church and prayed and it apeared
vppõ the bleſſed hil Golgatha, and ſhy-
ned to the holy hil Oliuet. A gaine vppon Iulian the Apoſtata who forſoke
his Chriſtianitie and ſacrificed vnto
idols, and vppon all his trayne accompa-
ning him, fell ſaieth Sozomenus a ſuer
of rayne, as he was going to Antioche
to roconcile him ſelff to the emperour
Conſtantius: and euery drop that fell e-
ther vppon his cote, or any other that
accompained him, made a ſigne off the
croſſe. At a nother tyme when the ſaied
Iulian counſelled the iewes to repayre
the temple of Hieruſalem deſtroied by
the Romanes, god to make them deſiſte

Epiſt. ad
Conſtãtiu
Imperat.

Lib. 5. cap.
50. Trip.

E 2   from

from that wicked purpofe of theirs, caufed the grounde where they had digged
a greate trench for the fundation to be
filled with earth ryfing out of a vallie.
And when this notwithftanding they
continued their woorke, god rayfed a
greate tempeft of winde, and fcattred al
the lyme and fande which they had gathred, and caufed a greate earth quake
and killed al that were not baptifed, and
fent a greate fyer out of the fundation
and bnrned many of the labourers. And
when al this nothing difcoraged them:
Theodorius In cœlo fignum fplendeus crucis falutaris ap-
lib. 6. cap. paruit, & Iudæorum veftes crucis fignaculo
43. Trip. funt impletæ. A bright glittering figne off
the healthful croffe appeared in the ele-
ment, and the iewes apparel was filled
with the figne of the croffe. And in diuerfe ages the lieke hath bene fene: but
this for oure purpofe may fuffife.

Nowe if any curious man wil afke to
what end al this tendeth, forfothe to no
other but to declare that god forefhe-
wing this figne by fo many figures in
the

the lawe of nature, Moyfes, and the prophetes, willeth all his highly to efteme
the thing which thofe figures fignified,
and prophetes denounced vnto vs, and
to beleue that as the figures wrought
temporall benefites to the Ifraelites, So
the trewth (that is the croffe it felf) fhall
woorke vnto vs his elect and chofen
children, beleuing in his fonne Iefus
Chrift, and hauing his figne printed in
oure forheades, the lieke benefittes, effectes, and vertues fpiritually: and much
more greater: It was fhewed to Conftā-
tine in gis greate anxietie and penfif pā-
ges and told him by the angells that in
that figne he fhulde ouercome his enemies, to inftructe vs that in al anxietie
of minde, and penfyfneffe of harte, the
croffe of Chrift fhalbe oure comforte,
and the figne a meane to ouerthroue
oure enemies: Chrift appearing to Conftantine and commaunding him to make a figne of the croffe to the liekeneffe
of that which he fawe in the element,
and furder willing him to vfe it as a pro-

tection ageinft his enemies in warre, geueth vs at this prefent daye to vnderftand (*quia Iefus Chriftus heri & hodie*
& ipfe in fecula becaufe Iefus Chrift is
yefterday, to daye, and he for euer) that
it is his pleafure to haue the figne of the
croffe made and fett vp in open places,
vfed in warres, and not conténed, burnt,
hackt, and hewed in peace. Is was fhewed from heauen at Hierufalem to declare that the faith and doctrine of the
Chriftians was both preached by men
and fhewed from heauen : and that it
confifteth not in the perfuafible woordes of humane wifdome, but in the fhe-
wing of the fpirite and pouer.

God caufed the droppes off rayne
that fell vppon Iulian the Apoftata and
his companie to make the figne off the
croffe in his and their garmentes, becaufe they fhuld vnderftand by that figne,
that the doctrine of the Chriftiās came
from god, and that it was neceffarie for
euery mā to be figned and marked with
the croffe . That it apeared in the element

mēt when Iulianus and the ieweswold
haue reedified the temple of Hierufalem,and filled their cotes with the ſigne
of the croſſe, god gaue them to vnderſtand that their labour was in vayne:
and made them go home to their owne
houſes confeſsing and acknowledging
that he was a trewe god whome their
progenitours,wipt, ſcourged, and hanged vppon the croſſe . And in them he
ierneth vs , that all thinges attempted
ageynſt god his will and pleaſure , ſhalbe fruſtrate:and the enemies of the croſ
ſe forced to confeſſe that ſigne which
before they deſpiſed : and tremble and
quake at the ſight of that which before
they maligned . For when Chriſte ſhall
come to the terrible iudgement , then
ſhall the ſigne of the ſonne of man ap-
peare in heauen , then ſhall all tribes off *Matth.24.*
the earth lament and moorne,then ſhall
they ſee the ſonne of god coming in
greate pouer,and maieſtie.The ſigne off *Auguſt.*
the ſonne of mā is the croſſe of Chriſt, *ſer.130.de*
which at that day with his brightneſſe *temp.*

E 4 ſhall

ſhall obſcure the ſunne, mone, and ſtar-
res, and ſhalbe borne before Chriſte vppō angells ſhulders, that they who haue
crucified oure lorde may knowe the
counſel of their iniquitie, and ſee into
hĩ whome with their nayles and ſpeare
they pearced. And this ſhal not only hap
pē vnto the iewes, but to all Chriſte his
De peniṫẽ. enemies. For as holy Ephrem ſaieth, In
cap.3. the end of the worlde at the ſeconde
coming of Chriſt, this ſigne of the croſ
ſe ſhal firſt of all appeare in the element
with great glorie and infinite legions
of angells, fearing and vexing Chriſtes
enemies, lyghtning and cōforting the
faithfull, and foreſhewing the coming
of the king and emperour off heauen.

Then thes croſſe crucifiers for ſhame
of their impietie towardes ſo mercifull
a lorde that redemed them with his death vppon the croſſe ſhall ſaye vn-
Luca.23. to the hilles, *Cadite ſuper nos*: Faulle downe vppon vs: and yet not be hard, becau
ſe they repented not in time of mercy
and grace: wherefore I exhorte them al
that

that by the malice of the deuil, and perfuafion of his minifters haue bene, or be
præfently enemies of the croffe of
Chrift, to returne with an humble and
contrite harte to their fauiour and mer
cifull lorde agayne, and by penaunce re-
enter into his fauour, whiles the eyes
of his mercy are open:Nowe is the time
of mercy:Nowe may he be founde of al
that wil feeke him : Nowe may we by
the afsiftance of his grace woorke with
feare and trembling, oure faluation:No- *Philip.2.*
we may we light oure lampes, and go
with him into the mariadg : Then (**I**
meane in the later daye) fhal be the time
of iuftice: Then wil he not be founde,
althought we feeke him with teares.
Then will he not heare vs although
we caull vnto him:Then wil it be nigh- *Ioan.9.*
te and no man fhall woorke. Then fhall
we haue no leyfure to light oure lam-
pes:but it fhal be faied vnto vs as it was
faied to the folifhe virgins, knocking at *Math. 25.*
the gate whé the brydegrome was gone
into the mariage. *Amen dico vobis nefcio*
vos

vos: verily I saie vnto youe:I knowe
youe not:therefore wache:becaufe youe
knowe nether the day , nether the hou-
re:Nowe to the third article.

THAT EVERY
CHVRCH CHAPPEL
AND ORATORIE E-
re&ed to the honour and
feruice of god fhuld
haue the figne of
the croffe.

3. Or declaratiō and proufe
of this article that eue-
ry churche, chappel, and
oratorie erc&ed to the
honour and feruice off

1. god fhuld haue the figne of the croffe, I
will declare it vnto youe , firft by a mi-
raculous dedication of a church by an
angell fent from god to that purpofe:
who made the figne of the croffe in fou-

2. re corners of the churche . Secondarely
by the example of S.Philip Chriftes A-
poftell

poſtell preaching to the gentils in *Scy-*
thia:and exhorting them to pluck downe their idol,and ſet vp a croſſe. Third-   3.
ly , by the authoritie of councells and
doctours, fouerthly by the lawes of Iuſtinian the emperour and cuſtomeof   4.
the churche : Touching the firſt , after
that the Apoſtles receuing the holy
ghoſt,had auctoritie to looſe and binde,
and comiſsion to go into al nations and
preache the glad tydinges of the ghoſpell, S.Bartholomewe went into *India,*
where was a greate temple and famous
idol caulled Aſtaroth, in Which the deuil by vayne illuſions,falſe miracles,and
prætenſed cures , had long time miſerably afflicted the people. The Apoſtell
entring into that temple , and tarrying
there for a time , did with his præſence
make the deuill ſo dūme and impotent
that he culd nether diſſolue the ridles
which were propounded vnto him,ne-
ther cure , ne helpe the lame Lazars,
whome he had tormented. And that he
made the wicked ſprite him ſelff acknowledg

knowledg and confeſſe: and before the king and al the people to detecte his impotency, howe he did hurte and was not hable to heale. And furder he compelled him to breake in pieces that and all other idolls in the tēple, ſo that there remayned not one. At which ſight the people cried: *Vnus Deus omnipotens quem præ dicat Bartholomeus:* That only god is om nipotent whome S. Bartholomewe præacheth . Wherevppon he taking occaſion to confirme that which god by grace beganne to woorke in them , and to delyuer that temple from that idoll, and people from idolatrie, lifted vp his handes to heauen , and deſyred god for his ſonne Ieſus Chriſte his ſake , that the multitude of lame Lazars and ſick perſons lying there hurte by the malice off the deuill might be cured and healed. And when he had ended his prayer, and the people ſaied Amen , *Apparuit angelus domini ſplendidus ſicut ſol , habens alas, & per quatuor angulos templi, circumuolans digito in quadratis ſaxis ſculpſit ſignum crucis, & dixit:*

& dixit: Hæc dicit dominus qui miſit me. Si-
cut omnes vos ab infirmitate veſtra munda-
mini, Ita mundaui templum hoc ab omni ſor-
de, & habitatore eius, &c. The angell off
god appeared bright as the ſonne hauing whinges, and fleing by the foure
corners of the temple, ingraued with his
finger in the ſquare ſtones the ſigne of
the croſſe, and ſaied: Thus ſaieth oure
lord god: Euen as al yowe are healed off
youre infirmities: So haue I purged this
téple frō al filthineſſe, and the deuil in-
habitour and dweller there. Furder god
commaunded me: that I ſhuld ſaye vnto
yowe, that looke what ſigne I haue ingraued in the ſtones, ſuch youe ſhuld
make in youre forheades, and al euill
ſhall flee from youe.

    Here good readers yowe may note
thre thinges, firſt howe god moued with
the prayer off his Apoſtel deliured the
people of India from the thrauldome of
the deuill and ſent his angell from heauen to fanctifie the temple polluted with
idols, which fanctification was done by
making

An angel ſent from heauen to dedicate a church and make the ſigne of the croſſe in the 4. corners.

making the figne of the croffe, which figne god cōmaunded to be ingraued in the fquare ftones at the foure corners of the téple: The fecond is, howe he wil led thē to make the figne of the croffe in their forheades. The third howe al e-uil fhall fle from thē that fo do: where-by yowe may lerne that euen from the beginning it hath not only bene godes wil, but alfo commaundement, that the figne of the croffe fhuld be fet vp in churches, and made in mens forheades, which heretikes irride and accompte: fuperftition and folly, as peraduenture they will this ftorie: but whatfoeuer it pleafeth them to faye, I truft euery good Chriften man ftaied by the grace of god in the vnitie of his churche, and grounded vppon that fure rock ageinft which hel gates fhall not preuayle, will more efteme the auctoritie of him that wrote it, then the leuitie of fuch as a-gayne faye it, efpecially feing it is, writ-ten by him that fawe oure Lorde in fleafh, and folloed Simon and Iūde in-

to

to *Perſia* and was at the death of S.An-
drewe, and made biſhop of Babylon by
the Apoſtells, Abdias I ſaie, who wrote *Lib.8.*
a litle diſcourſe of the Apoſtells liffes.

Concerning the example of the S.
Philip, the forſaied authour writeth in
this ſort : After Chriſtes aſcenſion S. *Lib.10.*
Philip preached the ghoſpel zelouſly
to the gentilles in Scythia:where when
he had bene kept in pryſon, and ſhulde
haue bene compelled to haue done ſacrifice before the idol of Mars , there
came out of the piller where the idoll
ſtode a great hydious dragon, and ſtra-
ke the prieſtes ſonne that myniſtred
fier at the ſacrifice, and the two tribunes
whoſe officers had the Apoſtel in pryſon: Beſides diuerſe were infected with
his venemous blaſtes , and began to be
ſick: which thinge the apoſtel eſpying,
ſaied vnto them . Heare my aduiſe and
counſel, and yowe ſhal haue yower health agayne: they which are dead , ſhall
be reuiued: the dragon which hath hur
te yo-

te youe,in the name of god fhalbe put
to flight:Then faied the fick men, Sire
what is beft for vs to do ? *Deijcite hunc*

Martem & confringite : Caft downe this
Idol Mars and breake him in pieces faied the Apoftel:*Et in loco in quo fixus fla-*
re videtur, crucem Domini mei Iefu Chrifli
affigite,& hanc adorate : And in the place
where he femeth to ftand faft,fet vp
the croffe of my lord Iefus Chrift, and
adore the fame : here marke good readers howe S. Philip Chriftes Apoftel
exhorteth the Scythians both to fet vp
the croffe , and alfo to adore it: which
if it were idolatrie or fuperftition as
as thes gaye ghofpellers,and newe pre-
tenfed reformers of Chriftianitie wold
make fimple foules beleue,S. Philip indued with the holy ghoft, highly efte-
ming the honour of god, and zeloufly
defyring the faluation of mans foule,
wold not haue counfelled the Scythians to haue done it , and in the mindes
of thofe late conuerfes for trewe honour and worfhipping of god , haue
planted

planted superstition and idolatrie. Nor
here cā they vse their sligt shift, and saye
that the Apostle cōmaunding the Scy-
thiās to set vp a crosse and adore it, mēt
only that they shuld set the passion off
Christ on high in their mindes, anu be-
thankeful to the lord for it:for the Apostle not only commaunded them to set
vp a crosse, but he apointed the place
where it shuld be set:that was in a stone
waull or piller,where faith in the passiō
off Christ culd not be fixed ne set, for
that the waull receueth no faith: vnlesse the melody off thes meale mouthed
mynstrels be so swete, that they can(as
the poetes fayned off *Orpheus*) moue
hard stones, or make brasen pillers vnderstand.

Touching the authoritie off coun- <sup>Coūcel-
les.</sup>
cels, we haue as ᵈ Iuo and ᵇ Gratian re- ^{a Lib.ʑ.}
cord in a Sinode kept at Orlians in Fraū <sup>b De confe
dist.1.</sup>
ce this canō. *Nemo ecclesiam ædificet ante-* ^{c Nemo,}
quā episcopus ciuitatis veniat & ibidem cru-
cem figat. Let no man build a church before the bishopp off that diocesse come,

F   and

and set vp a crosse: And in the second
Synode kept at Toures, we finde this

cano.2. canon. *Vt corpus domini in altari non in
armario, sed sub crucis titulo componatur.*
That the body off oure lorde consecrated vppon the aulter be not reposed and
set in the reuestry, but vnder the roode:
by which decre we perceue that then

a Roode there was a roode and crosse in the
in the
church church and the sacrament reserued, and
more thē
1000. ye- leyed vp reuerētly vnder the roode. Fur
res ago. der that the signe of the crosse was kept
and had in churches it may wel be
gathred by the sixt general councel

cap.73. kept at Constantynople in Trullo: and
by the whole discourse off the seuenth
generall councell kept a Nice. Where
thre hundred and fiftye bisshops men
off greate vertue, profunde knowledg,
and deape sight in diuinitie made this

Actio.7. decre. *Hijs se sic habentibus &c.* Thes thinges being so, we going the kinges high
way and standing to the doctrine off
oure holy and most gody fathers, and
obseruing the tradition off the catholick

lick church in which the holy ghoſt
duelleth, determe and define with al di-
ligence and care, that honorable and
holy images , made hanſomely in co-
lours , ſtones , boordes , or any other
matter be dedicated and ſet vp in holy
churches, *ad modum & formam venerandæ
trucis*, after the manner and foorme off
the holy and reuerend croſſe : and that
they be had in halloed veſſels , and ve-
ſtiments, and in waulles, tables, priuate
houſes , and high wayes , and eſpecially
the image off oure lord and god Ieſus
Chriſt oure ſauiour , and the image off
the immaculate virgin Mary mother of
god, and the images, of holy mē, that by
this beholding of painꞓed images , al
that looke vppon them , may come to
the remembraunce , and deſire of the
firſt ſamplers and patternes which they
reſemble : and with all exhibite vnto
them ſome courteſy , and reuerent honour : for honour and reuerence done to
an image redoundeth to the glory off
the firſt ſampler and patterne, and he

A decree that the croſſe and images ſhuld be in the churches.

Honour done to images is done to that vvhich they repreſent.

F 2   that

that adoreth and honoreth an ymage doth adore and honour that which is refembled by the image.

Here good readers yow fee by the determination of foure counceles, two prouincial and two general, that the figne of the croffe fhulde be had in churches. And by this decre of the councel off Nice yowe vnderftand that the image of Chrift and his mother and all other fainctes fhulde alſo be in churches and honored. And the fathers off the fame councel do excommunicate and accurfe all fuch as caftaway the figne of the croffe, or image off any fainct, or bring the fentences of fcripture fpeaking of idols, ageynft images, or caull images idols, or fay that Chriften men woorfhipp images as god. And what foeuer they binde in earth is bounde in heauen: which thing confidered, I truſt youe wil deteft their impietie who haue in moft lamentable wife defaced all images, throwen downe the croffe off Chrift, and in defpite of good Chriften men

They, that caft avvay the croffe and image off any fainCte is excōmunicated.

men reuerently worfhipping them, ha- Doctours
ue caulled them idols . As for doctours
we haue Ambrofe, Lactance . Auftyne,
and Pauline, S. Ambrofe faieth a church *Ser de cru-*
ce. 5 5. &
can not ftand with out a croffe, and 5 6.
that a croffe in the church is as it were
a maft in the fhip : iff a church lack a
croffe by and by the deuil doth difquiet
it, and the winde doth fquatte it, and beate it, *At vbi fignũ crucis erigitur, ftatim &*
diaboli iniquitas repellitur, & ventorum pro-
cella fopitur : but when the figne off the
croffe is fet vp, by and by both the malyce off the deuil is repelled , and the tempeft off winde appeafed. And thus much
S. Ambrofe there in effect : vppõ whofe
woordes we may build this argument.
That muft nedes be in the churche with
out which the church cã not ftand, but
as S. Ambrofe faieth a church can not
ftand without a croffe: Therefore a crof
fe muft nedes be in the church . Nether
here can oure aduerfaries cauil and fay
that the croffe off which S. Ambrofe
fpeaketh there, is the pafsion off Chrift
F 3   only:

only:for he saieth, *vbi signum crucis erigi-*
tur &c. when the signe off the crosse is
set vp the malice off the deuil is beaten
back:by which woordes he geueth vs to
vnderstand that ouer and aboue the passion off Christ, he talketh there off a
material church: and that in that material church the signe off the crosse is set
vp as a meane to resist and ouercome
the assaultes of the deuil,by the merites
of his passion that suffred death vppon
the crosse. Lactantius in his verses vppon the passion, maketh oure sauiour
Christ speake (as it were by a figure
caulled *prosopopeia*) after this sorte to al
that come into the church.

Quisquis ades medijque subis in limina tem-
pli.
Siste parum insontemque tuo pro crimine pas-
sum
Respice me:me conde animo,me pectore serua.
Cerne manus clauis fixas, tractosque lacertos.
Atque ingens lateri vulnus, cerne inde fluorē
Sanguineum, fossosque pedes,artusque cruen-
tos.

Whosoe-

Lactantius

Whofoeuer thowe art that comeft hither, and entrieft into the mideft of the church, ftand ftil a while and behold me that haue fuffred al this for thy fake being gyltleffe and innocent: ley me vp in thy minde: and keape me in thy harte: behold my handes faftened with nayles, and my armes ftreached out, and a great wounde in my fyde, and a bluddy ftreame flowing from thence, and my feete pearced, and al my body bloudded. Se good readers in *Lactantius* time there was a roode in the church, and the yma ge of Chrift fet vppon a croffe, with his armes ftreached, handes nayled, feetefaftened, fyde wounded, and all his body bloudded. For yf there had bene no ymage off Chrift in the church to whome *Lactantius* might attribute that talke by the faied figure, then muft oure enemies faye, that he made Chrift fpeake that from heauen: and that from then ce, he fhewed euery man that cometh into the church his torne body, and bluddy woundes; and that the authour

a Roode in the church.

F 4   mea-

meaneth not. For besides, that *Laƈtan-
tius* knewe to haue such a vision from
heauē it happened but to fewe, and that
off singular grace obtayned with long
fasting and continual prayer, (which all
that resort to the church vse not) he
commaunded the man that hath dili-
gently considered Christe hanging vppon the crosse: and earnestly beheld his
woundes, to faull downe vppon his
knees and worship the signe of the crosse: for he saieth there.

Flete genu: lignūqúe crucis venerabile adora,
bowe downe thy knee; and adore the
honorable wood of the crosse: by which
woordes he geueth vs to vnderstand,
that there was in the church a signe off
the crosse to which he shuld bowe his
knee: and a wood which he shuld adore

August. S. Augustine amongest other thinges
done with the signe of the crosse: sa-
Ser. 19. de ieth. *Crucis mysterio basilicæ dedicantur,*
sanctis. Churches are dedicated with the signe
of the crosse: which woordes may be
referred ether to the benediction which
the

the bifhop vfeth in the folemne prayers
made at the firft fundation, or to the
material croffe which euery biffhopp
muft fet vp at the dedication of euery
church. Furder he faieth in the place al-
le aged before, that Chrift *Cruce nobis in
memoriam fuæ pefsionis reliquit*. Left vs a
croffe in remembraunce of his pafsion,
Yf Chrift left vs a croffe in remembraunce of his pafsion, then we haue or
fhuld haue a croffe in remembraunce of
his pafsion. And I praye yowe where cā
we haue a croffe more conueniently to
remenbre his pafsion, thē in the church
wheter al men refort to pray, where the
facrifice of his body and bloud is and
fhalbe offred in remembraunce off his
death vntill his coming agayne ? *Pauli-* Paulinus.
uns writyng to *Scuerus* talketh much of
building churches, and fetting vp pictu- Epift.12.
res in the fame, and verfes ouer the
pictures, and faieth that did fet thefe ver
fes ouer the figne of the croffe.

Cerne coronatam Domini fuper atria Chri-
  fti

                              Stare

Stare crucem, duro ſpondentem celſa labori:
Præmia: tolle crucem, ſi vis auferre coro-
nam.

Behold here ſtandeth a croſſe of oure
ſauiour Chriſt with a crowne ouer the
church Porch, promiſing high rewar-
for oure great paines: take vp the croſſe
if thowe wilt beare away the crowne.
Agayne in the ſame epiſtle and diuerſe
other places he maketh ſuch mention
of the croſſe that no man who readeth
his woorkes, can ſaye but that in thoſe
dayes the ſigne of the croſſe was ſet vp
and had in the churche.

Iuſtinianus   Nowe by order it foloeth that I declare and proue this by the lawes of Iuſtinian the emperour. For diſchardge of
my promeſſe in this behalf I remitt the
readers to his newe and later conſtitu-
rit.de mo- tions:Where he ſaieth . *Illud ante omnia*
nach.§. *dicendum, vt omni tempore, & in omni loco,*
illud.
Col.1. *ſi quis ædificare venerabile monaſterium volu*
erit,non prius licentiam eſſe hoc agendi quam
Deo amabilem locorum epiſcopum aduocet, &
ille manus ad cœlum extendat,& per oratione
locum

*locum consecret Deo, figens in eo salutis nostræ
signum(dicimus autem adorandam & hono-
randam vere crucem)* This therefore before al other thinges we must saye, that at
all tymes, and in all countries, if any mã
wil build a monastery to the seruice and
honour off god, he hath no licence nor
leaue to do it, before he caull vnto hym
the welbeloued of god, bishopp off the
place: and he lyft vp his handes to heauen, and with prayer halloe the place to
the honour of god, setting vp there the
signe of saluation (we meane the crosse
trewly to be adored and worshipped) and
so let him beginne his building, leying
this decent and goodly fundation. In a
nother place he maketh this lawe . *Si*

Autent. de
ecclesiast.
tit. Col. 9.

*quis fabricare voluerit venerabile oratorium
aut monasterium, præcipimus nõ aliter incho-
andam fabricam nisi locorum sanctissimus e-
piscopus orationem ibi fecerit, & venerabilem
fixerit crucem.* Yf any man wil build a
chappel or monastery to the honour
and seruice of god we commaunde that
the frame be not begonne, except the
holy

holy bisshop of the diocese hath prayed there, and set vp a holy and reuerend crosse. In these two lawes of Iustinian the emperour, yowe see good readers a commaundement geuen in expresse woordes and playne termes, that no churche nor chappel shuld be builded without the signe of the crosse. Ageinst which the aduersaries of treuth and enemies of Christes crosse, haue nothing to reply, vnlesse they will absolutely say that nether crosse nether churche is necessary amongest Christen men, or flatly deny the authoritie of the emperour: and that were greate arrogancy and pryde: and not lauful for them nether. For reason willteh and the lawe saieth, that: *Qui admittit testem pro se non potest eundem repellere contra se*: He that admitteth a man to be witnesse for him, can not repel the same man, if he be witnesse ageinst him. Wherefore seing they haue vsed the authoritie of Iustinian, for prouf of their seruice in a barbarous tounge, where in deede it maketh nothing

L. Si quis C. de testi.

thing for them , being rightly scanned
and wel vnderstanded , of right they
can not denye his authoritie in this,
where in expresse woordes he maketh
ageynst them.

Touching the vse and custome off
the churche for hauing the signe of the
crosse,I nede not much troble the readers with many prouffes:euery man can
be witnesse and iudge in this,vnlesse by
fauour to his sect , and loue to heresie,
he be infensate, or vnsensible . Then as
the Philosopher willed all that douted
whether fier be hotte or no,to put their
fingers in to it and trie : So in lieke māner iff any man make any matter of am
biguitie off this , we may desire him to
take his eies in his handes,and looke in
all churches , chappells , and oratories
through out al countries where Christes religion is , and was in dewe reuerence before thes shifmes , whether
ther were or be any crosses or no . Certes he shalbe hable to finde none, no if
he had as many eies as *Argus*, vnlesse it
be a

be a temple of idols a Synagog of infidels, a congregation of miscreauntes, or assemble of heretikes. But yet to say somewhat I hope it shal not be altogether superfluous. Wherefore I will put yowe in remembraunce of the dedication of certen churches by *Helena* and Constantine the greate. The good vertous lady *Helena* when she had founde the crosse of Christ, made as *Socrates* reporteth, thre churches: One in the mounte of Caluarie where she founde the crosse: another in Bethlem where Christe was borne: The third in the mounte Olyuet from whence Christe ascended. In licke manner *Constantinus* builded a litle chappel in his palace, and caried a pauilion about with him made after the manner and proportion off a church, that nor he, nor his armie, might be destitute of a church, in which they might prayse god, make their prayers, and receue the sacrament. And shal we thinke that *Helena* commaunded by reuelation to seeke the crosse, and so highly este-

lib.1.c.17. Tripar.

Sozome.li. 1.c.8.hist. ecclesiast.

ly esteming it when she had founde it,
wold not set it vp in the churches which
she builded? Or that Constantine who
had the same signe shewed him frō heauen, who made it to be put in his banner, in his souldiers cotes, and had alwayes in his hand a crosse of gold, wold
not haue the signe of the same in his
chappel? No man of wisdome can thinke it trewe or liekely to be trewe. The
same god emperour Constantine made
diuerse other churches, and amongest
them one in the honour of S. Paule at
the suggestion of Siluester, and set a cros *in decretis*
se off gold vppon S. Paules cophyne *Siluestri.*
weying an hundred and fyfty pounde
weight: where by we may see that it was
his pleasure and delight to haue the cros
se in the churche.

But what nede so many woordes? to
end so euident a matter, I wil repete a
sentence out of a litle treatise made by
Ionas bisshop of Orlyans, and dedicated
to Charles the greate, where he saieth. *Ionas epis̄.*
Multa sunt quæ mos sanctæ ecclesiæ sicut à ma *Auñe.*
ioribus

ioribus tradita & derelicta sunt, quadam insi-
ta & natiua celebratione frequentat: Neque
enim noslro tempore vsus irrepsit figuram cru-
cis in basilicis statui, sed mos antiquæ obserua-
tionis legitimus id instituit. There be many
thinges which custome of holy church
doth off a certayne naturall ingraffed
custome obserue and vse, euen as they
were deliured and left vnto the of their forefathers. For the vse of setting vp
the signe of the crosse crope not in in
oure tyme: but the lauful custome off
old auncient obseruation did ordayne
and institute it: that the remembraunce
of it might not only print and fasten in
wise men and simple soules by the signe of the crosse a certeyne spirituall figu
re of it, but also the bodely and sensible
looking vppon it, might stedfastely fixe
the victorie of Christes paision in their
myndes: by which woordes yowe see
good readers that it hath bene an old
custome to haue the signe off the crosse
set vp in churches, and that this custome crept not in to the churche in Charles the

les the greate his dayes, who liued eight
hundred yeares ago, but long before his
time it was an old auncient obferua-
tion and cuftome . Wherefore I
conclude and faye, that euery
churche, chappel, and o-
ratorie erected to the
honour and ferui-
ce of god, fhuld
haue the fig-
ne of the
croffe.

G   The

A TREATYSE

THE SIGNE

OF THE CROSSE V-
SED IN AL SACRA-
MENTES, AND NO SA-
crament made and perfi-
ted rightly and in his
dewe order with
oute it.

4.

*Lib. 2. cap.
9. Trip.*

S Sozomenus a Greke
authour and one of the
compilers of the tripar-
tite historie writeth, *Probianus* a Pagan newly con
uerted to Christe, in so-
me parte behaued him self lieke a christen man: but the cause of oure saluation, that is the most holy crosse he
wold not worship and adore: whereup-
pon whiles he was in this determination and minde, *Diuina virtus apparens
signum monstrauit crucis quod erat positum
in altario eius ecclesiæ, & aperte palam fecit,
quia,*

*quia ex quo crucifixus est Christus, omnia quæ
ad vtilitatē humani generis facta essent, quo-
libet modo præter virtutem crucis gesta nō essent, neque ab angelis sanctis neque a pijs hominibus :* That is to say : The diuine pouer
apearing, shewed him the signe of the
crosse which was set vppon the aulter
of that church:and made it plainly ape-
are that euer sithens Christ was crucified, al thinges which were done for
the commoditie and weale of man, were done by no manner of meanes without the vertue of the holy crosse,nether
of holy angells 'nether of good men . S.
Cyprian saieth,what soeuer the handes
be which dip those that come to baptifme , whatsoeuer the breast is out of
which the holy wordes do procede , *O-
perationis authoritas in figura crucis omnibus
sacramentis largitur effectum.*The authori-
tie.of operation geueth effecte to al sacramentes in the figure of the crosse.

S. Augustine confirmeth the same,
saying,*Crucis mysterio rudes cathechisantur,
fons regenerationis consecratur,per manus im-*

A crosse
vppō the
aultar.

*Ser.de paf.
Dominl.*

*Ser. 19. de
sanctis.*

G 2   *posi-*

positionem baptizati gratiaru̅ dona recipiunt,
basilicæ dedicantur,altaria consecrantur , al-
taris sacramenta cum interpositione domini-
corum verborum conficiuntur,sacerdotes , &
Leuitæ ad sacros ordines promouentur , & o-
mnia ecclesiastica sacramenta conficiuntur:
that is to say : with the mystery of the
crosse the ignoraunt are instructed and
taught:the fonte of regeneration is hal-
loed:by imposition of handes such as a-
re Christened receue the giftes of gra-

Dedicati-
on off
churches.
Halloing
off aul-
ters.

ce:churches are dedicated: aulters halloed: the sacramétes of the aulter with the
putting in betwene of oure lordes wordes are made:priestes, and deacons pro-
moted to holy orders , and al sacramentes of the church perfited . And in ano-

Tract. 118.
in Ioan.

tger place he hath thes woordes : *Quid*
est quod omnes nouerunt signum Christi,nisi
crux Christ? quod signum nisi adhibeatur si-
ue ipsi aquæ qua regeneramur ,siue oleo quo
Chrismate inunguntur,sine sacrificio quo a-
*luntur, nihil eorum rite perficitur:*that is to
saye,What is the signe of Christ which
euery man doth knowe , but the crosse
off

of Chrift? which figne vnleffe it be put
to the forheades of faithful beleuers, or
to the water with which we are regene-
rate, or to the oyle with which men are *Holy oyle*
anointed in the holy Chrifme, or to the
facrifice with which mē are nourrifhed,
not one of al thofe is done rightly and
in dewe order . To this agreeth Chrifoftome, faying, The paffion of oure lord *Ho.55. in*
is the beginning and original of oure fe- *16. Math.*
licitie, with which we liue, and by the
which we be. With as good a will let vs
carry aboute with vs the croffe, as we
wolde a crowne: *Omnia enim quæ ad falu-*
tem noſtram conducunt per ipſam conſummā-
tur. Nam quū regeneramur, quum ſacratiſ-
ſimo alimur cibo, quum in ordine conſecrandi
ſtatuimur, vbique & ſemper id victoriæ in-
ſigne nobis aſſiſtit. that is to faye: For all
thinges which auayle to oure faluation
ar confummated and made perfect by
the fame croffe. For when we are rege-
nerate, or Chriftened, whē we are nourrifhed with the moft holy meate, when
we are placed and fett to be confecrated

G 3 in

in holy orders, that flag, banner, and figne of victorie alwayes affifteth vs.

In thefe authorities, and firft in the ftorie of *Probianus* note good readers the goodneffe of god driuing him by a vifion from heauen, to the woorfhipping of his croffe in earth, and that in thofe dayes there were aulters, and the figne of the croffe vppon them. And that thinges are done by angels and men, for the wealth of mans foule here vppon earth: but yet not without the figne of the croffe. Next in S. Cyprian note that mē haue authoritie by commiffion frō god to make, and minifter his facramentes, and that in the figure and figne of the croffe by that authority and operation, al facramentes haue their effecte. And note howe in S. Auguftines tyme, chur ches, fontes, and aulters were halloed, children after baptifme confirmed, and anoynted with holy oyle, and that al facramentes of the church are made with the figne of the holy croffe, and none rightly and in dewe order without it:

Churches fontes, and aulters halloed.

fur-

furder in Chrifoftome note, that al thin
ges auayleable to oure faluation are có-
fummated and made perfect by the croffe. And left they who enuye vs the effectes and fruictes of Chriftes bleffed fa-
crametes, make youe beleue, that al is to
be ment and referred to Chrifte his paffion only, confider that *Probianus* being
conuerted to Chrift, and beleuing alfo
that al thinges neceffarie to oure faluation
tion haue their operation and effect by
the vertue and merites of Chriftes paffion, had alfo the figne of the croffe fhe
wed him vppon the aulter. And that S.
Auguftine fayeth vnleffe the figne of
the croffe be put to the facrament of có
firmatió, holy orders, and the body and
bloud of oure lorde, nothing is rightly
done. And befides marke howe S. Chrifoftome afhrming al thinges to be confummated by the croffe, faieth in the
end: *Vbique & femper id victoriæ infigne no-*
bis affiftit, that banner or enfigne of victorie in all places and at all tymes affifteth vs: and in diuerfe places he vfeth

This wor-
de croffe
taken for
the figne
of the
croffe.

G 4   this

this worde(croſſe) for the ſigne off the
croſſe, as in his Demonſtration ageinſt
the gentills,he ſaieth . *Reges poſitis diade-*
matis crucem ſuſcipiunt mortis Symbolum:
In purpuris crux,in diadematis crux, in ar-
mis crux, in precibus crux, in menſa ſacra
crux, & in toto orbe crux, that is to ſaye:
Kinges leying downe their crownes take vp the croſſe,a ſigne of death:In their purple robes there is a croſſe : in their
crownes a croſſe : in their prayer bokes
a croſſe:in their armour a croſſe : in the
holy table a croſſe: and in al the worlde
a croſſe.

Here yowe ſee good readers by the
authoritie of S.Cyprian, Chriſoſtome,
and Auſtyne, and by the viſion ſhewed
to *Probianus* from heauen,that nothing
was euer done for the weale of man ſithens Chriſt ſuffred, with out the crof-
ſe: and that al the ſacramentes of the
churche are dewly perfited and made
with the ſigne off the croſſe, and neuer rightly and in dewe order without
it.

And

And here to take away occasion frō
al malitious Momes of cauillation, I
geue yowe to vnderstand that the crosse in celebration of Christes sacramentes is vsed for two causes specially. The
first is to put vs in remembraunce off
oure redemption by Christes death vppon the crosse. The second to declare
that all sacramentes haue their vertue
and effect of the merites of his passion.
And albeit the auncient fathers teache,
and the Catholike church commaūde,
that the signe of the crosse shuld be v-
sed in al sacramentes, yet it is not their
minde that any sacrament lacketh his
operation, effect and vertue, if or for ne-
cessitie, or by ouer sight, or by ignoraun
ce the saied signe be omitted, the intent
of the minister being sincere and good,
and wil to do is the catholick churche
doth. But when of self wil and set purpose the order off the churche is con-
temptuously broken, and the intention
of the minister euil, and faith worse (as
theirs is who be Swinglianes, Caluini-
ſtes

ſtes and ſuch leeke) there is dowte but
that they offend the goodneſſe of god,
and in omitting the ſigne of the croſſe
in the celebration of Chriſtes ſacramẽ-
tes, tranſgreſſe the ordinaunce of the ho
ly ghoſt, and tradition of the Apoſtels,
and auncient fathers, which they pretend to kepe, and reſtore vnto Chriſtendome agayne.

Nowe let vs conſider euery ſacrament
a parte. *Dionyſius Areopagita*, S. Paules
ſcholler declaring what reuerent ceremonies were vſed in baptiſme, amongeſt other ſaieth, that when any cometh

c. 2. eccleſ. to be baptiſed, the biſſhopp *Imponit eius*
Hierar. *capiti manum, conſignanſque illum, ſacerdóti-*
bus mandat vt virum ſuſceptorem deſcribant:
Leieth his hande vppon his head and
bleſsing him with the ſigne of the croſſe, commaundeth the prieſtes to aſſigne
ſome man to be his godfather. After-
warde the holy oyle is brought forth,

The vva- and the biſſhop *Trino crucis ſignaculo vn-*
ter of bap
tiſme hal- *ctionem inchoat.* Beginneth to anoynte
loed. him with thre ſignes of the croſſe. After
war-

warde he halloeth the water. *Terque in eas ad crucis effigiem sanctissimum fundens oleum,*and pouring oute the most holy oyle thrise after the manner of a crosse, dippeth him thrise in the water,and put teth on him a white garment meete for clenlynesse and innocecy (which nowe we caull a Chrisome S.Basile saieth We blesse the water of baptisme,and the oy-le of inunctio. *Insuperq; ipsum qui baptiza tur,*and the man also that is Christened. S. Ambrose saieth *Quum aqua salutaris fuerit crucis mysterio consecrata, tuc ad vsum spiritalis lauacri & salutaris poculi tempera-tur.*When the healthful water is conse-crated with the mystery or signe of the crosse,then is it made meete for to the vse of the spiritual bath, and healthfull cupp.S. Agustine saieth, *Baptismus,id est aqua salutis non est aqua salutis,nisi in Chri-sti nomine consecrata, qui pro nobis sanguinem fudit,cruce ipsius aqua signetur.* Baptisme, that is to laie the water of saluation is not the water of saluation,vnlesse after it be halloed with the name of Christ
who

holy oyle poured vppo the vvater.

cap.27. de Spirit.san-cto.

ca. 3. de ijs qui misle. initiantur.

Ho.27. li. 50.Ho. to 10.

who shed his bloud for vs , it be signed
and blessed with his crosse. Againe in o-
ne of his sermons he saieth. *Signo Christi*

*Sar.*119.
de tempo.

signatur baptismus,id est,aqua vbi tingimini.
Baptisme,(that is to saie,the water where yowe ar dipped) is signed with the signe of Christ.To this purpose also ser-
ueth S. Chrisostomes wordes, who rebuking his people for a superstitious
kinde of anoynting their childrens heades with durte taken out of bathes,say-

*Ho.*12.*in*
1.*Corinth.*

ieth. *Quomodo censes presbiteri manu frontē*
*signãdã vbi luto inunxisti?*Afterwhat sorte
thinkest thowe can that forhead be signed with the priestes hãd,where thowe
hast daubed durte?In lieke mãner *Raba-*

*Cap.*27.*de*
Inst.cleri.

nus an auncient father confirmeth this
ceremonie and vse of the crosse in most
expresse woordes . *Signatur* , saieth he;
baptizandus signaculo sanctæ crucis tam in
corde quam in fronte, &c . The man that is
to be baptised,is signed with the signe
of the holy crosse as wel in the breaste,
as in the forhead,that from that day forward the Apostata and false traytour the
deuil

deuil knowing the figne of his owne
deftruction in his old veffel may vnderftand that for euermore it is cleane alienated from him.

In confirmation which Melchiades *Epift.ade-*
caulleth a facrament, and which as S. *pifc.Hippa.*
Auguftine faieth, is in the kinde of vi- *Lib.2.cap.*
fible fignes, a moft holy facrament as *lit.Petilia-*
baptifme is, the churche taught by the *ni.*
example of Chrift, who imbrafing lit- *Mar.10.*
le children in his armes, and leying his
handes vppon their heades, bleffed thē,
and inftructed by the example of Peter
and Iohn who hearing that thofe of Sa- *Act.8.*
maria had receued the woord of god,
and were baptifed in the name of Iefus,
leyed their handes vppō them, that they
might receue the holy ghofte, and in-
formed by S. Paule doing the leeke at
Ephefus, doth in lieke manner wil and *Act.19.*
commaunde al bifhopes to bleffe the
children that are brought vnto them
and ley their handes vppon them and
vfe this forme of woordes. *Signo te figno*
crucis et confirmo te Chrifmate falutis in no-
mine

mine patris, & filij, & spiritus sancti, vt re-
plearis eodem spiritu, & haleas vitam æter-
nam : I signe the with the signe off the
crosse, and confirme the with the Chrisf
me of saluation in the name of the father, and of the sonne, and of the holy
ghoft, that thowe maieft be replenis-
shed with the same holy ghoft and ha-

Cōfirma-
tion no
nevve de-
uise. ue lif euerlafting: This sacrament is not
as it pleaseth, oure newe bold byblers
to bable, a newe deuise of mans inuen-

Cap. 4. ec-
clesiaft.
Hier. tion. For the holy father S. Denise doth
not only declare that this sacramēt was
taught by the Apoftells, and saye that
the Chrisme is *Sacrosanctum mysterium,*
eius ordinis atq; virtutis vt sacerdotalia cun
cta perficiat, Diuinum vnguentum quo pon-
tifex vtitur ad omnis sacræ rei cōsecrationem,
vnguentum cuius sacratißima consummatio-
ne sacræ regenerationis donum & gratia per-

The ver-
tue of the
Chrisme
or holy
oyle. *ficitur,* That is to saye A moft holy myftery, of that degre and vertue, that it
perfiteth al thinges appartayning to pri
eftes, a heauenly oyntment, which the
biffhopp vfeth to the consecration off
euery

euery holy thing, an oyntment with whofe moft holy perfection the gift and grace of baptifme is made perfect, but alfo he faieth it is: *Vnguentum prorſus deificum:Perfectio,& ſanctificatio,totius noſtra diuinitus indultæ ſanctificationis initium, atq; ſubſtantia, & perficiens virtus,* that is to fay.And oyntment altogether diuine and godly:perfection and fanctification:the beginning, the fubftaunce, the perfiting vertue of al holyneffe geuen vs from heauen.

Cap. 4.
Cap.2.eccle ſi.Hier.

Moreouer the holy Martir *Fabianus* in his epiftle to the biſhopes of the eaft caulleth côfirmation *Nouum Sacramentum*, a newe facrament, and faieth that oure lord Iefus after he had fupped with his difciples,and waſhed their feete,taught them to make the Chrifme, as oure predeceffours receued of the Apoftells, and left vnto vs,faieth he:And in the end of his epiftle he hath thes wordes, *Ipſa lauatio pedum noſtrum ſignificat baptiſmum quando ſancti Chriſmatis vnctione perficitur.* The waſhing of feete

To.1. Con.

doth

doth fignifie oure baptifme when it is
côfummated and made perfect with the
anoynting of the holy Chrifme.

Nowe that the holy fathers vfed alfo the figne of the croffe in this facrament, it apeareth by S. Denife faying:
When a man defirous off baptifme is
Chriftened, the prieftes put on him a co
te of innocency and bring him to the
biffhop, and the biffhop *Diuino ac dei-*
fico vnguento figneans, facratißimæ commu-
nionis participem facit. that is to faye, figning him with the diuine and moft
godly oyntment, maketh hym partaker
of the moft holy communion, the very body and bloud of Chrift, not the
prophane cômunion and polluted bread, which Caluine deuifed, and thes newe proteftantes brought from Geneua.
Of this outward figning and vfe of the
holy Chrifme in this facrament Tertul
lian writeth in this forte. *Caro vngitur*
vt anima confecretur: Caro fignatur vt anima
muniatur: caro manuum impofitione adum-
bratur vt anima fpiritu illuminetur: The
fleafh

Cap. 2. ec-
clefiaft. Hi
erar.

Lib. de re-
fur. carnis.

fleash is anoynted that the soule may be
sanctified: the fleash is signed, that the
soule may be defeded: the fleash is ouer-
shadoed by impofition of handes, that
the soule may be lightned with the holy ghoft. And S. Auguftine fpeaketh off
the fame in this forte, *Paffionis & crucis* *Lib. de ca-*
figno in fronte hodie tanquam in pofte fignan- *thech.rudi-*
dus es:ommefque Chriftiani fignatur. Thowe *cap.20.*
muft be figned, and marked in thy for-
head with the figne of the paffion and
croffe of Chrift as it were in a poft:and
al Chriften man ar fo marked. Rabanus
in like manner faieth, *Signatur baptiza-* *Lib.1.de*
tus cum Chrifmate in fummitate capitis per *inft. clerico*
facerdotem,per pontificem vero in fronte: The *ru.cap. 31.*
man that is baptifed, is figned with
Chrifme in the top of his head by the
prieft,and in his forhead by the bifhop,
that in the firft anoynting may be fignified the coming downe of the holy
ghoft vppon him to fanctifie an habi-
tation and dwelling place for god, and
in the fecond the feuenfold grace of the
holy ghoft with all plenty of holyneffe,
H know=

knowledg and vertue, may be signified
to come vnto man. For as S.Denise saieth, to him that is sanctified with the
most holy mystery of regeneration, the
inunction off the holy oyntment, making al ful and perfect, doth geue the co
ming of the holy ghost.

Wherevppon S.Cyprian considering
howe necessary this sacrament is for al
mankinde, saieth, *Vngi necesse est eum qui
baptizatus sit, vt accepto Chrismate (id est vnctione) esse vnctus dei, & habere in se gratiam
Christi possit.*It is necessary that he, that is
baptised be anoynted :that the Chrisme
(that is to saye the oyntment) being o-
nes receued, he may be the anoynted off
god : and haue in him the grace off
Christ. And the fathers of the councell
of *Laodicæa* made this decre: *Oportet bap-
tizatos post baptismum sacratissimum Chris-
ma percipere, & cælestis regni participes fieri.*It behoueth al that are Christened, to
receue after baptisme the holy Chrisme,
and be made partakers of the kingdome
of heauen. And S.Clement long before
(as it

e. 4 .Hier.
ecclef.

Lib.1. epi.
12.

Ca. 48.

(at it appeareth in his epiftle to *Iulius*
and *Iulianus* his fchollers) taught the fa ⟨*To.1. cōcil.*⟩
me,as a doctrine of S. Peters and other
Apoftells.His woordes be thes.All men
muft hafte with out delaye to be borne
agayne,and figned of the bifhop, (that
is to fay) to receue the feuenfold grace
of the holy ghoft. For otherwife no o-
ne can be a trewe Chriften man, and ⟨VVithout
cōfirma-
haue place emongeft the perfect, iff he ⟨tion nō
continewe without it of fet purpofe or ⟨mā hath
place emō
negligéce.And thus much S. Clement, ⟨geft the
with whome S.Cyprian agreeth faying. ⟨perfect.
Tunc vero fanctificari & effe filij dei poffunt, ⟨*Lib.1.E-
pift.2*
fi facramento vtroque nafcantur . Then ⟨Cōfirma-
trewly they may be fanctified and be the ⟨tion caulled a facra
fonnes of god, if they be borne with ⟨ment.
both facramentes . With him agreeth
Cornelius writing to Fabian off *Noua-*
tus the heretick: his woordes be thefe:
Nouatus vexed with an euil fprite, and
greuoufly afflicted with ficknes, was
chreftened with water caft vppon him ⟨*Eufebius*
in his bed.*Reliqua que baptifmū fequi folent* ⟨*Lib.6. cā.
14 . ecclc-
nec impleta funt,nec fignaculo Crifmatis con-* ⟨*fiaft.hiftor.*
H 2   *firmatus*

firmatus eſt, ynde nec ſpiritum ſanctū ynquā
promereri potuit . Al other thinges wich
are wounte to follo baptiſme, were nether fulfilled , nether he made a perfect
Chriſten man with the ſacrament off
confirmation , wherfore he culd neuer
deſerue, nor gett the holy ghoſt . The
ſame doctrine the bleſſed Apoſtells Peter and Iohn taught by their example in
Samaria:and S. Paule at Epheſus.For iff
in baptiſme thoſe off Samaria had receued the holy ghoſt in ſuch abundaunce
and plenty, as was neceſſary for them,
then wold not Peter and Iohn haue
prayed that they might receue the holy
ghoſt , nor then wold S. Luke haue ſa᷄-
yed,as yet the holy ghoſt was not come
vppon any off them.

Nowe then good readers,ſeying Dio
nyſius a greate lerned father,liuing at
the paſſion of oure ſauiour Chriſt , and
conuerted to the faith by S . Paule writeth ſo reuerently of the ceremonies v-
ſed in baptiſme,and eſpecially of the hal
loing of the water with the ſigne of the
croſ-

Act.8.
Act.19,

Act.8.

crosse, and speaketh so highly off the
Chrisme vsed both in baptisme and con
firmation, and declareth it to be the doctrine of the Apostells, And seying the
holy Martir Fabian testifieth the same,
and caulleth it *Sacramentum nouum*, a newe sacrament, And seying as S. Clement
saieth al men must hasten to be borne
agayne, and confirmed of the bisshop,
And no man can be a perfect Christen
man, iff the contynewe with out it of
purpose or negligence, And seying as S.
Cyprian and the fathers of Laodicene
councell say, euery man that is baptised
must be anoynted with Chrisme, and
confirmed, that he may be the anoynted of god, and partaker of the kingdome of heauen, I trust yowe wil more e-
steme, and better regard the authoritie
of thes auncient fathers, then the leuitie of these newe ghospellers, who caried about with euery winde and puff off
newe doctrine, be as S. Cyprian saieth, *Epist.ad*
begynners of schismes, authours of dis- *Nouatia.*
sension, destroyers of faith, betrayers of *Lib.1.E-*
pist.6.
H 3 the

the church,and Antichriftes: with who
me the fcriptures are more read then vn-
derftode:who going about to deface the
catholick religion commaunded by
Chrift,taught by the Apoftells,and cõ-
tinued in the church by the holy ghoft
fent from god the father to teach all
treuth, haue vtterly reiected the godly
ceremonies vfed in baptifme, and alfo
difanulled the facrament of confirma-
tiõ,with fuch flaunderous woordes,and
blafphemous workes, as no honeft eare
wold gladly heare, nor Chriften man
conceue in harte:And that not with out
the counfel of the lorde forfoth,whofe
workemé they are:who remébring what
a great foile and ouerthrowe he had by
the croffe,and knowing that in confirmation man is armed with the feuenfolde grace of the holy ghoft,loboreth bufely by his minifters to take away the
figne of the croffe,and difanul the facra
ment of confirmation. The croffe, becaufe he wold not be driuen away and
put to flight when he cometh to the
field

field to encounter, the facrament of confirmation, that his aduerfarie being vn-
armed, and fo for lack of armour leffe
hable to fight, might the eafier be ouercomed, and made abonde flaue of finne,
a veffel of iniquitie, ad pray for hel.

Wherefore good Chriften readers
feing thefe newe Euangelical doctours
caulling them felues reformers of religion, fetters foorth of the trewe faith of
Chrift, reducers of al thinges to the fta-
te and order of the primitiue church, ha
ue defaced al good religion, difaunlled
the facrament of confirmation taught
by Chrift, and deliured by the Apoftels,
prophaned the holy ceremonies taught
and vfed by the fathers of the primitiue
church, (as is before declared) youe haue
iuft caufe to difcredit al the reft of their
doctrine, and thinke, that as they haue
deceued yowe in prophaning fuch ceremonies, and bereathing yowe of fuch a
neceffary facrament, fo they do in al that
they boldely and bufely preach contrary
to the vniuerfal church and fea of Ko-
me,

me,whofe faith as as S . Hierome faieth is the catholick faith.

Therefore all ye fathers and mothers as ye intend to auoyd the ftreight ac-compt which fhalbe required of yowe at the terrible day for youre negligence in not purchafing to youre children the feuenfold grace of the holy ghofte by meanes of this facrament of confir-mation , and as yowe defire to haue the iffues of youre bodies to be the anoin-ted of god,children of election , veffells into honour,and perfect Chriften men: So ceaffe not to procure vnto them ftreyt after baptifme, or in fuch conue-nient time as yowe may,the feuenfolde grace off the holy ghoft to be their ftrenght and defence ageinft their ene-mies the worlde , the fleafh,and the de-uil.And if any newe mynifter, or fchol-ler of frier Luthers fchole,or Caluins ca ue, reclame ageinft it,or controlle youe for it,tel them to their teath , that they bringing in fectes of perdition,and blaf-phemiug the way of treuth , do coue-

toufly

toufly with faire woordes make mar-
chandifes of youe , and fel youe to the
deuil,into perpetual captiuitie and thrauldome in hel, and make youe by con-
temning the ordinaunce of Chrift,and
the holy ghoft in his church,to be children of wrath and euerlafting damnation with the reprobate . And auouche
euen to their faces,that this is the will
of god,the commaundemēt of Chrift,
the ordinaunce of the holy ghofte, the
tradition of the Apoftells , the doctrine
of the fathers of the primitiue churche.
as *Dionifius*,*Clemens*,*Cornelius*,*Cyprianus*,
Fabianus,*Melchiades* , *Ambrofius*,*Auguſti-*
nus,*Rabanus*,and the fathers of Laodicene councel recorde in the places alleaged
before: and as the holy ghoft teaching
al treuth and directing the church in al
her doinges,hath fuffred to be practifed
and vfed in al places of the worlde whe
re Chrifte his religion florifhed before
thefe fhifmes. Yf this do not fatiffie thē,
then may ye faye, they haue eares and
heare not: eies and fe not:hartes and be
leue

leue not, but ſtand obſtinate in their
owne fantaſies as men infatuated, and
geuen vp in to a reprobate ſenſe:which
god take from them at this pleaſure.
Certes if they repent not for their blaſ-
phemy ageinſt the croſſe of Chriſt,and
humble them ſelues to the churche,
li.4.c.1.ad which as S.Auguſtine ſaieth : *Per ſacra-*
Cathecu. *tiſſimum ſignum crucis eos ſuſcæpit in ytero,*
Hath by the moſt holy ſigne of the croſ
ſe conceued them in her wombe, and
ſay euery mã in his owne parſon as the
ſame holy father maketh a Chriſten
in pſal.141 man to ſay *Vſque adeo de crcue non erubeſ-*
co,yt non in occulto loco habeam crutem Chri
ſti,ſed in fronte portem : & non habeam nu-
dam frontem , tegat eam crux Domini mei,
I am not ſo farforth aſhamed of the
croſſe,that I haue it, not in a ſecret pri-
uie place but beare it in my forhead,
and let me not haue a naked forhead,
let the croſſe of my lord couer it, looke
as al that had not the poſtes of their dores ſpringled with the bloud of the lambe in Aegipt,when god paſſed ouer thẽ,
were

were killed by the exterminatour: And
as al that had not the letter Tau ſigned
in their forbeades, according as god ſpoke to his prophete Ezechiel, were ſtroken to death in the mydeſt off Hieruſa-
lē, Euen ſo euery man that hath not the
bloud of the lābe Ieſus Chriſt ſpringled
in the poſtes of his harte, and the ſigne
of the croſſe printed in his forhead, ſhal
be murdred by the exterminatour the
deuil, and ſtroken to æternal death by
the angel, when god ſhal paſſe ouer this
oure Aegipt, and ſeuer al that haue his
ſigne and marke from miſcreauntes, heretikes and infidells.

Nowe that the ſigne off the croſſe *ª Lib. 2.*
hath bene vſed in holy orders, which S. *contra e-*
Auſtyne, and *ᵇ* Leo the greate, caulle a *piſt. par.*
Cap. 13.
ᵈ Be bono
ſacrament, in which by inpoſition off *coniug.*
handes ſpiritual poure is geuen to exer- *cap. 24.*
ᵇ Epiſt.
ciſe the holy office of prieſthode, which *81.*
as S. Chriſoſtome ſaieth nor man, nor *Lib. 3. de*
angel, nor archangel, nor any creature, *ſacerdotib.*
or vertue aboue, but the holy ghoſt did
inſtitute and ordaine, and made mē re-
may-

mayning in fleaſh vppõ earth do the deu

Ignat.epiſt. ad Smir. tie of angels, which office whoſoeuer diſhonoreth, diſhonoreht god, and oure lord Ieſus Chriſt, the firſt begotten off al creatures, and by nature the only high prieſte of god, *Dioniſius* S.Paules ſchol- *Parte.2.* ler teacheth vs in the fifte chapiter of his eccleſiaſt. Hierarchie, where decla- ring the manner of conſecrating biſ- hops, and making prieſtes and deacons he ſaieth: *Cuilibet eorum a benedicente pon- tifice crucis imprimitur ſignum*. The ſigne of the croſſe is imprinted in euery one of them by the biſſhop bleſsing and con ſecrating them. And this impreſsion and making the croſſe vppon them, ſig- *Cap.5.par ie.3.* nifieth ſaieth he, the mortifying off all carnall luſtes and vacation from al fle- aſhly deſires, and a lif framed to the imi- tation of of god, alwayes beholding Ie- ſus Chriſt, who paſſed forwarde euen to death vppon the croſſe. Thes expreſ- ſe woordes of ſo auncient a father ioy- ned with that which was alleaged out of S. Chriſoſtome, and Auſtine in this matter

matter may suffise. Becaufe in so manifest a matter furder prouffe, and allega-
tion of authoritie wilbe of faithful catholick men thought superfluous, and
of faithlesse and incredulous creatures
nothing ynough, I wil to content the
one and not aggrieue the other, pluck
downe sayle, cast anchor here, and rest
in their authoritie as in a suer hauen.

Nowe to proue that the signe of the **The signe**
crosse hath bene in liek manner vsed in **of the**
côsecrating the blessed body and bloud **crosse v-**
of oure sauiour Christ in the sacrifice **sed in cô-**
of the masse we haue the example off **secration**
Christ, the testinonies of the fathers, **dy and**
and practise of the church : Iesus saieth **bloud off**
S. Mathewe whiles they were at supper **26.**
toke bread and blest it. And S. Marke say **14.**
ieth Iesus toke bread and blessing it brake it &c. The Euangelistes here vse this
woorde *benedixit* : he blessed it. That is
as *Albertus magnus*, a man of thre hun- *Tract.de*
dred yeares and more, reciting othermês *offi.misse.*
opinions touching that worde, allo-
weth best *Signo quodam manus benedixit.*

　　　　　　　　　　　　　　　　　He

He bleſſed it with a certayne ſigne of his hande. Which interpretatiō if we cōfer ſcripture, to ſcripture, and place to place (as in matters of ambiguitie we muſt ſaye the ghoſpellers for better vnderſtandīg of the ſenſe) we ſhal finde this interpretatiō to be right good, and euen that which oure ſauiour chriſt did at the inſtitutiō of this bleſſed ſacramēt, to teach vs what we ſhuld do in celebraing the ſame.

When Ioſeph had brought his ij.ſonnes Manaſſes and Ephraim to his father Iacob to be bleſſed, and placed the elder on his right hād, and the younger on his left (as it is ſaied before) Iacob ſtreaching out his right hāde, leyed it vppō Ephraim his head the yōuger brother, and his left hand vppon Manaſſes the elder, and ſo chaunging his hādes *Benedixit filios Ioſeph*, bleſſed the ſonnes of Ioſeph. This māner of bleſing with his hādes ſo chaunged and put one ouer the other, did expreſſe the ſigne of the croſſe ſaieth Damaſcene. Chriſt rebuking his diſciples for prohibiting younge children to be brought

Ge. 4**.

Lib. 4. ca. 12.

brought vnto him sayied, suffer litle o- *Marci.10.*
nes to come vnto me and prohibite thē
not:for of such is the kingdome of heauen. *Et complexans eos, & imponens manus*
super illos,benedixit eos.. And imbrasing thē
in his armes,and leying his handes vppon them blessed them. Againe Christ
ascending vp to heauen to send the ho-
ly ghost promised to the Apostells, cō- *Lucæ.24.*
maunded them to tarry in Hierusalem
vntil they were indued with vertue
from aboue. Then he led them out into *Bethania* : *& eleuatis manibus benedixit*
*eos.*And lifting vp his handes he blessed
them. Nowe then if in the foresaied pla
ces where this woorde *benedixit* is vied,
the blessing was geuē with the hande,
as Iacob with his hande blessed Ioseph
his childrē, Christe leyed his handes vp
pon litle childrē and blessed thē Christ
lifted vp his hādes and blessed his Apostels,why may not we affirme and saye,
that Christ instituting this sacramēt of
his body and bloud in his last supper,
and taking bread into his handes and
blef-

blessing it, lifted vp his hande, and with a certayne signe of the crosse blessed it, especially seing the auncient fathers do so ostentymes insinuate the same, and the holy ghost directing the churche in al her doinges hath all waies allowed this manner off consecration in this mistery and sacrifice.

Amongest the auncient fathers Chri sostome saieth: *Siue mysticus ille cibus su= mendus, siue aliqui in clerum coapatandi, siue quiduis aliud faciendum, vbique signum cru= cis nobis adest.* Whether that mystical meate be to také, whether any be to be admitted into the clergie, whether any other thing be to be done, in euery place the signe off the crosse is present with vs. And in another place he saieth: *In sacra mensa, in corpore Christi, in mysticis cœnis fulget crux.* The crosse shineth in the holy table, in the body of Christ, in the mystical suppers. And S. Augustine saieth: *Elegit crucem quæ leui motu manus exprimitur: Hoc enim signo crucis consecra= tur corpus dominicum, & omnia quæcunque sancti-*

Ser. de ve-
nerat. cru-
cis.

In demon-
stra. aduer-
sus gen.

Ser. 181. de
tempore.

sanctificantur, cũ inuocatione Christi nominis hoc signo consecrantur. Christ chose a crosse which is expressed with a light mouing of the hand. For with this signe of the crosse oure lordes body is consecrated, and al thinges which are sanctified, are consecrated with the signe of the crosse with caulling vppon the name of Christ. In another place he saieth. *Quo-* *Tract.118.* *modo ergo per id quod mali faciunt nihil, boni* *in Ioan.* *significatur, quando per crucem Christi quam fecerunt mali in celebratione sacramentorum eius, bonum omne nobis signatur?* After what sorte therefore is there no good signified by that which euil men, do, seing by the crosse of Christ which euil mē haue made in celebrating his sacramentes, al goodnesse is signed and signified vnto vs? And as it is alleaged before, he saieth in effect. *Signum Christi adhibetur sacrificio quo aluntur.* The signe of Christ is put vnto the sacrifice with which men are nourrished.

Nowe then good readers, if as S. Augustine saieth Oure lordes body is con-

I   secra-

secrated with the signe of the crosse, and
men in celebrating the sacramétes make
the crosse of Christ, and put the signe of
the crosse vnto the sacrifice with which
men are nourished, (that is the sacrament of the aulter) let oure newe master
mynisters tel vs, howe the body of Chri
ste is consecrated with the signe of the
crosse, or howe men cá make a crosse in
celebration of the sácramétes, or put the
signe of Christ, (which is his crosse) to
the sacrifice off the body and bloud off
Christ, vnlesse it be as the church vseth
by lifting vp the hande and making the
signe of the crosse ouer it?

Tit.20.
Pamplie. *Euthymius* writing ageinst the Arme-
nians, who neuer worshipped nor adored the crosse, before they had washed
it, and fastened a nayle in the midest of
it, and anoynted it with the bloud of the
sacrifice, saieth. *O stulti & mente capti: sic e-*
nim vos alloquar, Si crux manu designata res
omnès sanctificat quibus adhibetur, vt aquam
baptismi, & oleum, & vnguentum, & vultus
credentium, & panem mysticum, & sacrum
san-

sanguinem, cur apud vos figura crucis ex qua-
uis materia confecta, tanquam res aliqua com
munis & prophana, ablutione, & clauo, & san-
guine sanctificatur? Aut quo modo crux quæ
baptismum & sacrificium sanctificat ab ijsdem
ipsa sanctificetur? O folish men and blinde
in harte, for fo wil I caull yowe, Yff a
crofte made with the hand doth fanctifie al thinges to which it is put vnto, as
the water of baptifme, the oyle and oyntment, the faces of the faithful, the myftical bread and holy bloud, Why is the figure of the croffe, made of fome earthly
matter, fanctified amonge yowe with
wafhing, with dreuing in of a nayle, and
anoynting with the holy bloud, as
though it were fome common or prophane thinge? Or by what meanes can
the croffe which doth fanctifie baptifme, and the facrifice, be fanctified of the
fame? This holy father *Euthymius* being
a Greke, agreeth with that which I alleaged out of S. Auguftine: and faieth,
that a croffe made with the hand doth
fanctifie the myfticall bread and holy

A croffe
made
vvith the
hand fanc
tifieth all
thinges to
vvhich it
is put.

I 2   bloud,

bloud,a croffe made with the hand doth
fanctifie al thinges to which it is put vn
to.And yet thes newe ghofpellers wil ha
ue no croffe made in baptifme, no croffe made in confecrating the body and
bloud of Chrift,and fo forth,but accom
pte it fuperftition,and folly . *O ftulti , &*
menti capti . O folifh men and blinde in
harte:for fo wil I caull them . And feing
they nether follo the example ofChrift,
who toke bread in his hande and bleft
it , nor creditt the authoritie of the fathers who fay that with the figne of the
croffe the body and bloud of Chrift is
confecrated , nor harken to the practiffe
of the church, who by the direction off
the holy ghoft hath alwayes vfed this
manner of confecration , but doute off
that which euermore hath bene vfed, I
may faye Mo*dicæ fidei quare dubitaftis ?* O
ye off litle faith why haue ye dowted?
Efaie.21. *Q ui incredulus eft infideliter agit,*He that is
an incredulous creature dealeth vnfaith-
fully . To all fuch as are faithleffe,and a-
gre not to thetreuthe , tribulation and
indig-

indignation is alwayes redy, and euerlasting fyer, which is prepared for the deuil and his angels. Wherefor see as S. Pau
le saieth that there be no lõger in yowe
the naughty harte of incredulitie : but
according to the counsell of the wise
man, be wise touching matters of god,
in goodnesse: and in simplicitie of harte seeke hym:because he is founde off
those, who do not tempt hym, and apeareth to such as be not incredulous and
faithlesse to hym.

Nowe it remayneth, to be proued that
this signe of the crosse is vsed amongest
Christen men, in Matrimonie, Penaunce, and extreme vnctiõ: And first in Matrimonie they that knit that trewe loue
knot, (yf they were neuer maried before) after long prayer made by the prieste, are blessed with the signe of the cros
se. In penaunce after confession humbly
made, absolution is geuen, and the pæni
tent dimissed in the name of the father,
and of the sonne, and of the holy ghost:
which woordes the confessour neuer

Martialis Epist. ad Tolosa.

Hab.3.

Sapient.1.

pronoũceth with out making the signe
of the crosse. In extreme vnction euery
parte of the body that is anoynted, is also signed with the crosse. And al this
may by good authorities be proued: but
because S. Augustine saieth, Al sacramē-
tes of the churche are made with the sig
ne of the crosse, I wil not trouble the rea
ders with much matter, but briefly shewe that these be sacramentes off the
church, and the other wil necessarely
follo.

Firſt then that matrimonie is a sacra
ment, S. Ambrose declareth in his treaty
se vppon S. Paules epistle to the Ephe-
sians, and S. Augustine in his boke, *De*
nuptijs & ᵃ concupiscentia. in his boke, *De*
ᵇ bono coniugali, in his boke, *De ᶜ peccato o-*
riginali, and *ᵈ* Leo the greate in his .92. e-
piſtle, And S. Paule him selff writing to
the Epheſians, and commaunding euery man to loue his wiff as his owne body, and as Chriſt loued his church, saieth *Hoc sacramentum magnum eſt in Chri*
ſto & ecclesia: This is a greate sacrament
in

Cap. 5.
G Lib. 2.
Cap. 10.
b Ca. 14.
c Lib. 1.
Cap. 24.
d Cap. 4.

Cap. 5.

in Chrift and the churche. Nor here can
the ghofpellers haue any aduantage or
euafion, becaufe S. Paule writing in greke faieth it is *Mifterium magnum*, a greate
myftery: for myftery and facrament do
not fo far differ, but that, that which is
caulled a myftery may alfo be a facrament: as for example, baptifme, and the
facrifice off the body and bloud off
Chrift are caulled by diuerfe auncient
fathers a myftery, *ergo* be they not facramentes? a goodly reafon by S. Mary, not
much vnlieke to an old mother Mau-
kyns talk: who hearing her neighbour
faye that their S. Edmonde was a myn-
ftrel, faied nay by S: Mary goffhip he is a
minifter, as though in thefe later dayes
in the holy cōgregatiō, he that is a myn
ftrel can not be a minifter to, and *fimul
& femel* ferue both turnes for a nede. Wel
howe fo euer it pleafeth them to dally
with the fignification of the woorde, yf
they wil loke but to the definition of a
facrament, and confider what is required
in a facrament, they fhall finde nothing

I 4   lacke

lacke in matrymonie that is, or ought to
be in any other facrament : here is a vifible figne of inuifible grace: The vifible
figne is the externall coniunction and
knitting together of the mã and womã:
or that outward gefture and acte, by
which in the name of god they are vni-
ted to gether, and as they are by mutuall
confent knitting vp the knot, profef-
fe that they wilbe two in one fleafh,
and neuer breake that trewe loue knot:
This vniting and ioyning thẽ together,
reprefenteth vnto vs the myftical vniõ
of the diuine and humane nature, and
the coniunction of Chrift and his fpou
fe the church, not only in fpirite and loue, but alfo in nature, by taking ouer fleafh vppon hym: here is an inuifible grace, that is to fay, a gift of god by which
they are made more firme and ftable to
loue and concorde, more ftronger to fuf
fer aduerfitie, more wifer to inftructe
their children, and better hable to refifte
al corruption and vnclenlineffe, if they
haue before their eies the example off
good

good Toby and Sara: and refpect only
the honour of god and trewe end off
matrimonie:here is a matter, and thing
of a facrament, that is in indiffolubilitie
of the wedlock bonde: here be wordes
declaring the confent off the parties,
and knitting the perfons to gether in
the face of the churche by the office off
the priefte.

Pænaunce, caulled *Lauachrum lachry-*
marū, vitæ veteris expoliatio, fecūda poft nau
*fragiū tabula, animi renafcētia:*A bath of te
ares, a difpoiling of the old lif:the fecōd
boorde after fhipwrack, and a newe reui
uing or byrth of the minde, lighting vppon an humble perfon who with teares and penfiff panges lamétteh his finnes paft, and purpofet hwith al his harte
to forfake finne, and cleauing faft to the
promeffe of Chrift made to his Apoftells, faiyng:Receue ye the holy ghoft
whofe finnes ye forgeue are forgeuen
them, is with a fincere minde willing as
as Tertullian faieth, *Ieiunijs preces alere,*
ingemifcere, lachrimari, prefbiteris aduolui
                                          aris

Lib. de pœ-
nitentia.

aris Dei adgeniculari: To nourrish his prayers with fasting, to lament, to wepe,
to faull downe at the priestes feete, to
knele at godes aulters, and according to
the counsel of S. Cyprian, *Apud sacerdo-*
tes Dei dolenter & simpliciter confiteatur,
exomologesim conscientiæ suæ facit, animi sui
pondus exponit, doth sorofully and simply
confesse his faultes before the priestes
of god, make declaration of his côscien-
ce, shewe foorth the heuy burden of his
minde, and as Chrisostome faieth *Per*
species peccata dicit , telleth his faultes
particulary euery one in his kinde, and
after absolution geuen by the prieste,
intendeth to make such satisfaction as
by the aduise of his confessour shalbe
thought expedient and necessary, This
pænaunce I saye, is a visible signe of in-
visible grace. The visible signe is the external acte of the priest absoluing the
pœnitent. The inuisible grace is remission of sinne, which god effectuously
geueth by meane of this sacramēt to all
that vnfaynedly turne vnto him. The

marginal notes: *Ser. 5. de lapsis.*

marginal notes: *Ho. 46. Ad pop. Antioch.*

matter

matter of this facramēt is the external ac
te of the pœnitēt contayning thes thre
pointes, Cōtritiō, Cōfeſsiō, and Satisfa-
ctiō. The woordes are. *Egote abſoluo* , *&c.*
I aſſoyle the in the name of the father,
and of the ſonne of and the holy ghoſt,
which forme off woordes the churche
hath taken of oure ſauiour Chriſt ſpea-
king to S. Peter and ſaying *Quodcūq; ſol-* Math. 16.
ueris ſuper terrā erit ſolutū & in cœlis: What-
ſoeuer thoue doeſt vnbinde vppō earth
ſhalbe vnbounde in heauen, lieke as ſhe
hath takē thoſe wordes of baptiſme. *Ego*
te baptizo, &c. I baptiſe the of his wordes
ſpokē to the Apoſtells *Eūtes docete omnes* Math. 28.
gentes baptizātes eos in nomine patris, & filij,
& ſpiritus ſancti. Going for the teach ye al
natiōs, baptiſing thē in the name off the
father, and of the ſonne, and of the holy
ghoſt: and both are of lieke authoritie:
for the church that ordayned the one, or
dayned the other , and that of the wor
des of Chriſt . He that is deſirous to ſe
more touchinge this ſacramēt, let hī reade ſuch authours as haue thes later yeares

res traueled in prouig thefe facramétes,
and efpecially the boke of the feuen facramétes fet forth by the late king of fa
mous memory Henry the eight . In thé
he fhall finde fo much as may content
any Chriften man.

Nowe as for extreme vnction, becau-
oure cruel enemie the deuil alwayes lieth in wayte for vs, and neuer affayleth
vs more fearcely then in that terrible
agonye and conflicte which we haue
with death a litle before oure paffage
out of this worlde, Chrift oure fauiour
hauing fufficiently prouided for oure
faulfgarde al oure lif time, wold not for
his tender loue and infinite mercy, leue
vs deftitute of affiftaunce and help in
that extremitie of deathe: But ordayned
vs this facrament of extreme vnction,
as a fure defence ageinft all the force off
oure enemies. By this facrament the de
feafes of the bodie, and infirmities off
the minde by which the deuil vfurpeth
a tyranny ouer vs, are perfectly healed.
For as S. Marke faieth. The Apoftells
Vngebant

Vngebant oleo multos ægros, & sanabantur. 6.
Did anoynte with oyle many sick fol-
kes, and they were healed. The comodi
tie whereof the blessed. Apostel S. Iames
espying, gaue counsel to al Christen me
to caull for priestes in their extremitie
that they may praye ouer the and anoin
te the with oyle: His wordes be thes. *In-* 5.
firmatur aliquis in vobis, Inducat presbiteros
ecclesiæ, & orent super eum, vngentes eum o-
leo in nomine domini, & oratio fidei saluabit
infirmum, & si in peccatis fuerit remitten-
tur ei. Is there any sick amongest yowe?
let him bring in the priestes of the
church, and let them praye ouer him a-
noynting him with oyle, in the name
of oure lorde, and the prayer, of faith
shal saue the sick, and if he be in sinnes
they shal be forgeuen him. Behold here good readers the goodnesse off god
towardes vs: becauie we shuld not be
brought into perpetual slauery with Sa
tan, he hath prouided another externall
remedy for vs, that is the prayers off
priestes and anointing with oyle, which
                                    accor-

according to the counſel of Chriſtes
Apoſtel, the churche miniſtreth to al
faithful Chriſten men deſiring the ſame in caſe mortalitie, and daunger off
death . This is not as oure aduerſaries
ſaye,a vayne ſuperſtition and deuiſe off
man : yowe ſee howe god by his Apoſtel S.Iames hath ordayned this to the
comforte of man. In this ſacrament here
is a viſibile ſigne of inuiſible grace. The
viſible ſigne is the externall vnction.
The inuiſible grace is the releaſe from
ſynne. The matter of the ſacrament is
oyle ſanctified by the biſhop: the which
as it hath thre properties , to make men
nimble to labour, to nouriſh light , and
cauſe mirth, So doth this extreme ano-
yntingwith oyle,delyuer men from pay
nes gotté by ſickneſſe of body, and ſinnes of the ſoule:and geueth light , ioy,
and ſpirituall myrth, if the patient be
ſtronge in faith . Here be wordes pronounced by the prieſte anoynting the
ſick,and deuoutely praying that it may
pleaſe god of his infinite mercy by that
                                    inun-

(margin note) Extreme vnction inſti tuted of god by his apoſtle S Iames.

inunction of oyle to forgeue the fick
man al his offenfes cōmitted any manner of wayes ageynft his diuine maie-
ftye.

Moreouer both extreme vnction and
al the other facramentes afore mentioned, ar not only accompted and named
facramentes of the churche by diuerfe
holy and aunciēt fathers, but alfo by the
coūcell of Floréce, and this laft Synode
of Trent: where for the difcuffing off
matters brought in controuerfie by heretikes, and declaration off treuth in
pointes of religion , the beft lerned
and floure of al Chriftendome were
affembled in the holy ghoft (who promefed that when two or thre were affembled to gether in his name he wolde
be in the mideft of them) both determined thefe matters of controuerfie
in religion, to the vtter confufion and
ouerthrowe of heretikes , and alfo pronounced a terrible curfe, to al that fhuld
beleue or teach the contrarye . Wherefore as the holy father Hilarius writing
ageyn-

ageynft *Auxentius* a notable Arrian wil
led euery man to be ware of him, faying
*Abſiſtite ab Auxentio Satanæ angelo, hoſte
Chriſti vaſtato, perdito fidei negatore, quam
regi ſic eſt profeſſus vt falleret, ſic fefellit vt
blaſphemaret,* Flee from *Auxentius* an angel of Satan, a wicked enemie of Chriſtes, a deſperate denier of faith, which
he hath in ſuch ſorte profeſſed to the
king that he might deceue him , and
hath ſo deceued that he might blaf-
pheme, So iff any newe myniſter exhorte yowe to follo hym, and forſake the catholick faith of the churche,
I deſire yowe as yowe loue youre owne ſoules, flee from hym, as from the
angel of Satan, the enemie off Chriſt
the deſpoiler of the churche, the denier
of faith, which in pretence and colour
he profeſſeth, to deceue yowe, and de-
ceueth yowe to triumphe ouer yowe:
And as that holy father *Hilarius* ſaied
when *Auxentius* made conuenticles a-
geinſt him, caulled him heretick, and
brought him in diſpleaſure with the
prince,

prince, *Congreget nunc ille quas volet in me Synodos, & hæreticum vt iam sæpe fæcit publico titulo proscribat, & quantam velit in me potentium iram moliatur, mihi certe ille nunquam aliud quàm diabolus erit, quia Arrianus, Neque pax aliquorum vnquam optabitur, quàm eorum qui secundum patrum nostrorum apud Nicæam trattatum, anathematizatis hæreticis, Christum verum deum prædicauerunt,* Let hym nowe gather to gether ageinſt me as many Synodes as he wil, let hym proſcribe me and with a paper on my back proclame me heretick, let him purchaſſe me as much diſpleaſure of noble men as he liſt, he ſhal neuer be accompted other off me then a a deuil becauſe he is an Arrian : nether at any time we will wiſh for the frindſhip and peace of any other then theirs, who according to the treaty and determination of oure fathers of Niçe did accurſe all heretickes, and pronounced Ieſus Chriſt to be trewe god: Euen ſo, when any newe Enangeliſt chardg yowe with the concluſions of their con-

uocations, and caul youe in al assemb-
bles, sermons, and meetinges, papistes,
and threaten the indignation off the
prince, for staying and withstanding
the procedinges, say vnto him. Talk
of youre congregations as long as thoue list, caul vs papistes as longe as thowe wilt, threaten the displeasure of the
prince, as longe as thowe mayest. Sue-
erly to vs *Nunquam aliud quam diabolus*
eris, quia Caluinianus. thoue shalt neuer be other then a deuil, because thowe arte a Caluiniste: Nether at anytime
we will wishe to haue frindship and
peace with any other then with those,
who according to the determination of
oure fathers assembled at Florence and
Trent haue accursed al heretickes and
pronounced that there be seuen sacramentes in the catholick churche, ordayned by Christ and his Apostelles, as meanes to help man to æternal saluation
in heauen.

The

THE APOS-
TLES AND FATHERS
OF THE PRIMITYVE
CHVRCH BLESSED THEM
selues with the signe off the crosse,
and counselled all Christen men,
to do the same, and that in
those dayes the crosse
was set vp in euery
place conueni-
ent for it.

IN this article thre pointes remayne to be pro-
ued. The first is that the
Apostles and fathers off
the primityue churche
blessed themselues with the signe off
the crosse. The seconde that they coun
selled euery good Christen man to
do the same. The thirde that in their
dayes, a crosse was set vp in euery conuenient place. To discourse of the first,

K 2   and

and runne ouer the lyffes off all the A-
poſtles , and fathers of the primityue
churche,it were a longe labour, vnplea-
ſaunt for the reader and impertinent to
my purpoſe : For that I am deſiours in
this treatiſe, to be ſhorte:not longe and
tedious.Wherefore I wil only ley before
youre eies the examples of certayne, by
whome ye may be eaſely induced,to cō
iecture and thinke the lieke of other. S.
Paule beinge brought to the place of ex
ecution,where he ſhuld ſuffer martyrdo
me vnder the cruell tyraũt *Nero*,for his
cōſtāt faith in Ieſus Chriſte,and treuth
of the ghoſpell,which he had preached,
turned him ſelf to the eaſt, and lyftinge
vp his handes to heauen prayed a greate
while,and when he had ended his prayer and geuen peace to his bretherne
whiche folloed him , and taken his leue
of them all , *Flexis genibus cruciſque ſigno ſē*
muniens ceruicem præbuit percuſſori. Faul-
linge downe vppon his knees,and bleſ-
ſinge him ſelf with the ſigne of the croſ
ſe,held owt his necke to the burreau or
hangeman

Abdias li-
bro. 2.

hangeman.

When S.Andrewe had done manye myracles and conuerted diuers to the faith in *Patras* a citie of *Achaia*,it fortuned that *Maximilla* the lieutenauntes wyffe inftructed in the faithe did fo digently attend vppon the Apoftle , whiles her hufband was in *Macedonia* , that at his returne home he had almoft taken her and a greate company of other men and woomen hearinge the worde off god in his palace with the Apoftle: which thinge S.Andrevze forfeinge, fel downe vppon his knees and prayed in this forte . Suffer not lorde the lieutenaunt to come into this place, before al be departed hence: which when he had done , the lieutenaunt before he coulde come in,was by necefsitie driue to go in to a fecret place to the fecretes of nature:and whiles he taryed there,S. Andrewe leying his hades vppon the that were with him , and fygninge them with the croffe, fuffred them to depart. *Noui- fsime autem fe fignans & ipfe difcefsit* . And *Abdias. lib 3.*

laſt off al bleſsinge him ſelff departed thence.

When S. Iohn had in *Epheſus* by his worde only forced the temple and Idol of *Diana* to faulle downe and fitter in pieces, as duſt, which the wide bloweth from the face of the earth, *Ariſtodemus*, chiefe myniſter and ſuperintendent o- uer the idols, poſſeſſed with a wicked ſprite rayſed a greate ſedition amon- geſt the people, in ſo muche that they were redy to fight. Then ſayed S. Iohn O *Ariſtodemus*, what ſhall I do to take this rancour and malyce owt off thy harte. Marry ſayed he, yf thow wilt that I beleue in thy god, I will geue the poyſon to drinke, whiche yf thow drin- ke and doeſt not dye, then ſhall it appe- are that thy god, is the trewe god. S. Iohn ſayed, if thow geue me poyſon to drinke, after that I haue caulled vppon the name of my god, it ſhall not be hable to hurte me. To be ſhorte he to ke the pot of poyſon, and bleſsinge it with the ſigne of the croſſe, made his prayer to god to god,and his prayer being complete and ended . *Os suum & totum semetipsum armauit signo crucis, & bibit totum quod erat in calice.* He bleſſed his mouthe and al his bodie, with the ſigne of the croſſe, and drunke vp al,that was in the pot S. Clement apoynted by S.Peter to be his ſucceſſour,teaching what a biſhop praying with the prieſtes and hauinge a goodly cope vppon his backe , ſtandinge at the aulter ſhulde ſaye, ſaieth. *Trophæo crucis ſe conſignans in fronte,dicat Gratia omnipotentis Dei,& charitas Domini noſtri Ieſu Chriſti ſit cum omnibus vobis* . Let the biſhop ſigning his forhead with the ſigne of the croſſe ſaye. The grace of almightye god,the loue of oure lorde Ieſus Chriſt,be with yowe al. S . Anthonie , going to viſite the holy father and good Eremite Paule ſawe by the waye a monſter caulled of the poetes *Hippocentaurus* in the vpper parte lieke a man, in the nether parte lieke a horſe . *Quo viſo ſalutaris impreſſione ſigni armat frontem,* *&c.* Whiche monſter being ſene he armed

H 4   med

Abdias lib 5.

Lib.8.cap. 16.conſt. Apoſt.

Hiero. in vita Pauli Eremita.

med his forhead with the imprefsion of
the healthfull figne, and by and by the
monfter runninge fwyftly ouer the fielde, vanifhed out of fight. S. Martin biffhop of Toures in Frauce, a mã of greate
vertue and holines, as *Sulpitius Seuerus*

In vita. D.
Martini. writeth, *Se aduerfus diabolum figno crucis*
& orationis auxilio protegebat: Defended
him felf ageynft the diuell with the figne off the croffe and healpe off prayer.

Sozo.lib.
9.cap.46
Trip. *Donatus* biffhop of *Euoria Epyri*, when
a terrible hydious dragon lyfted vp his
heade, and was redie to deuoure him,
made before his face the figne off the
croffe with his finger, and killed the
dragon.

To this if it pleafe yow to adde the
example of a woman, *Paula* noble a womã of Rome, of fuch ardẽt zeale to god,
feruent loue to her neyghbour, and ex-

Ad Eu-
ftoch. Epi-
taph. Pau-
læ. ceffiue liberalitie to the poore, that as S.
Hierome writeth, the whole worlde
fpoke off her, al prieftes woundred at
her, al vertuous virgins wiffhed for her,
and al religious perfons, lamented her
when

when she died, of whom he writeth no
thinge for flatterye, but taketh Christe, and all his sainctes to witnesse, that
whatsoeuer, he speaketh of her is far
lesse then she deserued, blessed her selff
with the signe of the crosse: and coming
in her peregrination to Hierusalem, as
S. Hierome there describeth, *Postrata ante crucem quasi pendentē Dominum cerneret,
adorabat*: Fawlinge flat before the crosse, as though she had sene oure lorde
hanging there, did worshipp it. Marke
good readers how this good ladye, did
both blesse her self with the signe off
the crosse, and also worship it. And this
historie is so notable, both for the per-
son that did it, and the authour that
wrote it, that if there were no other, I
suppose it woulde moue yow to thinke,
that is nether superstition to blesse you
re self with the signe of the crosse, nether
idolatrie to worship it. For if it had bene either superstition or idolatrie, nether woulde that vertuous ladye *Paula*,
renouncinge the worlde, and sekinge
the

It is no su
perstition
to blesse
oure sel-
ues vvith
the signe
of the
crosse.

the honour of Chrift, and trew feruice
of god, haue bleft her felf with the figne
off the croffe, nor worfhipped it: nether
woulde S. Hierome beinge much conuerfant with her, and writing the difcourfe of her lif, and reportinge nothing
of her but that which was trewe, and
caullinge Chrift to witnes, that he fayned nothing in ether parte, but wrote
as it becomed a Chriften man off a
Chriften woman, a trew hyftorie, not
a panegyrical oration, S. Hierome I fay
woldnot haue reported this amongeft
her other godly vertues, and fpoke that
in her commendation which was (yff
it be trewe that heretickes fay) to her
fhame, and accompted that for vertue,
which was vyce, and that for trew religion which was vayne fuperftition.

Now that the Apoftles and fathers
off the primityue churche counfelled
all Chriften men, to bleffe them felues,
it well appeareth bothe by that, which
Abdias writeth of S. Paule, Andrewe,
and Iohn, recited before, (for their doinges

inges be vnto vs as inſtructions,and examples as counſells) and alſo by the expreſſe wordes off diuers auncient fathers. Holy Ephrem ſaieth : *Pingamus in* De pæni-
ianuis,atque in frontibus noſtris & in ore,& tentia.
in pectore , atque in membris omnibus v iui-
ficum ſignum . Armemur inſupe rabili hac
Chriſtianorum armatura.Ea enim victrixeſt
mortis,fidelium ſpes , lux orbis terræ , paradiſi
reſdtatrix hæreſium proſligatrix , dæmonum
expulſatrix: Let vs paynt in oure gates, The croſ-
and printe in oure forheades,faces,bre- ſe putteth
aſtes , and al partes of oure bodie, the reſi.
lyuely ſigne , let vs be armed with this
inuincible armour of Chriſten men:for
this is the cõquerour of death , the hope of faythefull,the light oft the world,
the key off paradiſe , the abandoner off
hereſy,the expeller of diuells, the healpe of religious,the piller off faythe, the Euery
comfortable warde, and perpetual glo- Chriſten
ry off the faythful : *Hanc o Chriſtiane ar-* man muſt
maturam diebus ſingulis, horis, & mometis, ſelſt.
in omni loco circumferre non deſinas. Ceaſſe
not ô Chriſten man , to carry about
       with

with the this armour in euery place,
day and night, howre and moment:and
do nothing withowtit , but whether
thow fleape or wache , iournye or contynewe at worke , eate or drinke,fayle
ouer fea or ryuer,*Hac te lorica circumtege,*
membraque tua omnia falutari figno exorna,
atque circumfepi: neque accedent ad te mala.
Couer thy felf rownde with this cote-
armour,adorne and befett all partes off
thy bodye rounde abowte with the figne off faluation : and no euill fhall come vnto the.

Ho.55. in
16. Math. Chrifoftome fayeth *In fronte ac mente,*
magno ftudio crucem inferamus: hanc non
fimpliciter digito in corpore , fed magna fide
in mente prius formare oportet . Let vs with
great ftudy and earneft zeale , fet in oure forheades and myndes the croffe: we
muft not fimply and only , with oure
finger make this croffe in oure bodyes,
but firft off all with greate fayth in oure
myndes.And in another place rebukin-
ge the fuperftition off certeyne,that toke durte owt off hot batthes and a-
noynted

noynted their childrens heades, he hath
thes wordes. *Nolite hec fratres, sed a primis* Ho.11. in 1. Corinth.
annis filios vestros spiritualibus armis munia-
tis: & cruce sibi signanda frontem erudiatis, &
priusquam ipsi per se facere possunt, vos id
facite. O bretherne do ye not this, but Fathers and mo-thers.
with spirituall armour defend youre
children euen from their tender yeres, must te-ache their children to blesse them sel-ues.
and teache them to make the signe off
the crosse in their forheades : and before they are hable to do it them selues,
do ye it for them. S. Hierome in his epi- To. 1.
stle ad *Demetriadē* saieth , *Crebro signaculo*
crucis munias frontem tuam, ne exterminator
Ægipti in te locum reperiat: Defend thy
forhead oftentimes with the signe of
the crosse , lest the destroyer of Aegipt
finde place in the. And writinge to *Eu-* De custo. vir.
stochium, he saieth A*d omnem actum, ad om-*
nem incessum, manus pingat crucem. whatsoeuer yowe do , whether soeuer yowe
go, let youre hand make a signe of the De restitu-dine catho. cōuersatio-nis.
crosse: S. Augustine instructinge and te-
achinge men sinceritie of lyffe and ho-
nest conuersation , sayeth *Facite quæ pre-*
cepta

tepta sunt, habete Christum semper in mente,
signum eius in fronte facite , scitote quia mul-
tos aduersarios habetis, qui cursum vestrū im-
pedire festinant, ideo omni loco, omni hora cru-
cis signo vos armate . Do those thinges
which are commaunded : haue Christ
alwayes in minde : make his signe in
yower forheades : vnderstande ye that
yowe haue many enemies which hasten
to staye youre course , therefore in euery place and at al times , arme youre selues with the signe of the crosse. *Pruden-*
tius sayeth.

Lib. Cathe
merinon.
hymno an-
te somnum
Fac cum vocante sommo
  Castum petis cubile,
Frontem locumq; cordis
  Crucis figura signet.

That is in effecte to saye , see when
sleape coming vppon the, thowe goest
to bed , thowe make the signe of the
crosse in thy forheade and in thy breast.
And why? marry sir
  Tali dicata signo
Mens fluctuare nescit. The minde dedicated or earnestly fixed vppon such a signe can

ne can not be inconstant and wauer.

Thus did these holy fathers, teach the people committed to their charge, and al other that desire to liue in quietnes of minde, and securitie from thefiery dartes off the deuill, and that not of them selues; but as they had receaued and lerned of their forefathers. For longe before the forenamed authours, *Prudentius Ephrem*, Chrisostome Hierome, and Augustine, Tertullian declareth that al Christen men commonly vsed to make the signe off the crosse in their forheades: his woordes be thes. *Ad omnem progressum atque motum, ad omnem aditum & exitum, ad vestitum & calceatum, ad lauacra, ad mensas, ad lumina, ad cubilia, ad sedilia, quacunque nos conuersatio exercet frontem signaculo terimus.* When so euer we go forth and moue forwarde, when so euer we come in or go owt, when so euer we put on oure apparel, and drawe on oure shewes, whe we wash, whe we sit downe at the table, when we haue light brought in when

we

we go to oure chambers, and sit downe, what so euer we haue to do, we make thesigne of the crosse i oure forheades. Lo good readers, in the time of the Apostels the signe of the crosse was vsed, and hath continued euer sence. In Tertullians time with in two hundred yeaies after Christe, men commonly blest thē selues with the signe of the crosse. In holy Ephremes tyme they did the lioke, the yere of oure lorde 380. They did so in Chrisostomes time, the yere of oure lorde, 431. They did so in S. Hieromes time the yeare off oure lorde god. 422. They did so in S. Augustines tyme, the yeare of oure lorde. 430. They did so in *Cyrillus* his time in the yeare of oure lorde 436. They did so in *Prudentius* his time *Anno Domini*. 465. and that by ernest requeft or rather expresse commaundemēt of these holy fathers . And shall we so far discredit , and disauthorise these graue, vertuous, and lerned men , as though they knewe not the scriptures, and trewe interpretation off the same?

As

As though they knewe not lyght from
darknesse, veritie from heresie, trewe religion from vayne superstition ? Alas
god forbed . Yf euer any men had the
trew meaning , and right sense of scripture, it must nedes be , that they had it,
who with humilitie made their owne
senses and fantasies captiues to the serui
ce of Christ, a nd with deuoute prayer,
holye life, and good intent, sought it of
the holy ghost, kept them selues in the
vnitie off the churche , and were nigh
the Apostles tyme , whose traditions
and doctrine were then freash in mens
mindes, and deliured as it where from
hande to hand: In these later dayes whē
the world is in declination, to seke the
trewth and trewe meaninge off godes
worde, of such as of greate singularitie,
and high pride contemne al other that
were before them, and vaunte them selues as trew reformers of Christen religion, sincere preachers of the ghospell,
and restorers off godes worde (as
thought Christ before their dayes had

2. Corinth, 10.

                        L   forsaken

forfaken his churche, and fent no trewe
fetters forth of his honour, no fincere
preachers of his trewth, no right interpre
ters of his will) and haue fuch affiaunce
in their owne wittes, that what fo euer
other men write or fpeake, contrarie to
their fantafie, they prefer their owne,
and vouchfauf not to caul for the grace of the holy ghoft, and fprite of inter
pretation, in humilitie of harte by fafting and prayer, but lyue diffolutely, in
the luftes of the fleafh, and more defire
to mayntayne their worldly wealthe,
carnal lybertie, and fenfual luftes then
the honour off god, and faluation off
mens foules (as al thes miniifters do) of
fuch I faye to feke the treuthe and trewe meaninge off godes worde, it is extreme follye. For We reade that *In no-*
Epift. Iudæ *uiſſimis temporibus venient illufcres, fecun-*
dum defideria fua ambulantes in impietati-
bus. In the later dayes there fhal come
deceuers walking after their owne defires in impietie and vngodlineffe: and
becaufe we fhuld the better beware off
them

thē, the bleſſed Apoſtle gaue vs a note
and marke to knowe them:and as it were ſaieth,will yowe vnderſtande who be
thes deceuers ? *Hi ſunt qui ſegregauerunt
ſemetipſos.* Thes are they who haue ſepa-
rated them ſelues:as the pacchers vp of
the Apologie haue openly profeſſed
them ſelues to haue done. And this ſeparation and goyng away from others
in the vnitie of Chriſtes churche is one
of the tokens that the later daye is at
hande ſaieth S. Paule. Beſides we reade *2.Theſſa.2*
that in the later daies charitie ſhal waxe
cold,impietie abounde , and that many *Math. 24.*
falſe Prophetes ſhal come in to the worl
de and deceue many . And that many
ſhal go from the fayth and geue eare to *1Timoh. 4*
the ſprites off errour , and deuiliſh doctrine off deuilles ,who in hypocriſie
ſpeake lies. Yff then thes be the later
dayes(as vndoutidly they are) and more later then when Tertullian,Ephrem
Cyrillus , Hierome , Auſtine, *Prudentius*
and other holy fathers wrote, thē muſt
it follo that nowe deceuers walking af-

ter their owne luftes in al impietie be
come in to the wordle, nowe charitie is
cold, nowe iniquitie aboundeth, nowe
falfe prophetes begone abrode, nowe
many go from the faith, and harken to
the fpirites off errour and deuilyfh doctrine of deuilles, couered vnder mynifters goundes, and fo confequently all
that is taught by them contrarie to the
fathers off the church, is nether the
trewth nor trew meaninge off gods
worde, but cockel, chaff, and darnel, and
they *Inimici qui fuperfeminant* the enemies that fowe ouer that which is fowed,
and as S. Paule fayeth, *Adulterantes verbū
dei*, corrupting the worde of god, *illufo-
res iuxta proprias concupifcentias ambulantes*,
deceuers walkinge accordinge to their
owne concupifcences, and luftes, *Mur-
muratores querulofi fecundum defideria fua
ambulantes, animales, fpiritum non habentes.*
Murmurers alwayes complayninge, wal
kinge after their owne defires, al worl-
delye, not hauinge the holy ghoft: for
the holy ghoft fleeth from the diffembler,

Math.13.

2.Cor.2.

2.Pet.3.

Epift.Iudæ

Sapien.1.

bler,and refteth only vppon the humble
and meke,which vertue can neuer be in
an heritike.

Yff any curious man befides thefe
playne and expreffe wordes of the doctours require fcripturealfo,we faie with
Tertulian that cuftome increafer, con-
firmer,and obferuer of faith,taught this
vfe of the croffe:and that this cuftome *Lib. de co-*
came of tradition : *Quo modo enim vfur-* *ro. militis.*
pari quid poteft , fi traditum prius non eft,
for how can a thinge be vfed , if it were
not firft deliured ? And traditions are
not fo lightly to be paft vppon , or caft
a way as oure newe mafters make men
beleue. For as S.Bafile faieth. *Si confuetu-* *Cap. 27. de*
dines quæ fcripto proditæ non funt tanquam *fpiri. fan.*
haud multum habentes momenti reijciamus,
imprudentes & ea damnabimus quæ in Euan-
gelio neceffaria ad falutem habetur:imo verius
ipfam fidei prædicationem, ad nudum nomen
contrahemus . Yf we reiect and caft a way
cuftomes which are not writté, as thinges of no greate valewe or price, we
fhall condéne before we be ware , thofe

thinges which in the ghofpel are accompted neceffary to faluation:yea rather we fhall bringe the preachinge of
faith to a naked name: Euen as we fee it
come to paffe nowe a daies.For in their
congregation , who haue reiected the
cuftomes and traditiõs of the Apoftles,
and auncient fathers , yowe maye heare and fee the name of the ghofpel, but
no euangelical fruictes, much bable of
the lorde,but no good workes in Chrift,
in talke much vehemency, but in deede
no charitie, in apparence an outwarde
fhew of lerninge, but in effect no fown-
de doctrine, a rhetoricall floriffh, but no
profounde knowledge. For as the fame
holy father Bafile fayeth . The doctrine which is preached in the church , we
haue partly owt off the written fcripture, and partlye we receaued off the traditions of the Apoftles , brought vnto
vs in myfterie : which both haue lieke
force and efficacy to piety.And no man
doth contrarie, or agayne faye them,
who hath any meane or fimple knowledge,

Cap.27.de
fpiri.fancto

ledge, in the lawes off the church.

Yff then such as haue agayne sayed
and reiected, the customes and traditions of the church haue no meane sight
in the lawes of the church (which lawes
are the worde off god) for as Leo the
greate teacheth, *Dubitandum non est, quic-*
quid ab ecclesia in consuetudinem deuotionis
est retentum de traditione Apostolica, vel de
spiritu sancti prodire doctrina, It is not to
be dowted, but what so euer is retayned
off the church in to custome off deuotion, cometh ether off the tradition off
the Apostles, ether of the doctrine of the
holy ghost) it must nedes follo, that
they them selues be *cæci & duces cæcorum*,
blinde and guides off the blinde, and so
faull bothe in to the deeke. But to talke off traditions off which S. Ciprian
sayeth *Non minus ratum est, quod dictante*
spiritu sancto, apostoli tradiderūt, quam quod
ipse Christus tradidit, That is off no lesse
authoritie which the apostles by the
suggestion off the holy ghost haue deliured, then that which Christ him selff

Ser. de ieiu-
nio pente-
cost.

Ser.de ab-
lutio.pedK.

L 4　　　delyured,

delyured, it perteyneth not to my purpofe, and therefore it omit it, and enter
in to the treatye off the thirde parte off
this article, that in the time of the Apoftles, and fathers of the primitiue church
the figne of the croffe was fet vp, in e-
uery place : And this is in parte proued

In he
third ar-
ticle. alredy in the third article, and thither
for that parte I remitt the reader . For
furder prouffe *Martialis,* one off the.72.
difciples fent owt by Chrift to preache,

Epift.ad
Burdega. faieth : *Crucem domini in quem credidiftis,*
deum verum & dei filium in mente, in ore,&
in figno tenete . Keepe the croffe of oure
lorde, in whome yow haue beleued, the
trewe god, and fonne of god, in youre
mynd, in youre mouthe, and in a figne.
With this figne the heauenly victorie is
geuen vnto vs , and by the croffe the
baptifme of god is fanctified. And what
ment Chriftes difciple thinke yowe
when he commaunded the Burdegalen
fians to haue the croffe of oure lorde in
a figne, but that they fhuld haue the figne of the croffe? In good faithe of fober
wittes

wittes it can be no otherwife taken: lett
hereticks wringe and wreft as longe as
they lift, to wife men they fhal neuer be
hable to perfuade the contrarie. Nowe
that it ftayed not here, but was fet vp,
and had in reuerence in other places,
and other ages, it apereth by *Athanafius*
who afkinge the queftion why all faith
full Chriften men, make croffes like
vnto the croffe of Chrifte, and make
not hinge lieke to the fpeare, reede, and
fpóge, beinge holy as the croffe: anfwe-
reth and faieth : *Crucis certe figuram ex*   *Queft. 39.*
duobus lignis componentes adoramus &c. we   *ad Anti.*
certes makinge the figure of the croffe,
of two pieces of wood adore and worfhip it, but if any infidell accufe and bla-
me vs, as though we adored and worfhipped wood, we maye eafely feparate
and diffolue thofe ii pieces of wood, and
defacinge the forme and figure of the
croffe by accomptinge them but mere
wood, perfuade the fame infidel, that
we worfhip not the wood but the figure
and figne of the croffe : of the fpeare,
reede

reede and fpōge we can not do, nor fhewe the fame.

Ah fee good readers in the tyme off
Athanaſius, biſſhop of Alexandria , who
ſtowtely refiſted Arrius , and al the Ar-
rians, and woulde not yeld one Iota to
thē, faithful Chriſten mē made croſſes
lieke vnto, the croſſe of Chriſte, and adored the fame . And Athanaſius him ſel-
ffe, was one of thofe faithful Chriſten
men. For he faieth, we make croſſes, we
worſhip and adore the figne of the croſ
ſe: which he woulde not haue done,
had he then adiudged it ether idolatrie,
or fuperſtition. Nowe when they were
made, yf any incredulous creature dowte, whether they were fet vp in priuate,
or publicke places or no, let him thinke
with him felf whether any man maketh
a fine veluet cote to ley vp in his preſſe,
or caufeth his fathers or derely beloued
frendes image to be paynted and portraicted in a fayre table to be caſt in a
corner, fet in an angle , or leyde in a cole houfe, and as he iudgeth of the one,
so let

ſo let him imagine of the other.

Furder in the citie of *Alexandria* in the time of *Theophilus* when the famous Idol *Serapis*, was throwen downe, and deſtroyed: *Vnuſquiſque ſignum crucis in po ſtibus in ingreſſibus, in feneſtris, in parietibus, columniſque depinxit.* Euery man paynted the ſigne of the croſſe, in poſtes, in entres of howſes, in windoes, in waulles, and pillars. And that it was ſo in *Cyrillus* time it wel apeareth by that which Iulian the Apoſtata, obiecteth to him and all Chriſtians, for making and worſhipping the ſigne of the croſſe. At Conſtantinople in Chriſoſtomes time, they had the croſſe ſaieth he *In domibus, in foro, in ſolitudine, in vijs, in mari, in nauigijs, in veſtibus, in armis, &c.* In houſes, in markets, in wildernes, in highwayes, in the ſea, in ſhippes, in garmentes, in armour. Euery man did ſo zelouſly take vnto him that maruelous and wonderfull gift. And in a nother place declaringe the vertue off the croſſe he commaundeth vs to ſet it, *In penetralibus, in parietibus, in*

Ruſſinus lib.2. de ecclesiast. hiſto. cap. 29

Cyrillus. 6 cōtr. Iulia.

In demonſtra. contra gentiles.

Ho. 55. in 16. Math.

bus,in feneſtris. In oure parlours , in oure
waulles,and in oure windoes.

Furder that it was ſet vp in Aphrica in
S.Auguſtines time , it appeareth by the
ſermon he made De *cruce & latrone.* His
wordes be theſe . *Antea crux nomen con-
dēnationis erat,nūc vero faſta eſt res honoris,
prius in dānatione malediſti ſtabat,nūc in oc-
caſione ſalutis ereſta eſt.* Before the croſſe
was a name of cōdēnatiō,nowe it is ma
de a matter of honour:before it ſtode in
dānatiō of a curſe,nowe it is ſet vp in oc-
caſiō and ſigne of ſaluatiō,Here I praye
youe(good readers what other ſenſe or
meaning can be gathred of thes wordes
of S.Auguſtine,but that he maketha dif
feréce betwene the croſſe in the old lawe , and the croſſe in the newe lawe?
And declareth that as then the material
croſſewas a name of ignominie,ſo nowe
the material croſſe is a name,yea and *res*
a thing off honour,and as thē the materi
al croſſe ſtode in many places in damna
tion of a curſe , (that is to ſaye as a curſed ſigne of dānatiō)ſo nowethe materi
al

al croſſe is ſet vp in moſt places as a ſigne of bliſſe:For he ſaieth. *Crux in occaſio-
neſalutis erecta eſt.* The croſſe is ſet vpp in
occaſiõ or ſigneof ſaluatiõ,which wordes can not be racked to a Metaphorical
ſenſe , nor to the time of Chriſtes paſſion only in the mounte off Caluarie :
For he ſaieth , *Nunc erecta eſt* . Nowe at
this preſent, in the tyme of grace it is ſet
vp:and Chriſten men haue the ſigne of
it , as in another place more playnly he
declareth,ſaying. *Habent Chriſtianorum* Lib.de vi-
arcana,illud dominicæ crucis quaſi quoddam ſitat. infir-
venerabile monumentum,quod de crucis ipſius mo.cap. 3.
imaginatione crucẽ cognominant, &c . The
ſecret myſteries of the Chriſtians haue
that of oure lordes croſſe , as a certayne
honorable monumẽt,which of the imagination of the croſſe it ſelfe, they caul
a croſſe: which we acknowledge to be
moſt worthy off al honour , and in remembraunce of Chriſte crucified, wor-
ſhipp the ſame. De vita Cõ
ſtan. lib.3.
Beſides all theſe we reade in *Euſebius*
howe Conſtantine the great ſerued
Chriſt

Chriſt the ſonne of god boldely, and
was nothinge aſhamed of the name off
a Chriſtian, but eſteming it a greate honour and renowne, openly ſhewed him
ſelf to be one in deede . *Nunc vultum*
ſuum ſalutari ſigno communiens, nunc victo-
riale trophœum oſtentans, quod & in picta ta-
bula quadam ſublimiſſima, & præ foribus im-
perialibus ſuſpenſa, omnium oculis viſendam
proponebat . Some tymes defendinge his
face with the ſigne of ſaluation, ſom-
tymes ſhewinge foorth the victorious
enſigne and banner, which he ſet foorth
to be ſene of al men in a certayne high
paynted table , hanged vp before his
courte gate. But what nede I ſeeke ſuch
and lieke authorities, ſeinge Chriſoſtome in one worde telleth vs, that , *In to-*
to orbe crux . The croſſe is in all the
worlde, where Chriſte, and Chriſtes
faith and ghoſpel was receaued and prea
ched. And now a maruelous caſe. They
that profeſſe them ſelues trewe Chriſtians, trewe preachers of Chriſtes faith,
and ghoſpel, haue deſpiſed Chriſtes croſ
ſe, caſt

De vita
conſtantini
lib.3.

The em-
perour
Conſtãti-
ne ſet the
ſigne off
the croſſe
on high
in a table
at his co-
urte ga-
te.

In demon-
ſtra:contra
gent.

se, cast it owt of churche, chappel , and
oratorie, pluckt it owt of priuate houses,
scraped it owt of windoes , and waulles,
pluckt it downe by high wayes , and
with fier and faggot , axe and hacchet,
destroyed it euery where : much resem-
bling the impietie of those Iewes, who
in despite of Christ, crucified his image
in a citie caulled *Berythus* as Athanasius saieth , and not far degenerating
frō the wickednes of certayne heretikes
in *Tyrus* who coming into the church
of oure lady, stoned a crosse as *Epipha-*
nius writinge to the fyft Synode of a Cō To. 2. ꝯcil.
stantinople declareth . They that pro-
fesse them selues foloers of the Apostles
and fathers of the primitiue church, accompte their doinges folly , and superstition . They which acknowledge thē
selues schollers, countermaūde their masters, which thinge howe wel it agreeth
to their vocation, iudge yowe good readers. Certes in this poynte , and almost
al others, they follo the Apostelles and
auncient fathers, as the oxe foloeth the
plowe,

plowe, the horſe the carte, the hare the
hounde. Wherefore as in this yow finde them fayle, ſo may yowe right well
thinke they do in all their aſſertions
which they do as blindely and boldely
aſſeuer e ageynſt the doctrine of the catholike churche, the the piller of treuth
and ſpouſe of Chriſt. Wherefore for
Chriſtes ſake thinke deliberatly vppon
it: And yf yow be carefull of youre owne ſoules and myndfull of æternal ſaluation, forſake them by tyme, geue thē
ouer in playne field, requoyle to the citie that ſtandeth vppon the hill, flee to
the caſtel that ſhal neuer be ouer throwen by hell gates, repayre to the rich
ſtore howſe, in to the which as *Irenæus*
Lib.3.cap. writeth Apoſtoli pleniſ ime contulerunt om-
4.aduer- *nia, quæ ſunt veritatis.* The Apoſtles haue
ſus hære. moſt plentifully brought al thinges ap
pertayninge to the treuth. There ſhall
ye finde reſt, for youre ſoules, and obtayne the crowne of glory, which ye ſe-
ke and labour for.

Diuerſe

DIVERSE HO-
LY MEN AND VVO-
MEN GOT LITLE PIECES
OF THE HOLY CROSSE, AND
inclofed them gold, or filuer, and
ether left them in churches to
be worfhipped, or hanged
them aboute their nec-
kes there by to be
the better war-
ded.

Or prouffe of this article
we haue diuerfe notable
ftories, and to begynne
with that vertuous lady
Helena Conftantines mo
ther who was cõmaun-
ded by reuelation from god to go to
Hierufalem and feke the precious croffe
of Chrift, hid vnder a heape of ruble
and ftones, in the moũte Caluarie where the Iewes to abolyfhe the memory of

Chriftes

6

A TREATYSE

Chriftes paffion, had builded a temple
to the harlot *Venus*, *Eufebius* in his ec-

Lib.10.c.8
ecclefiafti.æ
hifto.

clefiafticall hiftorie, faieth, *Helena Con-
ftantini mater partem ligni falutaris detulit
filio,partem thæcis argenteis conditam dereli-
quit in loco,quæ etiã nunc follicita veneratione feruatur.*That is to faye.*Helena* Conftantines mother, brought parte of the
healthful wood to her fonne, parte fhe
left in the place inclofed in filuer cafes:
which is kept at this prefent day with
greate veneration and reuerence.

In lieke manner *Procopius*, an old
greeke hiftoriographer declareth, and
Nicephorus owt of him, that the inha-

Lib.17.cap
15..Eua.
grius
Lib.4.cap.
26.ecclefi.
aftiçæ hifto.

bitantes of *Apamæa* a cytie of *Afia* the
leffer,had a piece of the holy croffe, and
vfed the fame as a defence,ageynft their
greate enemy *Cofroes* king off *Perfia*
who with fier and fworde had deftroyed Antioche:his wordes be thefe.*Quũ
Apamæi Antiochiam incendio vaftari cogno-
uiffent,Thomam Apamæorum epifcopum ro-
gauerunt,vt falutiferum & viuificum crucis
lignum præter folitum proferret & proponeret,*
vt fi

vt si extrema periclitanda essent, solam morta-
lium salutem contuentes cōplecterētur, & alte-
rius vitæ compendiũ, preciosa cruce ad melio-
rem ipsos ducente sortem acciperent : fæcit hoc
Thomas: protulitque viuificum lignum &c.

When the Apameians knewe the cytie
off Antioche to be destroyed with fier,
they desired Thomas their bysshop to
bring foorth the healthfull and lyuely
wood of the crosse, and sett it in the
sight of the people, otherwise thē their
vsual manner was, that yf they shulde
be in extreme daunger, they seing the
only saluation of men, might embrace
that, and receaue the blysse of the other The croslyf, the crosse leadinge them to better foorth to
chaunce. Thomas did so much at their the peorequeft, and brought owte the lyuely vvorshipwood of the crosse, and certeyne ordy- ped.
narie dayes, set it forth to the peoples
sight, that all the cytie, might resorte vnto it, and frō Christ, by meane of that,
haue helpe. And so as the hystorie spe-
cifieth it chaunced in dede. For at that
tyme they were delyuered from al feare

of warre, and daunger of kinge Cosroes
pouer, and tyrannye.

Paulinus bisshop of *Nola*, had a piece
off the holy crosse sent vnto him from
Hierusalem, by a blessed woman caulled
Melania. And when his frend *Seuerus*
buildinge a church, and lackinge holy
relickes (required to the consecration of
euery church,) complained by letters to
Paulinus, *Paulinus* sent him a litle peice of
the holy crosse, and amongest other
thinges, in his epistle he hath these
Epist.11. woordes. *Accipite magnum in modico mu-*
nus: & in segmento pene atomo hastæ breuis,
sumite munimentum præsentis, & pignus æ-
ternæ salutis. Non angustetur fides vestra car-
nalibus oculis parua cernentibus, sed interna
acie, totam in hoc minimo vim crucis videat:
dum videre vos cogitatis lignum illud, quo sa-
lus nostra pependit. Receaue ye a great re-
ward in a litle: and take in the paringe of
a shorte splinter, almost no bigger then
a gnat the defence of this præsent, and
pledge off eternal health. Let not youre
fayth be strayted seinge litle thinges
with

with youre carnal eies, but let it behold
with the inward eie, al the force of the
crosse in this litle, whiles yowe thinke
yowe see, that very selff same wood, in
which oure saluatiō did hange, and this
I send yow saieth he, *vt crucem & corpo-*
re possideretis, quam tenetis & spiritu, & pro-
positi virtute portatis. That yowe might
haue, and possesse with youre body the
crosse, which yow kepe in sprite, and be
are in good harte, intent, and mynde. S.
Gregorie writinge to Recharede kinge
of the wisigothes after he had specified,
the principall poyntes of his letters, saieth, *Crucem quoque latori præsentium dedi-*
mus vobis offerendam, in qua lignum domi- Lib. 7.
nicæ crucis in est, & capilli beati Ioannis Ba- Epistola.
ptistæ, ex qua solatium nostri saluatoris per Epist. 126.
intercessionem præcursoris habeatis. We haue
also geuē to the bearer of thes presentes,
a crosse to be delyured vnto yowe, in the
which is a piece of the wood of oure lor
des crosse, and heare of S. Iohn Baptist,
owt of the which yowe may haue the
cōforte of oure sauiour by the intercef
M 3   siō off

fion of the forerunner of oure lorde.

But what nede I feke old hiftories?
Chrifoftome writinge ageynft the gentills declareth this in moft expreffe and

Men de- playne wordes . *Ipfum hoc lignum* fayeth
firous to he,*in quo pofitū eft fanctum corpus domini &*
haue pie
ces of the crucifixum , quare nam habere totus orbis ita
holy crof- *contendit ut qui paruum quiddam ex illo ha-*
fe.
bent, hoc auro includant,tam viri quam mu-
lieres,& ceruicibus fuis aptant , hinc valde ho-
neftati & magnifici ,muniti & protecti licet
condemnationis fuerit lignum? Why then
doth al the whole worlde , fo earneftly
defire and labour to haue that very felff
fame wood,in which the holy body off
oure lorde , was put to death and crucified,in fo much that they who haue a
litle piece of it,inclofe it in golde,as wel
men as women , and make it meete for
their necks , by that right highly hone-
fted and honoured , defended and garded , although fome tymes it was the
wood of condemnation?

Now then yf in thofe dayes fuch was
the deuotion of good men and women,
that

that they fo earneftly defired and labo-
red to haue fome litle piece of the holy
croffe, and when they had got any par-
teofit,inclofed it in golde or filuer, and
left it in churches to be reuereced,or hā-
ged it aboute their neckes, by meane of
that to be defended , and as Chrifoftome fayeth,many were *protecti & muniti* Men de-
defended and garded , and the croffe it fended by
felf was of fuch power , that it warded the holy
them from their enemies,who reuerent- croffe.
ly adored and worfhipped it,what cawfe
is there,why we fhuld not haue the lieke deuotion , zeale , and defire to feeke
fome part off that holy croffe , and yff
happely we get any piece of it,why fhuld
we not fet it in gold,filuer,and precious
ftone?why fhuld we not leue it in churches to be reuerenced ? why fhuld we
not hange it aboute oure neckes therby
through the goodnes of god , to be the
better warded? Why fhuldnot we thinke
it hath nowe that vertue , efficacie and
pouer,which it had then ? *Nunquid ab-* *Efaie.50.*
breuiata eft manus domini? Is the hande oft

Mala.3. oure lorde fhortened?no no . *Ego domi-*
Hebr.13. *nus qui non mutor.Iefus Chriftus heri & ho-*
die,ipfe & in fecula. I am thy lorde which
am not chaunged.Iefus Chrift is yefterday,andto day,andhe for euer.

But peraduenture fome wil faye it
may be, that as god permitted defeafes
to be cured,and deuills expelled by the
napkins,and partlets,that were brought
Acto.19. from the body of S . Paule: So Chrift
becaufe that wod of the holy croffe
fometymes touched his moft tender fle
afh and precious body, permitteth the
forfaied effectes to be wrought by it.
Marry that the lieke vertues be done by
a fimple croffe made of other matter, as
gold,filuer,precious ftone,or fuch lieke,
or expreffed in the ayer,with mans håde
ouer the thinge that is to be figned,it is
not proued, nor it appeareth by the authorities alleaged before. For anfwere I
faye,that euery litle piece and portion
of that holy croffe,vppon which Chrifte the light of the worlde and faluation
of man dyed,is a rich iewel,and in-
eftima-

estimable threasure, which whosoeuer
hath may accōpte him self most happy.
And as Christ by touche of his tēder fle
ash gaue the wood of that crosse, a spe
cial vertue and pouer:So by faith and in
uocatiō of his holy name,he gueueth the
lieke to other crosses, or made of some
earthly matter or expressed by some mās *Lib.2.ad*
hande.For as *Athanasius* declaringe how *Maca:de*
before the cominge of Christ deuils mi *incar.*
serably afflicted men, and howe when
Christ was come they were discomfited
and ouerthrowē,saieth .*Signo crucis tātū*
*ytēs homo,oēs horū fallacias pellit.*Man vsin-
ge only the signe of the crosse putteth
awaye al their subtiltie and craft.And in
the same place,to make the matter more playne he hath thes woordes. *Veniat*
qui harum rerum experimenta quærit addif-
cere,ipsiusque dæmonum pompæ, diuinatio-
num fallaciæ, & magiæ mirabilium,ytatur si-
gno,(yt ipsi dicunt)ridiculæ crucis Christum
solummodo nominans,videbit per ipsum fuga-
ri dæmones,vaticinia conticescere, & magiam
*omnem omneque veneficium destrui.*Let any
man

man come that defireth to learne experience of thefe thinges, and of the very
pompe of the deuils, fubtilty of diuination,and ftraunge fightes by wichcraft:
let him vfe the figne of the folifh croffe
(as they faye) but only naming Chrifte, he fhall fee the deuilles to be put to
flight by it, al diuination ceaffe, and all
magick and wichcraft deftroyed : Furder S.Auguftine faieth . *Quod faciebat in*
terris corporis Chrifti præfentia, hoc facit cum
fideli inuocatione nominis Chrifti, victoriofæ
crucis infignita memoria . Looke what the
præfece of Chrift did in earth, the fame
doth the memorie of the victorious crof
fe expreffed in a figne, with the faythful inuocation of the name of Chrift.
And as *Euthymius* writeth . *Per virtu-*
tem crucis dæmonum expelluntur caterua, &
ægrotationes variæ curantur,ea gratia & vir
tute que femel in prototypo & primogenio fuit
efficax,ad ipfius quoque crucis effigies , vna
cum fimili efficacia procedente.By the figne
of the croffe companies of deuills are
expelled, and diuerfe defeafes healed:
the

Ser. de an-
nūtia.

Tit 19.par
te 2. pano-
plie.

the same grace and vertue which was ones effectuous, in the first saumpler and patterne, proceding also with lieke efficacie, to the very figures and signes of the crosse, which thing *Cassiodorus* In expos. semeth to approue, saying. *Sicut terres-* Psalmi 1. *tris aqua decurrens vita est lignorum virentium, si aqua spiritalis signum crucis inundat: quæ salus esse cognoscitur fidelium animarum* As earthly water dropping downe, is the lif of greene trees, so spiritual water doth floweinto the signe of the crosse, which is knowē to be the saluatiō off faithfull soules. Thus good readers yowe see by thes holy fathers, howe the signe of the crosse by faith in the merites of Christes passion, and caulling vppon his holy name hath vertue to expel diuells, destroye wychcrafte, cure deseases, and worke in some pointes, that which oure sauiour Christ did here in earth, according to his holy wil and ordinaunce.

That

THAT A CROS-
SE VVAS BORNE AT
THE SINGING OR SAY-
ING OF THE LITA-
nie which we om-
monly caul pro-
cefsion.

7.

Lib. 8. *cap.*
8. *'ecclefia-*
fticæ hifto-
rie.

Or the treuth of his article we haue in *Sozomenus*
this notable hiftorie: At
what time the Arrianes
in the raigne of the good
emperour *Theodofius* were fet befide their churches in Conftantinople, they ma
de their affemblees without the waulles of the citie: (as the Hugonotes did of
late *in* Fraunce) and when the congregation was gathred to gether, they diuided them felues into companies, and
fonge pfalmes and hymnes made in ry-
me after their owne guife, with additi-
ons for prouffe and defence off their
owne

owne doctrine, as they did of late vnder
the greate patriarch Iohn of *Geneua*, and
do nowe vnder oure newe Rabbines in
Englãd, which thíg the good bishop and
and vigilaunt pastour Chrisostome espying, lest some of the catholikes allured
with the plasaunte casure of their miter,
and swete founde of their rime, shulde
go to their assemblees, diuised also certen hymnes in myter and made them
sing them in the same tune that the Arrianes did: whereby it came to passe that
the catholikes far passed them in numbre, and in solemnitie of procession. For
saieth *Sozomenus, Argentea crucis signa v-*
na cum cereis accensis præcedebant eos. Before
the catholikes went two siluer crosses
with tapers or torches burning : Loe
(good readers) Chrisostome an auncient father, and one of the most famous
doctours of the greke church and re-
nõmed for vertue and lerning through
owt the worlde, had the signe of the
crosse and tapers with light caried in
his churche off Constantinople before
his

Crosses
and ta-
pers cari-
ed in pro-
cession.

his people in proceſſion. And note with
al, that the Arrianes at the ſynging off
their hymnes had no croſſe, euen as oure heretikes wil haue none nowe a dayes at the ſynging of their Lordes prayer, and that becauſe nether their lorde
nor they can abyde the ſight of the croſ
ſe. For yf they could, they could not be

De pœnitē- heretikes. For *Crux eſt hæreſiũ expulſatrix.*
tia. cap. 3. ſaieth holy Ephrem: the croſſe is an expeller and driuer away of hereſie.

Wel ſtep a litle furder, and come to
Iuſtinianes time, who liued more then
a thouſand yeares ago. In him yowe
ſhal finde two lawes meete for this
purpoſe: The one is in his boke intitled
Codex, The other in his Nouelles or later cõſtitutions : In his Code he ſaieth.

De epiſcop *Laicis facere Litanias interdicimus ſine cleri-*
& cler. l.
ſed nemo. *cis: quæ ſine orationibus & cruce fieri non de-*
bent. We prohibite and forbed al laye mē
to make any proceſsion, without prieſtes, which ought not to be made with
oute praiers and a croſſe. Marke the emperours wordes good readers, he ſaieth.

Litaniæ

Litaniæ non debent fieri sine cruce. The Litanie ought not to be saied, nor procession made without a crosse. Wherefore oure newe masters must resume the crosse agayne in their litanie, or els haue none at al, iff Iustinianes lawe be of any authoritie amongest them, and for that I thinke they woulde not much passe: But let vs loke to his later constitutions where he saieth more at large, *Omnibus* *Laicis interdicimus Litanias facere sine sanctis episcopis, & qui sub eis sunt reueredissimis clericis. Qualis enim est Litania in qua sacerdotes non inueniuntur & solemnes orationes faciunt? Sed & ipsas honoraudas cruces cum quibus & in Litanijs ingrediuntur non alibi nisi in venerabilibus locis reponi, & si quando opus vocauerit ad Litanias celebrandas, tunc solum ipsas sanctas cruces accipere eos qui consuete eas portare solent, & cum episcopo & clericis Litanias celebrare.* We prohibite and forbed al laye men to make any procession with out the holy bishops and most reuerend priestes that are vnder them: For what manner of Litanie or procession

De sanctif. Episco. ca. 32. col. 9.

fion is that where no prieftes are founde?and where the prieftes make not folemne prayers? Furder we chardge and
commaunde that the honorable croffes
with which they go in procefsiō be not
put and layed, but in fome femely and
decent place. And whenfoeuer nede
fhal require and caul to fing or faye the
Litanie,that then they only take he ho
ly croffes who were commonly accu-
ftomed to beare them, and fo with the
biffhops and priftes make a folemne pro
cefsion.

Here alfo good readers yowe fee by
this lawe off Iuftinian the emperour,
that more then a thoufande yeares ago,
Chriften men had croffes in the churche, and vfed the fame in finging and
faying the Litanie.Befides youe fee that
thē(as by the wordes of the lawe it may
be gathred)they went aboute in procef-
fion,and fate not ftil in the quier, and
caried the croffe with thē, not fixed it
ftil in one place at that time. And this
beganne not in Iuftinians time,but lōg
before

before, as by other wordes of the lawe
it may wel be gathred. But I wil not
grate vppon wordes, nor ſtand nowe
vppon examination of them, ſeing o-
therwiſe they manifeſtly confirme the
trewth of this cauſe. Wel let vs come
lower, yea euē to oure owne countrie.
When the religious father, Auguſtine
ſent from Rome by S. Gregory to con-
uert vs to the faith (whome next vnto
god we muſt thanke that we were delyured from the captiuitie of the deuil,
and made partakers by faith of the meri
tes of Chriſtes paſsion) when I ſay
this holy father and his company came
into England, they came to the king,
not, as he ſuſpected, *Dæmoniaca, ſed diuina*
virtute, præditi, infected with deuiliſh
trumpery, but indued with heauenly
vertue: *Crucem pro vexillo ferentes argen-*
team, & imaginem domini ſaluatoris in tabu-
la depictam: litaniaſque canentes pro ſua ſimul
& eorum pro quibus venerant ſalute æterna
ſupplicabant. bringing a croſſe of ſiluer
for their banner, and the image of oure

Beda lib. 1.
cap. 22.
hiſtoriæ
Angli.

N   lord

lord and fauiour painĉted in a table: and
finging the Litanie they made earneſt fup
plication to god for the æternal faluation
of thé felues , and others for whofe fake
they came . And it was reported as Bede
faieth that whé they aproched nigh vnto
the citie with the croſſe and image off
the greate and mighty king Iefus Chriſt,
they fonge with a goodly fwete voyce,
this antemne:*Deprecamur te domine in omni mifericordia tua ʹʹt auferatur furor & ira
tua a ciuitate iſta, quia peccauimus* . In al thy
mercy we befeeke the O lorde that thy
indignatiō and fury may be také fró this
citie, and fró thy holy houfe,becaufe we
haue finned.Beholde good readers theho
ly fathers that came fró Rome wel nigh
a.1000 . yeres ago to delyuer vsfrom idolatrie,and fight ageinſt Satan prince off
darknes and lorde of idolatours , came
with their lordes image painĉted in a table,and their maſters banner ſpred to the
vewe and fight off the people , the croffe I fay. And they came not as falfe Prop
hetes,and men feduced with mad fanta-
fies

fies, but they came as the ftorie faieth *Diuina virtute præditi,* indued with heauély
vertue. And to plante the religion off
Chrift, they brought the image and croffe of Chrifte. And oure newe brothers
prætending to come into the field and
fight ageinft Satan for their mafter
Chrift, and reftore his faith againe, are
afhamed of their mafters enfigne, and
dare not fpred his banner: but labour as
bufely as they can, to haue it owt of the
field and fight of al Chriftes fouldiers.
Howe thinke youe? be thes faithful war-
riers? be thes trewe mé to their lorde? be
thes lieke to fight for Chrift, and reftore
his religion and faith, that can not abyde the fight of his image? nor figne off
his croffe? No No. neuer good fouldier
was in deadly hatred with his mafters bã-
ner and enfigne: but ioyious and glad rather whé he might fe it. But let vs retur-
me to oure purpofe. For furder declara-
tiõ and prouf that the croffe was vfed in
procefsion, we reade that at what tyme
the relickes of the holy Martir *Anafta-*
N 2   *fius*

ſius were brought owt of *Perſia* into *Cæ-*
ſaræa in Paleſtine, the people being maruelous glad of it, went foorth and met
them in oure Ladies church: *Illinc cum*
cruce & ſupplicatione egreſsi, læti & gaudentes
cū gratiarū actione ſacris reliquijs occurrerūt.
From thence they going foorth with a
croſſe and proceſsion, met the holy re-
likes ioyfully and with thankes geuing.
Behold againe mentiō made of procef-
ſion with a croſſe : and tranſpoſing the
holy martirs relickes from one place to
another, to the greate reioyſing off the
people. And as then oure forefathers v-
ſed the ſigne of the croſſe in proceſsion,
So hath the church alwaies continued
the ſame, to put vs in remembraunce,
that as euery good ſouldier muſte haue
an eſpecial regard to the capitaines banner and enſigne, vnder whome he ſerueth: So it behoueth vs (caulled by faith
to be the children off god, and apointed
to be Chriſtes ſouldiers) to haue oure
eies euermore fixed vppon his enſigne
and banner, and neuer remoue oure har-
                                    tes

tes from the côtemplation of his bitter
pafsion vppon the croffe:and to put vs
in comforte that we fhal ouercome al
the mighty force,and fearce affaultes off
oure aduerfaries with that figne , fo terrible by the merites off Chriftes death
to al wicked fprites, that when they
fee it,they ceaffe their rage,and
flee for feare owt of the fielde . And this for this a-
ticle may fuffife.

N 3   Many

MANY STRA-
VNGE AND VVOVN-
DERFVL MYRACLES
VVROVGHT BY THE
figne off the croffe.

8.

S oure fauiour Chrift conuerfant here vppon earth to bring men in belieffe that he was the trewe fonne off god, wrought by his omnipotency, might and power diuerfe miracles, by diuerfe external meanes, as by the hem off his cote he healed a woman off her blouddy flix, and diuerfe other fick perfons by the touch off his hande, and ipetle off his mouth he reftored the fight of the blind man, and opeaned the eares off the deaff, and by a playfter made off durt he healed fore eies : Euen fo by the fame omnipotency, might, and pouer he hath to aduauncement of his

honour,

Math. 9.
Mar. 6.

honour, and confusion of his enemies,
sithens his ascension wrought by diuerse
external meanes, diuerse straunge and
wounderful myracles, as by the shado-
we off S.Peter, napkins of S.Paule, ashes *Act.5.*
off his Apostles, tumbes off his Martirs, *Act.19.*
and signe of his crosse, as by good re-
cordes, and faithful histories may be
proued. But because it is not incident to
my purpose to treate of al such miracles,
as hath bene wrought by euery one off
the foresaied meanes, I wil leaue the
treaty of them to other, and declare only such as hath bene wrought by the
signe of the crosse, and not al those nether, but certen. And seing I am here
for the multitude in as greate perplexi-
tie where I shal beginne, as he is that sit
teth at a table furnished with many delicate dishes, whereof he shal first taste,
or as one that cometh into a garden set
rounde aboute with freash fragraunt
floures, which he may first gather, I wil
leaue al curiofitie, and as the hungrie
man to serue his appetite, fedeth vppon
N 4   that

that wich ſtandeth nereſt vnto him,
and he that cometh into a garden anoyed peraduenture with ſome noyſome
ſauour before, plucketh the firſt floure
he ſeeth: Euen ſo I hungry and deſirous
of their ſaluation who haue erred, and
anoyed with the venemous blaſtes off
their blaſphemous mouthes who haue
rayled ageynſt this holy ſigne, to help
them and eaſe my ſelf, wil take ſuch examples as be nereſt vnto me, and pluck
the floure which I firſt finde.

Euſeb. lib.
10. cap. 7.
& . 8. ec-
cleſiaſticæ
hiſto.

At what tyme the vertuous lady *Helena* willed as the ſtory mentioneth by
reuelation from god to ſeeke the croſſe
of Chriſt in *Hieruſalẽ*, founde after lõg
digging in the mounte of Caluary thre
croſſes ſo confuſe that nether by the
title which Pilate ſet vp in Hebreue, greke, and latyn, nether by any other meanes they could diſcerne which was the
croſſe that bore oure ſauiour Chriſt, a
noble woman of the citie conſumed
and ſpent with long ſickneſſe did lie at
deathes doore. *Macarius* then biſhop
off

of *Hierufalem* feing the good lady *Hele-na* ftaggring at the matter, and al her trayne difcomforted, faied vnto them bring hether the thre croffes which are founde, and god fhal open and reuele vnto vs, which is the croffe that caried oure fauiour Chrift. They did fo : and when the croffes were brought, *Maca-rius* went with *Helena* into the chamber where the forefaied noble woman lay, and being there, fel downe vppon his knees, and prayed in this forte. O lord who by thy only begotten fonne vouchfauffideft togeue faluation to al mankinde, by his death vppon the croffe, and haft infpired the harte of thy hand maydē in thes later dayes to feeke that bleffed wood in which oure faluation did hange, fhewe I befeek the, wich of thes thre croffes ferued to the glory of god, and which to the feruile punifhement of the theafes, that this ladye which lieth here half dead, may be brought from death to liff agayne, as fo ne as the wood of faluation hath touched

ched her . And when he had ended his prayer, he put vnto the sick woman one of the thre crosses , it auayled nothing: he put vnto her the second, no help came: he put vnto her the third, and as sone as euer it touched her, she opened her eies , rose out of her bed , and receuing strenght agayne , was more lustier and lyuelier then when she was in her best health, and wēt vp and downe the house, and magnified the greate mercy , and mighty pouer of god.

A vvomã half dead reuiued by the crosse.

By this example note good readers that god inspired the harte of that good lady *Helena* to seeke the crosse vppon which oure sauiour Christ was crucified, and that by touch of that holy wood, the noble woman which had no vse of her senses, no knowledg what was done about her, but ay as one half dead , was reuiued , and made lusty and strong agayne. Nowe if god would not haue Christ his crosse reuerenced , he wold not haue inspired that womans harte to haue sought it but rather haue

suffred

suffred it to haue lien couered with ruble and durte as it was before. And if he
wold not haue men vse it as a meane to
magnifie his holy name, and declare his
mighty pouer by doing some straunge
cure, and myracle, he wold neuer so my
raculously by the touch of it, haue reuiued that half dead and mortified gentil
woman. For god worketh nothing in
vayne.

Afterward to geue vs to vnderstand
that not only the whole crosse, but euery litle piece and percel of it, for that it
was ones imbrued with the water and
bloud of oure sauiour Christe, hath the
lieke efficacy and force, god wrought a-
nother straunge miracle by a litle splinter of the crosse: In *Nola* a greate citie
of *Campania* in Italie, a religious mans
cel was set a fier in the night by a litle cole or sparkle faulling into the stra-
we, and put the churche and citie in gre
ate daunger. The bishop *Paulinus* and
his clergy went to the church and prayed: the citizens came with al hast and
speade

speade to help. This not withstanding,
the fier increased: At the lenght the bisshop remembring him self, went home
to his house,and hauing a piece of the
holy crosse, brought it foorth, and held
it vp in to the fier,and by and by the flame which no water could quench, ceassed his rage and went no furder. This
story is written by *Paulinus* him self the
bisshop of *Nola*, a man for his lerning,
innocency of lif,and zeale to god,high-
ly commended of S.Ambrose:Hierome
and Austine:his woordes although they
be long, yet becaufe they ar effectuous,
and eafy to be borne away,for that they
are written in verfes, I wil not let to recite them here.After he had bene in the
churche and prayed with his clergy he
saieth:

Vide quæ præfigun-tur lib.Epistola.eius

Ipse domum remeans , modicum ,sed grande
saluti
De crucis aeternæ sumptum mihi fragmine lig-
num
Promo,tenensque manu aduersis procul inge-
ro flammis.

Vt

In 10. Natali Fælicis Mart.

*Vt clypeum retinens pro pectore, quo tegerem
    me,*

Arceremque hostem collato vmbone relisum:

*Credite : nec donate mihi , sed reddite Chri-
    sto*

Grates,& iustas date laudes omnipotenti.

*Nostra salus etenim cruce Christi & sangui-
    ne constat.*

*Inde fides nobis , & in hac cruce nixa , peri-
    clo*

*Profuit , & nostram cognouit flamma salu-
    tem:*

*Nec mea vox aut dextra illum, sed vis crucis
    ignem*

Terruit, inque loco de quo surrexerat ipso,

Vt circumseptam praescripto limite flammam,

*Sidere , & extingui fremitu moriente coe-
    git:*

*Et cinere exortam cineri remeare procel-
    lam.*

*Quanta crucis virtus , vt se natura relin-
    quat?*

*Omnia ligna vorans, ligno crucis vritur ig-
    nis.*

*Multa manus crebris tunc illa incendia va-
    sis*

fis
Aſpergens,largis cupiebat vincere limphis. .
Sed licet exhauſtis penſarent fontibus im-
bres,
Vi maiore tamen,laßis ſpargentibus,omnem
Vicerat ignis aquam ,nos ligno cxtinximus
ignem:
Quamque aqua non poterat vicit breuis ha-
ſtula flammam.

Thes verſes may be engliſhed thus.

I my ſelf going home agayne to my
houſe,brought out a piece of wood taken for me out of a ſmal ſplinter of the
æternal croſſe , litle for the quãtitie,but
greate for the vertue : and holding that
in my hãde,I thruſt it out into the fyer
ouer right ageynſt me, keaping it as a
buckler before my breaſt to defend my
ſelf,and put away my enemy.Beleue me
and geue not me but thankes to Chriſt,
and worthy prayſe to almighty god:for
oure ſaluation conſiſteth in the croſſe
and name of Chriſt:faith deriued vnto
vs from thence, and leaning faſt vppon
this croſſe auayled much ageinſt that
peril

peril of fier: and the flame knewe and acknowledged oure faluation, and nether my voyce, nether my hand, but the force and pouer of the croffe feared the fier, and compelled it as a flame compaffed with in a certen prefcript place, to ftay and dye without any cracking or noyfe, in the felf fame place where it beganne? O howe greate is the vertue of the croffe that nature doth forfake her felf? The fier that burneth al kinde off wood, is burned and confumed away with the wood of the croffe. Many men endeuoured with cafting off water to quench the fier, but although they did caft water as faft out of the fountaynes, as rayne faulleth by fhewers from heauen, yet for al that, when they had caft water with al their might, tyl they were wery, the fier ouercame the water. We with wood put out the fier, and the flame which water could not quench, a lit le fplinter of wood did ceaffe.

A ftraunge cafe good readers, that wood the matter and nourifher of fyer,

shuld

A church and a religious houfe preferued frō burging by the crofse.

ſhuld put out the fier , and that a litle
ſplinter ſhuld quench that, which the la
ye mē could not do with water, nor the
biſſhop and his clergy with prayer : and
yet done it was . The authour that writeth this ſtory was biſhop of the citie
where i twas done,preſent hī ſelf at the
doing of it,and the only man that held
the croſſe in the fier. Of his credit there
is no doute : in his time he was ſo famous for his vertue and lerning, that as
I ſaied before,S.Ambroſe , Hierome and
Auguſtine right highly commended
him:and whome they cōmend we may
not improue,whome they authoriſe,we
may not diſcredit.

  Moreouer as by litle parcells of the
holy croſſe thes and diuerſe other ſtrau͜-
ge thinges haue bene wrought : So by
the ſigne of the croſſe and caᵤlling vp-
Lib.1. hæ- pon the name off Chriſt, many other
reſi.3'o. myracles haue bene done.*Epiphanius* de
contra.E í i clareth that when a fayre beutiful gen-
onitas. til woman by *Sycyria* waſhed her ſelf in
a bath,a younge man that made loue vn
to her,

to her, came in as she was bathing, and
offred her violence. She blest her self in
the name of Christ, and the younge
mans attempt was frustrated. Afterward
he vsed wichcraft to obtaine his purpose but al preuayled not. For as *Epipha-*
nius saieth, *Per signaculum Christi, & fi-*
dem mulier auxilium percæpit, nec valuit in-
cantationis vis vbi erat nomen Christi, & si-
gnaculũ crucis. By the signe of Christ,
and faith, the woman receued help, nether did the force off inchauntement
auayle, where the name of Christ, and
signe of the crosse was.

A wwomã
præserued
from rape
and vvych
craft by
the crosse
and name
of Christ.

Palladius reporteth out of *Hyppolitus*
an auncient writer (who was familiar
with the Apostles) that a mayden off
great nobilitie and excellent beutye
brought vp in spiritual exercise at Corinth, was accused to a iudge off the gen
tils in tyme of persequution: and because she could not be reduced frõ the pro-
fessing of Christes faith, and cõfessing
his holy name, she was caried to a common brothelhouse to be abused. *Verum*

ca.14.8.in
histo.pa.

O   hæc

A vvomã brought falfout of the ste-vves by the grace of Chriſt and ſigne of the croſſe. *hæc ſe totam crucis ſigno muniens, egreditur ex illo loco omnino incorrupta, & impolluta:* but ſhe defending her ſelff with the ſig-ne off the croſſe, came out of that place altogether vnſpotted and vndefiled: and by the grace of Chriſt was præſer-ued.

In Carthage a nother deuoute wo-man caulled *Innocentia,* one of the chie-feſt and peres of the citie, had a cancker in her breaſt, a deſeaſe, as the phiſiti-ons ſay) incurable : therfor that mem-bre where it groweth is wounte to be cut from the body, or the venemous in-fection eaſed with ſome pleaſaunt and ſweete lenitiues, that the patient may li-ue more at eaſe : for death foloeth that deſeaſe although it be lõg. Which thing the gentil woman learning by a ſkilful phiſition alwayes frendful to her, and *Lib.22.c.8 de ciuitate dei.* her familie, with humble prayer com-mitted her ſelf to god. Then as S. *Augu-ſtine* ſaieth, ſhe was admoniſhed in her ſleape a litle before Eaſter, that what ſo-euer Chriſtened woman came vnto her firſt

firſt as ſhe ſtode waching at the bapti-
ſtery or fonte, in that ſide where the
women ſtand, *Signaret ei locum ſigno cru-*
cis Chriſti :facit,& continuo ſanitas eſt ſequu-
*ta,*ſhuld bleſſe and ſigne her breaſt where the cancker was, with the ſigne of the
croſſe of Chriſt : ſhe did ſo, and by and
by ſhe was whole.

In the yere of oure lorde.3 9 6. a great
dragon lying vnder a brydge by the high
way in *Euoria Epyri* did much anoye
the inhabitauntes:and toke for his pray
oxe, horſe,ſhepe,gote,man,woman and
al that paſſed by:*Donatus* a holy and vertuous man, then biſſhop there as it was
ſaied before, came to the bridge with
out ſworde,darte,ſpere, or any kinde of
weapon to deſtroye this terrible, and
oughely beaſt.When the dragon eſpied
him, he thruſt out his head as though
he wold haue deuoured him . Then ſayeth *Sozomenus, Ille vexillũ crucis ante faci-*
em eius in aere in deſignãs os eius expuit,beſtia
vero mox ſputum ore ſuo ſuſcipiens expirauit.
He making with his finger a ſigne of the
O 2 croſſe

A cãcker
in a vvo-
mã breaſt
healed by
the croſſe

Lib. 9. *cap*
4 6. *Trip.*

A dragon
killed
vvith in
the croſſe

croſſe in the ayer , ſpet in the dragons mouth. The beaſt receuing his ſpetle into his mouth,died out of hand.

S. Martin as *Sulpitius Seuerus* teſtifieth in his lif, compelled with the ſigne of the croſſe certen gentils carying a dead corpes to burying after their ſuperſtitious manner , to ſtand ſtill,as ſtiſt as ſtakes .Agayne as the ſame authour reporteth when certen gentils had ſet woorkemē to hewe downe a greate tree, and placed him vnder the tree , becauſe it ſhuld faul downe vppon him , and ſo bryſe and ſquatte him to death , as the tree was faulling , he made the ſigne off the croſſe , and turned the tree another waye,and put the gentilles in daunger.

In the mideſt of a ſkyrmiſh which Conſtantine the greate had with his enemies,it happened that his whole armie being amaſed with a ſodayne noyſe, tumult,and larum , he that bore the ſigne of the croſſe vppon his ſhulders (for ſo Conſtantine had ordayned that it ſhulde be alwayes caried) began for feare to

In vita D Martini.

re to be maruelous hoful and penſif,and
that he might the better runne away,
deliured the ſigne of the croſſe to ano-
ther:when this other man had taken it
of him,and he that fled away was nowe
out of the protection and warde off the
ſigne of the croſſe, he was thruſt thorough the ſmal of the bely with a darte,
and ſo defeated of his liff.And when he
was thus puniſhed for his fearful mynde, and faithleſſe harte, the other that
toke the banner off ſaluation of him,ſa-
ued his owne lif:and whereas there were many dartes caſt at him, he euer eſca-
ped. The ſtaff where the banner or ſigne of the croſſe did hange,euermore receued the dartes which were caſt at him.
And this was a maruelous and ſtraunge
thinge,.that the enemies dartes being
caſt at the man,lyghted euermore vppon
the ſtaff ,.and neuer hurte the man him
ſelff.A goodly ſtorie to teach al ſouldiers and men off armes to haue the ſigne off the croſſe in better reuerence,
and greater pryce then of late yeres they

Conſtan-
tines ſtan
derd be-
rer vvar-
ded from
his enemi
es dartes
by the
croſſe,

O 3   haue

haue had. He that douteth of the treuth
of this ftorie, let him reade *Eufeb. in vita
Conftan. lib.*1. *Zona.to.*3 *Chro. Sozome. lib.*1.
cap. 4. *ecclefiaft. hiflo. Eutrop. lib.* 11. *rerum.*
Ro.

And as this may be a goodly præfident to al fouldiers, So may the ftory of
Theodofius be to al princes and capitay-
mes in warre. This noble emperour after he had difcomfited the cruel tyraunt
Maximus was by two trayterous men
Argobaftes and E*ugenius* put both in greate daunger of his empire, and loffe of his
liff. For they had gathred a great army of
French men ageynft him, and fo craftely
leyed imbufhmentes in the ftreight and
narro paffages of the Alpes, (where *The-*
odofius was, that there was no way for
him to iffue out and efcape. Then he
faulling downe flat with his body vppon the grounde, and fixing his mynde
on high in heauen, with dropping teares
prayed vnto oure fauiour Chrift, and after he had continued a whole night in
prayer, and left behinde him plenty off

teares

teares in witnesse that he desired aide
from heauen, with stoute courage, and
greate confidence toke his sworde in his
hand, and as *Orosius* writeth *Sciens se esse* *Lib.7.c.35*
non solum signo crucis tuendum, sed & victo- *aduersus*
riam adepturū, signo crucis se muniens signū *paga.*
victoriæ dedit, ac signo crucis signum prælio
dedit, ac se in bellum etiam si nemo sequeretur,
victor futurus immisit. Knowing that he Theodo-
shuld not only be defended with the sig- sius bles-
ne of the crosse, but also get the victory, selt vvith
arming him self with the signe of the the crosse
crosse, he gaue a signe of victorie, and the battail
with the signe off the crosse he gaue a and
wach woord to fight and as one that shul ouercame
de be conquerour, went to the battail al- mics.
though none of his souldiers wold folloe. And se what happened. One of thee
nemies cāpe caulled *Arbitrio* taking *Theo*
dosius in the schoute, moued with the re-
uerēce of the emperour there present, not
only deliured him out of daūger, but also
aided him with a garrison off men. And
when he came to the place of fight, there rose a great hurling wind in the ene-
O 4 mies

mies faces , his fouldiers weapons and
dartes were caried in the ayer higher thē
any man culde reache, and neuer fuffred
to faul vntil they ftroke their enemies.
The hurling winde did maruelous fearcely beate the enemies faces and brea-
ftes , and yff they did caft any darte or
fhote owt any engine of warre,they were driuen backe with the winde,and made to pearce the enemies that caft them.
In fuch forte that the whole armie fub-
mitted them felues to the emperour *Thē-
odofius* , *Eugenius* was taken , and flayne,
and *Argobaftes* murdred with his owne
hande.

Nowe iudge yowe god people whether the croffe of Chrift,by which god
rayfed the half dead and mortified woman in *Hierufalem* , and præferued
a religious houfe from burning in *Nola* , or the figne of the croffe by which
god defended a gentil woman from
violent rape , and wicked whichcraft
in Sy*cyria*;and præferued a nother from
corruption in the brothelhoufe at Corinth

rinth, healed a lady of a cancker in her breaſt in Carthage, deſtroyed a hydious dragon in *Euoria*, defended S. Martin from the faul of a tree, made the ſuperſtitious gentills ſtand ſtil, warded Conſtantines ſtanderdbearer from al his enemies dartes, and myraculouſly deliured the emperour *Theodoſius*, is ſo contemptuouſly to be reiected, ſo blaſphemouſly abuſed, at is hath bene thes later yeares by heretikes? Yf any man hath a precious ſtone of ſome ſtraunge vertue, or an herbe in his garden medicinable for this or that defeaſe, he keapeth them warely, nor ſuffreth his ſtone to be broken, nor herbe roted out of his garden. And alas ſhal we Chriſten men breake the croſſe of Chriſt, a precious pearle of much vertue, efficacy, and pouer? Shal we roote out of oure gardens that holy ſigne? a fouerayne herbe ageynſte al ſorowes, griffes, and anguiſhes of minde? medicinable ageinſt al coniuration, inchauntement, focery, and wichcraft? for ceable ageinſt al fantaſies of the fleaſh,

aſh,wiles of the worlde, and tentations
of the deuil? O lord what impietie were
it. The wicked caytiffes that deſpite
Chriſt,and his religion can do no more
And ſhal not we Chriſtians differ from
ethnikes? Or ſhal we be worſe then pay
nims? O merciful god: what dayes are
theſe? What people are we? The hea-
thens by credible reporte,and letters off
ſuch as haue traueled into the newe In-
dians,euen at this preſent do cauſe euery Chriſten man that cometh vnto thē
to make a ſigne of the croſſe,and leue it
in their houſes,and the iewe (as it apeareth by the ſtory recited before out off
S.Gregory) cauſed the ſigne of the croſ
ſe to be made in his body. And we redemed with the croſſe of Chriſt , and re-
generate by the water of baptiſme ſanctified by the ſigne of the croſſe,ſtrēght-
ned by the ſacrament of confirmation,
and nourriſhed with the body and bloud off Chriſt conſecrated with the ſame ſigne,can nether abyde to haue it in
oure ſight,nor made in oure forheades,
nor

nor vfed in the facramentes , nor fet vp
in high wayes and other places . *O tem-*
pora , O mores:I befeeke god,thes newe
mynifters and præfented reformers off
Chriftianitie , go not about to abolifhe
the name of Chrift, and bring vs to Pa-
ganitie. I wil tel yowe a prety ftory . It
chaũced ones that a ruffine and roifter
of the citie of Millan cauiled Andrewe
Lampugnam being difpleafed with the
duke cõfpired with two other royfters *Claudius*
to kil him . Not withftanding he durft *Paradin in Symbolis*
not do it,nor come nigh the duke , he *heroicis.*
was fo afrayed of his comely perfonage
and princely looke. At the lenght he de
uifed away to be fure of his purpofe:and
that was this . He caufed the duke to be
liuely painĉted and fet foorth in a table.
And when he had him liuely painĉted,
he came with his dagger as oftentimes
as he fawe the dukes image , and ftroke
it:and fo continued dayly ftreking of it
vntil he had gotten fuch audacitie by
ftreking the image,that he came vnto
the duke,as he was in the church,in the
mideft

mideſt of his garde , and ſtroke him to death. So in good ſooth theſe heretikes couertly conſpyring to ouerthrowe the religion of Chriſt , and take away the memory of his paſſion , but fearing the maieſtie of Chriſt, and the fayre and aniable countinaunce of his deare ſpouſe the churche , and therefor not openly daring to ſet foorth any ſuch doctrine, leſt their enterpriſe ſhuld be diſcried, and they diſcredited , haue thought it beſt for their purpoſe to come with their daggers , and peck at the croſſe , and ſtreke at the image of Chriſt, and hurle it downe vnder prætence of idolatrie. And ſo whē they haue hardened them ſelues, by pecking at the croſſe, and ſtreking the image of Chriſt, they wil come to the churche, in the mideſt off al faithful Chriſten men after their firſt determination, and longe purpoſed malice, and ſaye in effect, there is no Chriſt at al : Tel me I praye yowe if a man come into the chamber of præſence , and pluck downe the cloth of eſtate , and breake

The intēt of ſuch as throvve dovvne the croſſe.

breake the princes armes in pieces, is it
not his intent to haue that prince depo
fed, and beare the fouerainte no longer
ouer him? No loyial and faithful fubiect
can thinke the contrary. And may not
we thinke that thes ghofpellers pluc-
king downe the figne of the croffe,
which is Chriftes cloth of eftate, the ar
mes and recognifaunce off his kingdome, which euery Chriften man muft
fixe in his harte, and beare in his forhead, (if he minde to haue any comforte
by the merites of Chriftes paffion, vppon the croffe) meane any other thinge
then *Nolumus hunc regnare fuper nos?* We
wil not haue this man raygne ouer vs? *Luce. 19.*
yes certes. And vnleffe god of his goodneffe ftreke of this *Hidra* his head, and
quickly kill this creaping cancker,
the euent wil fpedely follo: Which
god forbed, and graunte that the enemies of his croffe may repent and be afhamed of their impietie, and reftore vnto
vs agayne the outwarde fight of the crof
fe, by which men haue more vehement
impref-

impreſſions , and deper meditations
of the paſſion of Chriſt in a day , then
by al the collations they make in a yea-
re:which thing the wily ſerpent Satan
eſpying laboreth by his miniſters,by his
marchantes , by his brokers , and al his
black garde to bring men in hatred with
the ſight of, croſſe. And the firſt leſſon
that he geueth to al his deare derlinges
is, that they ſhal deſpite and hate the
croſſe of Chriſt:and image of the bleſſed virgin Mary his mother , and tread
them vnder their feete. He that wil ſee
euident prouffes of this,let him reade a
litle boke ſet foorth by the famous vni-
uerſitie of Colonie caulled *Malleus Ma-*
leficarum and *Alfonſum De caſtro De pu-*
nitione hæreticorum. There ſhall he ſee by
the playne confeſſion of diuerſe men
and women whome Satan had entrap-
ped and moſt miſerably abuſed, the veritie of this auouched.

    But as S. Auguſtine when he had e-
uident prouffes by hiſtories that *Romu-*
lus killed his brother *Remus,* or cauſed
him

Lib.1.cap
de lamijs.

him to be killed faied that notwithſtan
ding al that . *Hoc multi impudentia ne-* *Lib.3 cap.6 de ciuitate Dei.*
gant,multi pudore dubitant,multi dolore diſ-
*ſimulant:*Many of impudécy denie this,
many for ſhame doute of it, many for
ſorowe diſſemble it : So peraduenture
many hearing thes ſtraunge myracles,
wrought by the croſſe,wil ether of im-
pudency denie thé, and ſay they be lies:
or for ſhame off their former doinges
doute of them, and thincke it ſtraunge
that it ſhuld be ſo:or for ſorowe diſſemble it,and not be knowé that euer they
read any ſuch thing.Yf it be ſo,we deſire
the impudent to conſider that firſt they
denie the omnipotécy of god,as though
he could not worke any ſuch myracles,
by any ſuch external meanes:ſecódarely
the authoritie of ſome of the beſt and
moſt approued hiſtoriographers of the
churche,as *Euſeb.Sozomenus, Oſorius,Eu-*
tropius and others:and thirdely thre holy, vertuous and lerned fathers, S . Auguſtine , Pauline, and *Sulpitius, Seuerus*
Whoſe credit,hath euer, and ſhal to the
worldes

worldes end, counteruaile the moſt proude and præſumptuous kereti.k that euer wrote. The douteful men that thinke it ſtraunge that it ſhuld be ſo, we deſire to remembre, that *Non eſt abbreuiata manus Domini.* The hand of god is not ſhortened. *Ieſus Chriſtus heri, & hodie, & ipſe in ſæcula.* Ieſus Chriſt is to day and yeſterday, and he for euer. And that as god, *Dedit homini primordia & infantiam ſuam ex alijs de ſe conijcere, & authoritatibus muliercularum multa de ſe credere,* Would haue man (as it were) coniecture off others what beginning he had, and what he did in his infancy, and beleue the authoritie of women in many pointes touching him ſelf: So vndoutydly he willing to haue the glory of his name magnified for euer, and his mighty pouer knowen from generatiō to generation, would haue vs beleue thoſe that lyued before vs: and willeth his myracles to be declared by the father to the ſonne, and by the ſonne to his childrē, and ſo foorth from to man, that they may knowe what

woun-

Eſa. 59.
Heb. 13.
Lib. 1. Conſeſſio: cap. 6.
Exod. 10.
Ioelis. 1.

wounderful thinges he hath done. And
becaufe we fhuld not be ignorant, he geueth euery man commaundement to re
membre the old daies, and thinke vppon
the generations and ages that be paft: and
that we may at no tyme prætend igno-
raunce, he faieth, *Interroga patrem tuum et* Deute. 32.
annunciabit tibi: maiores tuos & dicent tibi:
Afke thy father, and he fhal fhewe the:
thy elders and they fhal tel the. And as he
would haue vs afke oure forefathers, fo
he would haue vs beleue them, and owe
fuch reuerence vnto them, that we fhuld
credit that they report vnto vs, efpecially fuch holy and auncient fathers as al
the worlde haue in admiration, authoritie, and high credit, as *Auguftinus, Paulinus, Sulpitius Seuerus, Eufebius, Sozomenus,
Orofius, Eutropius* and fuch other are, or
els it were to no purpofe to bid vs afke
them, yff we fhuld not beleue them whē
they tel vs.

The diffembler we defyre to confider,
that as S. Cyprian faieth, *Seipfum fallit &* Lib. 1. E-
decipit, qui aliud corde occultat, aliud voce de- piftola 2.
P   *nunciat:*

nunciat:he doth deceue and begylde him
felf that hideth one thing in his harte,
and fpeaketh another thing with his
Iacob. 4. mouthe. And that, as *Scienti bonum & non*
facienti, peccatum eſt illi : He that knoweth
howe to do wel and doeth it not offen-
deth, So he that knoweth the treuth, and
for forowe that it cōuinceth his eri our,
wil not acknowledge the treuth, doth
highly offend god who is treuth, and
ſtandeth in daunger of that terrible cur-
Eccleſiaſt. 1 ſe, *Ve duplici corde, & labijs ſceleſtis, & pecca-*
tori terram ingredienti duabus vijs, O be vn
to the doble harted and deape diſſem-
bling man, and to al wicked lippes, and
the ſynner that goeth vppon the earth
*Prouerb.*3 two manner of wayes . For, *abhominatio*
domini omnis illuſor , & cum ſimplicibus ſer-
mocinatio eius, Euery diſſembler and dece-
uer is abhorred of god : and his talk is
with the ſimple. And when they haue
couched thes conſiderations narroly in
their mindes, we doute not, but that in fi
ne they wil take modeſty for impuden-
cy, faith for incredulitie , treuth for diſſi-
                                        mu-

mulatiō, and simplicite for doble dealing
with god and man: and so repent for their former mysdoinges and in treuth and
simplicitie of harte seeke the fauour off
ouer merciful lorde agayne, and returne
to the vnitie of his churche and saue
their soules . Which god graunte they
may. Nowe to the nynthe article.

VVHAT COM-
MODITIE EVERY
CHRISTEN MAN HATH,
OR MAY HAVE BY THE
signe off the crosse.

S *Germanus* bisshop off
Cōstantinople declaring
what commoditie euery
Christen man hath by the
images off holy men who
serued god trewly, and resisted the tyranny of princes, assaultes of Satan, iniquitie and sinne, euen to death, saieth, *Ima-*
gines sanctorum sunt fortitudinis eorum deli-

9.
*Act.*4.
*Nyce.*2.

P 2   *neatio,*

neatio, sanctaeque virtutis, & dispensationis fi-
guratio, & ad glorificandum deum cui in hac
vita seruierunt, admonitio & instructio, The
images of holy men are a lyuely description of their stoutenesse, and a repræsen-
tation of holy vertue, and dispensation
of grace geuen vnto them, and a warning
and instruction to teache vs to glorify
god: Euen so may we saye nowe, that the
signe off the crosse and ymage of Christ
crucified set before oure eies in church,
chappel, high way or otherwise, is vnto
vs a liuely description of his stoutenesse
in bering the blowes of the iewes beating his face, tearing his fleash, streaching
his armes, pearcing his feete, and with a
sharpe pointed spere opening his side.
Who in al those tormentes neuer gaue
signification of sorowe, neuer opened
his mouth to expresse his woo, but gaue his chekes to al that would hale and
teare them, and his face to al that wold
spet and spattre it, and lieke an innocent
lambe was led to the bouchery with out
any noyse or strogling at all: This signe

The commoditie of images and figne of the croffe.

is a

is a repræfentation off his infinite mercy *The crof-* *fe is a re-* and loue towardes vs , who being the *præfenta-* fonne of god æqual with his father in *tion off* *the mercy* diuine pouer and maiefty , although we *of Chrift* were drowned in fynne , and by nature *in rede-* *ming vs.* the childrē of wrath, alienated from the conuerfation of Ifrael , ftraungers of his *Ephe.2.* teftamentes, hauimg no hope of promef fe,and with out a god in this worlde, ma de vs his deare frendes by fheading his precious bloud,became oure peace ,made both one , broke the midle part off the wauil,toke away al enemitie and recon- ciled vs to god by his croffe.

This figne is an admonition and in- *The crof* *teacheth* ftruction to teach vs to glorifie god the *vs to* father:who loued vs fo entierly that he *glorifie* *god for* gaue his only begottē fonne *Iefus* Chrift *fending* to death for vs,and when we lyued after *his fonne* *to redeme* the pleafures of the world and luftes off *vs.* the fleafh , as the prince of the ayer allu- red vs,and were dead in finful liff, being rych in mercy , reuiued vs agayne with Chrift , and rayfed vs vp with him ,and made vs fit on high with him in heauen.

Againe iff any man think him selfto be somewhat , wherein dede he is nothing, and vppon a proude præsumption brag as the Pharisey did, that he is not

Luce.18. *Sicut cæteri homines* , as other men are: or vppon a litle knowledg which is the gift of god geuen to euery man according to his measure, glory that he is wiser, then al other, more lerned then al other , more expert in scriptures , doctours , and antiquities , then al other , or in his owne fantasie condeneth other mens iudgmétes , and craketh to the people , that the

The crosse teacheth the proude and contentious man humilitie. doctrine which he teacheth contrary to al other , is sure , founde , and grounded vppon the worde of god, that man I say, looking intentiuely vppon this signe, may lerne humilitie , and say with S. Paule, *Absit mihi gloriari nisi in cruce Domini*

Gal.6. *nostri Iesu Christi*. God forbed thad I shuld brag, or glory in any thing but in the crosse of oure lorde Iesus Christ. And

1.Cor.2. *Non me iudicaui scire aliquid inter vos nisi Iesum Christum, & hunc crucifixum:* I haue not iudged my selff to knowe any thing amonge

amonge yowe, but *Iesus* Chrift and him crucified.

Befides euery contentious man ful of fingularitie, turning but his eie to this figne with fome godly meditation, may lerne that he ought to do nothing for contention, nothing for vaine glory, but *Phil. 2.* in humilitie thinke other mē better, and wifer thē him felf. And although he were the beft lerned and moft wifeft in al Chriftendome, yet as Chrift when he was in the forme of god, thought it no no robbery for him to be æqual with god, but abafed him felf taking the fhape of a feruaunt, made to the lickneffe of men, and in behauiour founde as man, humbled him felf, made obedient to his father euen to death, yea death vppon the croffe, fo fhuld he thinke it behoueth him to be obedient vnto the church, directed by the holy ghoft præfident in the fame, and euer more geuing fuggeftion what is beft to be done, euen to the vtter abandoning of his fingularitie, and mortifiyng of his felff wil: and haue al

P 4 waies

waies in memory that the spirite of god
resteth vppon the humble, and resisteth
the proude.

O bstinate sinners who are glad whē
they haue done euil, and rejoise in wic-
kednesse,and saye to them selues,we ha
ue made a bargen with death, and coue-
naunt with hel:we wil follo oure owne
fantasies, and do after the imaginations
of oure owne hartes,may in a moment
by sight of this signe haue remorse off
cōsciēce, and saye to thē selues:Behold
it pleased god to reconcile vs vnto him
by his only some Iesus Christ, pacify-
ing al that is in earth beneath,and in hea
uen aboue by the bloud of his crosse.
And whē we were his enemies;inwrap-
ped in the workes of iniquitie,he recōci
led vs in the body of his owne fleash by
death, to make vs holy, immaculate,
and irreprehēsible before him. And alas
behold we liek villaines follo thelustes
of oure fleash, lewde wil and fantasie,
and heape sinne vppon sinne,and lease
the fruicte of his death and passiō.O let

Prou.2.

Iere.18.

Coll.1.

vs

vs chaunge this wicked lif, and caft a wa
ye oure iniquities,and make oure felues
a newe fpirite and a newe harte, and in
fafting,weaping, wayling and praying,
turne to oure lord god,and he wil receue vs oure iniquitie and naughty lif fhal
not hurte vs: and thus many a foule is
faued,and made foner by fight of the ho
ly croffe to leue al wickedneffe and fin-
full liff, then by any other meanes. For,
Quis (faieth *Athanafius*) *Ita hominibus fo-*
litos affedtus e præcordijs exemit, vt fcorta pu-
dice agerent ? Homicidæ non amplius ferrum
tenerent?Pauidi robur conciperent? Quis bar-
baros,gentefque alias in fuis fædibus perfuafit
immanitatem deponere, & pacifica meditari,
nifi Chrifti fides,& fignaculum crucis? Who
hath fo taken out of mens hartes their
wounte affections,that harlottes wolde
liue chafte?murderers kepe their weapõ
no longer? Feareful men conceue courage?who hath perfuaded barbarous people, and other nations to ley awaye al
immanitie in their owne countries,and
to mufe only vppon quietneffe and peace,

De huma-
nita.verbi.

The fig-
ne of the
croffe ma
keth vvic
ked men
thinke vp
pon god.

ace,but the faith of Chriſt and ſigne of
the croſſe?as much to ſaye Noman.

Furder diuerſe brought by conſide-
ring the burden of ſinne that preſſeth
their conſciences,in daunger of deſpe-
ratiō , by the malice of oure enemie the
deuil, take by ſight of this ſigne goodly
comforte:and that which wordes could
not print in their heades, the contēpla-
tiō of this ſigne doth ſo printe in their
mindes, that they triūphe ouer the deuil,and ſaye although we were dead in
ſinne,yet Chriſt hath reuiued vs agayne,and forgeuen al oure iniquities : He
hath taken away the obligation of debt
and faſtened it vppō his croſſe, and ſpoi
ling the dominion and pouer of oure e-
nemies hath brought them foorth in
open ſhewe,and triumphed ouer them.
Beſides it is a good inſtruction to teach
vs,that as Chriſt the ſonne of god could
not paſſe through this vale of miſerye
without blaſphemous wordes , wooful
paynes,and horrible perſequutions,and
death vppon the croſſe : So we ſhal ne-

uer

*The croſ-
ſe cōfor-
table in
deſpera-
ſion.*

Coll. 2.

*The croſ-
ſe tea-
chet vs,pa
tiently to
ſuffer al
perſequu-*

uer paſſe this wreached world, and co--tion,and
me to Chriſt,vnleſſe we patiently hea-aduerſitie
re al ſlaunderous wordes ,abide tribulation , ſuffer perſequution , and take vp
his croſſe and follo him.

Here if the enemies of the croſſe wil An obie-
ſaye we may lerne this and al before mē ction.
tioned by reading the ſcriptures,and hearing good preachers, and therefor for
any ſuch conſideration the ſigne of the
croſſe is not to be ſuffred amongeſt
Chriſten men, I anſwer , and acknowledg it to be trewe,that men maye haue Anſvver.
goodly inſtructions by reading the ſcriptures, and hearing good preachers:but
notwithſtanding the conſequent hol-
deth not.For firſt euery mā can not reade ſcripture,nor vnderſtand it when he
reade it: and euery man can not al times
ſo conueniently heare a good preacher,
as he may ſe the ſigne of the croſſe, if it
might be ſuffred to ſtād. And what kno
we we when god wil geue his grace, or
when Chriſt wil come, whether late in Mar. 13.
the euening , or at midnight or at the
cro-

crowing of the cock, or early in the mor
ning. But imagine that euery man can
reade and vnderſtand the ſcripture, and
at al times heare a good preacher, yet
muſt they nedes confeſſe that as Hora-
ce ſaieth:

Segnius irritant animos demiſſa per aures,

Quám quæ ſunt oculis ſubiecta fidelibus:

Things let downe by the eares do
more ſlowely ſtyrre vp mens mindes,
then ſuch as are ſubiect and leyed præſent, before the faithful eies: which thin
ge although daily experience teacheth
to be trewe, yet for furder prouffe I wil
recite and example or two.

Iulius Cæſar being in Hiſpaine, and ſe
ing certē noble faictes and exploictes of
Alxāder, the greate fayer and tindely pa-
incted, muſed a greate while with hī ſelf
and ſighed. And whē his frendes woundred at it, Alas ſaied he, do ye not thinke
there is iuſt cauſe why I ſhuld ſighe, ſeing, *Alexāder* at this age ſubdued ſo many natiōs, and I haue done no noble a-
cte. And frō that day forward ſaieth the
ſtory.

Thinges
ſeene do
moue mo
re affecti-
ons then
that
vvhich is
harde, or
read.

ſtory . *Ad præclaras res gerendas expeditior
& fortior effect us eſt*. He became more re-
dier and more ſtouter, to al faictes of armes, exploictes of warre, and noble actes.
Scipio Aphricanus was wounte to ſaye
that he was by no māner of thing more
ſtirred to vertue, actiuitie, and princely
prowes, then by the examples of his forefathers. *Quorum imagines in foro depictas
videbat*, Whoſe images he ſawe painted
in the market and publick place off aſſemble: *Gregorius Niſſenus* in his oration
writen of the picture which repræſented the ſtory of Ahraham offring vp his
ſonne Iſaac, ſaieth: *Vidi ſæpius inſcriptionis
imaginem, & ſine lachrymis tranſire non po-
tui, quum tam efficaciter ob oculos poneret hi-
ſtoriam*. I ſawe oftētimes the image whe
re the whole hiſtorie was deſcribed, and
I could not paſſe by without teares , ſeing it, did ſo effectually repreſent and ley
before my eies the trewe ſtory : which
wordes a father of the ſeuenth general
councel kept at Nice hearing recited, ſaied. *Si tanto doctori hiſtoria inſpecta peperit
vtilitatem*

Actio.4.
Nica.2.
vtilitatem, quanto magis rudibus & idiotis
vtilitatem & commoditatem afferet. Yff a
ſtory beheld and looked vppō, brought
to ſuch a famous doctour greate commoditie, and with al made him wepe?
howe much more, wil it bring commoditie and profit to the ſimple and ignoraunt? Another ſaied, *Si Gregorius vigi-*
lantiſſimus ad diuina oracula inſpecta hiſtoria
Abrahæ fleuit, quanto magis Oiconimia incar
nati Domini noſtri Ieſu Chriſti a nobis inſpe-
cta ad lachrymas & vtilitatem contemplantes
adhortabitur? Yf Gregory moſt vigilaunt
and ſtudious in reading the worde off
god, wept whē he ſawe the ſtorie of A-
brahā? howe much more wil the whole
diſcourſe of oure ſauiour Chriſtes liff
here incarnate vppon earth being ſene
of vs, moue al that behold it to teares
and other furder commoditie?

By theſe examples yowe ſee I truſt
god readers, that an image painctedin a
table, or otherwiſe portraicted, doth mo
re ſtyrre the mindes of men to vertue,
then the bare lettre read in boke. *Iulius*
Cæſar

Cæfar was vndoutidly lerned, and much conuerſaunt in reading the ſtories off emperours and noble princes: *Scipio* not ignoraunt of the noble faictes of the auncient Romanes: Gregory, not ſimply occupied in reading the ſcriptures, yet in al their reading, they were neuer ſo ſtirred to vertue, and moued to pittie, as they were by the ſight off images. Wherfore it muſt nedes be trewe, that if al men could reade, yet al that they reade, in their bokes can not ſo much moue them, as that which they ſee with their eies.

Againe if a man were in place where he might oftentimes heare a good preacher zelouſly diſcourſing vppon the paſſion of Chriſt, yet a litle briegment, and ſhorte demonſtration of it expreſſed in imagrie, muſt nedes be profitable. For if as *Germanus* biſhop of Conſtantinople ſaieth They who haue oftentimes harde many worthy thinges reported of holy men, if they ſee them repræſented againe an in image, do caul to

Epiſt. ad Tho. epiſto. Claudi. na betur to. 2. Con. act. 4 Nica. 2.

remem-

remembraunce al that they haue harde
and feene, and the ignoraunte take occafion to afke and lerne, and befides are
ftyrred by them more vehemently to loue and praife god, in fuch forte that by
both thefe, they that fee and heare the
noble actes of holy men, are conftrained
to glorifie oure father which is in heaue:
Much more muft we feing the liff, and
paffion of oure fauiour Chrift fet foorth
in painting, or ymagrie, caul to remem-
braūce that which we haue read, and harde: and better bere it awaye : and if we be
ignoraunt, there may we take occafion
by the obiect to afke and lerne, and be
erneftly ftirred to loue, praife, and glorifie god, for his infinite mercy in fending
his only begotten fonne to redeme vs.
Wherfor if there were no other caufe
why images, and efpecially the croffe of
Chrift fhuld be permitted in churches,
chapppells, and other places for Chriften
to behold, yet becaufe they quicken the
memory which in many is fickle help
ignoraunce, which in fome is lurde, ftirre

vp

vp loue which is waxen cold, helpe hope which is almoſt dead, moue deuotion which in al men decayeth, reuiue
faith which almoſt fayleth, they myght
right wel be ſuffred amongeſt Chriſten
men, without any diſhonour to god, or
hinderaunce to Chriſten religion . For
there be ſaieth S. Auguſtine, *Quædam ſig-* *Cap. 3. de*
na exteriora pigritantis etiam fidei excitato- *viſit. infir.*
ria, & quaſi quandam compunctionem pene-
tralibus ſuis figentia, quæ & Chriſtianitatis
religio vult obſeruari. Certen external ſignes ſtirrers vp of the ſlouthful and ſlug-
giſh faith, and faſtening as yt were a certaine compunction in mens hartes,
which the religion of Chriſtianitie wil
haue obſerued. For this ſtirreth vp oure
ſlouthful faith.

And as the holy father Cyril arch-
biſihop off *Alexandria* writeth, yt ma- *Lib. 6. con*
keth vs remembre howe oure lorde and *tra Iulia.*
maſter Chriſt, although he might haue *Apoſta.*
remained in forme egal al manner off
wayes with his father, and ſit in the
high throne of Maieſtie, yet he thought
Q   it

it no robbery for hym to be æqual with god, but humbled him felff, taking the ſhape of a feruaunt vppon him, contemned al ſlaunder and ignominie, and ſuffred death vppõ the croſſe, that he might take away the pouer and corruption off ſinne, and howe he alone died, and was rayſed againe to deliuer mankinde from the ſnares off death, to deſtroy the tyranny of ſinne which was prædominãt in vs, to pacifie the lawe which raged in the partes off ouer body, to make vs woorſhippers off god in ſpirite and treuth, to mortifie the luſtes of the fleaſh, and make them the children of god, ſanctifie them with the holy ghoſt, who beleue in him, to ſpoyle Satan and al the malignant pouers vnder him, off their vſurped tyranny ouer men. *Hæc omnia recordari nos facit ſalutare lignum.* Al thes thinges the healthful wood doth make vs remembre. And furder counſelleth vs to thinke that one is dead for al, that al men liuing, may no longer liue vnto them ſelues, but vnto him

The croſſe bringeth to onre remembraunce al the merites off Chriſtes paſsion.

him who is dead , and risen againe for them.

Againe in the same place , he saieth: *Preciosi ligni crucem facimus in memoriam omnis boni , & omnis virtutis* . We make a crosse of the precious wood in remembraunce of al goodnesse and al vertue: and thus much *Cyrillus* . By whome youe see good readers that the signe off the crosse maketh vs remembre the merites of Christes passion , and al other benefites wrought by his mercy to mankinde: and that in those dayes men made the signe of the crosse in remembraunce of al goodnesse and vertue . And nowe oure newe masters as though they were more profundely lerned in scriptures then *Cyrillus*, and more zelous to the honour off god then the Christians of that age , by the aduise of their lord Satan transfiguring him self into the angel of light, throwe dow ne the crosse, to bring men a litle and a litle out of remembraunce of Christe his passion, and rote out of their mindes

The crosse made in remẽbraunce of al vertue and goodnesse.

al ver-

al vertue and goodneſſe , and ſo by de-
grees driue them to paganiſme, and make them beleue, *Non eſt Deus*,there is no
god. Therefor good people ſtay by tyme. And as *Cyrillus* reſoning ageinſt Iu
lian the *Apoſtata* (who with greate ex-
probation entwited Chriſten men with
the woorſhipping of the croſſe, and ma
king the ſigne of the ſame in their forheades,and ſetting it before their dores)

Lib. 6. con tra Iulia. ſayed ſtoutely, *Vis igitur vir ſtrenue vt lig
num quod nos ad recordationem omnis virtu
tis inducit abijciamus & relinquamus,pueriſ-
que & mulierculis tua proponamus ?* Wilt
thowe therfore o ſturdy man that we
caſt away and relinquiſh the wood that
bringeth vs in remembraunce of al vertue , and propoſe to children and women thy trifles?So ſay yowe to al thes
miſcreantes , and heretikes entwiting
youe with tbe hauing,and worſhipping
off the croſſe of Chriſt , will yowe ſires
that we caſt away the ſigne of ſaluatiõ
that repreſenteth vnto vs the paſſion of
Chriſt,and bringeth vs in remembraun

ce

ce of al vertue and goodneſſe, and ſet
vp before mens eies (of whome the gre
teſt multitude can not reade) ſuch ſen-
tences as youe cōmaunde vs? painċting
the waulles with ſcriptures, and canc-
kring youre hartes with hereſy? bearing
the bible in youre handes, but no good
fruiċt in youre mindes? euer talking of
the ſprite, but alwayes walking in the
fleaſh? No: god forbed: we haue lerned
thes leſſons of S. Paule. *Depoſitum cuſto-*
di. State et tenete traditiones, quas didiciſtis, ſi
ue per ſermonem, ſiue per epiſtolam noſtram.
Doĉtrinis varijs & peregrinis nolite abduci.
Kepe that which is left with youe. Stan
de and kepe the traditious which yowe
haue lerned ether by my talke, or by my
epiſtle. Be not led and caried away with
diuerſe and ſtraunge doĉtrines. The ſig
ne of the croſſe hath bene left vnto vs
in the churche to be kept, and had in re
uerence, euer ſithens the Apoſtels time:
therefor we muſt kepe it. It hath bene
deliured vnto vs as a tradition and doĉtrine of the Apoſtels: therefor we muſt

1. *Timo.* 6
2. *Theß.* 2.
Heb. 13.

Q 3   hold

hold it. I is a ftraunge doctrine that the
figne of Chrift fhuld be taken away frõ
Chriften men, and fo vilanoufly abufed, and neuer practifed but by heathẽs,
paynims, Apoftatats and heretikes: therefore we muft not be led and caried a-
way with it. We lerne by S. Bafile that
honour done to an image is referred to
him that is reprefented by the ymage,
and contrary wife difhonour done to
an image, is done to hym that is reprefented by the image. We are taught out
of holy *Athanafius*, that Chrift wil deny him before his father in heauẽ who
denieth his image in earth before men,
much more then iff we deny his croffe.
Wherefor it ftandeth vs vppon not to
follo this youre newe deuifed doctrine.

Seing then the figne of the croffe, is
a liuely defcription of the ftouteneffe
of oure fauiour Chrifte, in fuffring the
vilany of the iewes, a reprefentation of
h is mercy in redeming vs, an inftructiõ
to teach vs to glorifie god for fending
his fonne into the worlde, and reuiuing

vs

Li.ad Am philoch.ca. 18.

Ser. de fan ctis patri- bus & pro phetis.

vs from ſinne, by the bloud of his croſſe, a myrrour to lerne humilitie in, a leſ
ſon ageinſt contention, a lewre to re-
claime obſtinate ſinners, a comfort a-
geinſt deſperation, an admonition to pa
tience in perſequution, a quickening of
the memory, an occaſion of knowledg,
a meane to ſtirre oure hartes to the loue of god, no man redemed with the
croſſe of Chriſt, and deſirous of æternal ſaluation purchaſed by his death vppon the croſſe, can iuſtely be offended
with the ſigne of the croſſe, and accom
pte him ſelf a frend of Chriſtes, what
ſoeuer excuſe, pretence, or cloke he hath
to the contrary. For that Chriſten
men may worſhip and adore the
ſigne of the croſſe without a-
ny diſhonour to god, or feare of idolatrie, in this
next article it ſhal-
be declared.

(?¿?)

Q 4   THE

THE ADORA-
TION AND VVORS-
HIPPING OF THE
CROSSE ALLO-
wed by the old
auncient fa-
thers.

10.

Lthough good readers I haue in diuerse places of this treatise as occasion serued put yowe in re-membraunce that the signe of the crosse shuld be worshipped and adored , and that without any dishonour to god, or feare of idolatrie,as in declaring the story off

Artic.3. Christes Apostel S.Philip cōmaunding the Scythians to hurle downe the i-dol off *Mars,* and set vpp the crosse off

Artic.5. Christ and adore it,and in referring the facte off *Paula* and others ,yet because the aduersaries of treuth and enemies of
Chri-

Chriftes croffe perfuade the contrary,
and haue no other reafon to make men
defpite and throwe downe the croffe,
but feare and miftruft of idolatrie, I wil
declare vnto yowe by the old auncient
fathers and general councelles, that the
figne of the croffe may be woorfhipped
and adored:and that in Chriften men
worfhipping and adoring the fame there can be no miftruft nor feare of idolatrie.

As touching the firft the holy father
Chrifoftome making a whole fermon
of the worfhipping of the croffe faieth.
Venit nobis anniuerfarius dies omni religione
colēdus, & illuftris fanctorum ieiuniorum, qui
& ter beatam vitalemqué conferuatoris no-
ftri crucem profert, & ad venerandum propo-
nit . The anniuerfary day is come to be a
woorfhipped of vs with al religion and
holyneffe, and the folemne day of holy
fafte, which bringeth foorth the moft
bleffed and liuely croffe of oure fauiour
Iefus Chrift, and fetteth it foorth to be
worfhipped . By thes woordes of Chri-
foftto-

The invē
tion off
the croffe
kept for
a holy
day.

foſtome yowe ſee good readers that in his time there was a ſoléne holy daye or dayned in the honour of the croſſe, and kept yerely: and the croſſe ſet foorth to be worſhipped: and beſides yowe ſee here that the faſt which yowe were wounte to caulle the croſſe dayes, was then ſolemly kept. Furder in the ſame ſermon he ſaieth. *Quia hodiernus dies precioſæ crucis veneratoni conſtitutus eſt, huc a-deſte: eam cum metu, & deſiderio amplectamur.* Becauſe this præſent day is ordayned for the woorſhipping of the precious croſſe, come ye hether, let vs with feare and deſire imbrace the ſame. Againe in the ſame ſermon he proueth by the ſcripture that the croſſe is to be woorſhipped and adored: for god ſaied to his prophete make the ſigne *Tau* in their forheades who moorne and lament for their abhomination and ſinne: kil man, woman, and child: But come not nigh to them who haue that ſigne: and Salomon ſaieth. *Laudate ſignum quo iuſtitia oritur.* Praiſe the ſigne out of which iuſtice

Croſſc
Daies.

Ezech. 9.

ſtice ſpringeth: and thus much Chriſoſtome there. In his cōmentaries vppon
S. Paules epiſtle he ſaieth. *Quód apud eos* *Ho. 12. in*
qui crucem adorant, & arcana myſteria com- *, Epiſt. 1. ad*
municant, hæc ignominia præualet maximè *Corinth.*
deplorandum. It is much to be lamented
that this ignominy, (that was a vayne
ſuperſtition which they had to daube
their childrens forheades with durte taken out of bathes) præuayleth amongeſt
them who adore the croſſe, and com-
municate the ſecret myſteries. Beholde
here he ſaieth, his people do adore the
croſſe.

Athanaſius, for his great lerning and
ſtouteneſſe in Chriſtes cauſe ageinſt
the Arrianes caulled *Lumen orbis* the
light of the worlde, ſaieth, as it was alleaged before. *Crucis certe figuram ex duo-*
bus lignis componentes adoramus: We certes making a figure of the croſſe of two
pieces of wood do adore it. S. Baſile ſpe- *Epiſt. con-*
aking of the bleſſed virgin Mary, pro- *tra Iulian.*
phetes, Apoſtels, and Martyrs ſaieth: *Apoſtatã.*
Hiſtorias imaginum illorum honoro, & pa- *vt allega-*
lam *tur actio*
4. Nice. 2

I am adoro : *Hoc enim traditum nobis a san-*
Ctis Apostolis non est prohibendum, sed in om-
nibus ecclesijs historias imaginum illorum eri-
gimus. I honour the stories of their images, and openly adore them: for this being deliured vnto vs of the Apostles is
not to be forbedden, but in al oure chur
ches we set vp ther stories. *Lactantius*
Arnobius scholler writing vppō the paffion maketh Christ speake to euery one
that cometh into the church in this forte . *Flecte genu , lignumque crucis venerabile*
adora. Bowe downe thy knee and adore
the reuerend wood of the crosse. *Pauli-*
nus bishop of *Nola* writing to *Seuerus,*
and deſcribing howe myraculously the
crosse of Christ was founde by *Helena,*

Epist. 11.
Aulters
gilded.

faieth : *Consecratur condita in passionis loco*
Basilica, quæ auratis corusca laquearibus , &
aureis diues altaribus, arcano positam sacrario
crucem seruat, quam episcopus vrbis eius quo-
tannis quum pascha Domini agitur adoran-
dam populo, princeps ipse venerantium propo-
nit. The churche builded in the the place of the passion, is halloed , which shy-
ning

ning bright with goodly gilted beames
in the rouffe, and rych with gilded aulters, kepeth the croffe leyed vp in a fecret priuy chappel, which the bishop off
that citie fetteth foorth euery yere at E-
after to be adored of the people, and is
him felf the firft and chefeft man off all
that adore and worfhip it. S. Auguftine
one of the moft famous doctours in
Chriftes churche, declaring that Chriften men haue the figne of the croffe a-
mongeft them, acknowledgeth it to be
worthy of honour, veneratio, and wor-
fhip, and faieth. A*d memoriam crucifixi ve-* Cap.2.de vifitatione
neramur . We woorfhip it in remembra- infirmorū.
unce of oure lord Chrift crucified. Damafcene a lerned father writing of the
croffe faieth . *Adoramus figuram precioſæ* Lib. 4.cap
& viuificæ crucis, &c. We adore the figure 12.de orth.
of the precious and liuely croffe, albeit fide.
it be made of another matter, not worfhipping the matter it felff, for god forbed that, but the figure, as the figne off
Chrift. And a litle after in the fame place he faieth, *Adorandum eſt ſignum C i i*

The figne off Chriſte is to be adored.
which woordes expreſſe a kinde of dew
ty that euery Chriſten man oweth to
the reuerent worſhipping of the ſigne of
the croſſe of Chrſt . The fathers of the
6. general councel kept at Cōſtantino-
ple in *Trullo* to declare what reuerence
euery mā ſhuld haue to the ſigne of the
croſſe made this decree . *Quum crux vi-*
uifica illud nobis ſalutare oſtenderit, nos omne
ſtudium adhibere oportet, vt ei per quam ab an
tiquo lapſu ſaluati ſumus, eum qui par eſt ho-
norem habeamus . Vnde & mente & ſermone,
& ſenſu adorationē ei tribuentes, crucis figu-
ras, quæ à nonnullis in ſolo ac pauimēto fiunt,
omnino deleri iubemus , ne incedentium con-
culcatione victoriæ nobis trophæum iniuria af
ficiatur. Seing the croſſe which made vs
liue, ſheweth and repræſenteth vnto vs
that ſaluation, it behoueth vs to implo-
ye al oure endeuour and ſtudy that we
geue vnto that by which we are redemed from oure old faulle , that honour
which is meete and conueniēt. Where-
vppō we with minde, worde, and ſenſe,
geuing,

The croſ-
ſe ſhuld
not be
trod vppō
ergo
nether
burnte
nor cut in
pieces.

geuing adoration vnto it, commaunde that the figures or fignes off the croffe which of fome be engraued in the grounde, and pauiment, be clene taken away, left by the treading off thofe that paffe by, oure triumphant figne off victorie be iniuried. The feuenth general councel kept a Nyce, proueth and ap proueth the vfe of images, and figne off the croffe in churches and other places, and by the authoritie which Chrift gaue his Apofteles, and left in his churche to lofe and binde, excommunicateth al that impugne the vfe of images : he that doth difcredit this may fe there the who le difcourfe at large.

Nowe iudge yowe good readers whe ther according to the minde of thes ho ly fathers the figne of the croffe, fhulde not be worfhipped and adored. S. Chrifoftome fpeaking of the folemne holy day ordayned in remembraunce off the inuentio of the croffe, faieth that day is *Omni religione colendus.* To be woorfhipped with al holyneffe and religion, and therefore

The auncient fa-thers vvcordes touching he adorat

therefore the defireth his people to come to the churche and woorſhipp the
croſſe:and as he ſaieth . *Crucem adorant.*
they do adore the croſſe. *Athanaſius* ſaieth. *Crucis figuram adoramus* . We adore
the ſigne of the croſſe . S . Baſile ſaieth.
*Hiſtorias imaginum illorum honoro, & pa-
lam adoro.* I honour and opely adore the
ſtories of their images:and men are not
to be forbedden ſo to do, becauſe it is a
tradition of the Apoſtles ſaieth he : and
if ſo holy and auncient a father adored
the images of ſainctes, which were but
creatures,much more he adored the ſigne of the croſſe, and image of Chriſte
his creatour. *Lactantius* ſaieth to him
that cometh into the churche, *Lignum
crucis adora* . Adore thowe the wood off
the croſſe. *Paulinus* ſaieth *Epiſcopus crucem populo adorandam preponit* . The biſſhop ſetteth foorth the croſſe to be adored of the people. S . Auguſtine ſaieth.
*Monumentum crucis omni veneratione dig-
num arbitramur, & ad memoriam crucifixi
veneramur,* We thinke the ſigne off the
croſſe

worthy of al veneration and woorſhip,
and in remembraunce of Chriſt crucified we woorſhip it. Damaſcene ſaieth
Adorandum eſt ſignum Chriſti. The ſigne
of Chriſt is to be adored. The fathers of
the ſixt general councel, ſpeaking of the
croſſe, ſaye: *Eum honorem qui par eſt ei ha-*
beamus adorationem tribuentes .Let vs geue that honour vnto it, which is meete
and cōuenient, geuing adoratiō vnto it.
And yf thes wordes. *Honorare , adorare,*
venerari , veneratione dignum arbitrari,
honorem habere, adorationem tribuere, to honour , to adore , to worſhip , to thinke
worthy of worſhip, to geue honour, to
attribute adoration, vſed of the holy fathers do not importe a kinde of worſhip
and adoration dewe to the ſigne of the
croſſe, let oure newe maſters deuiſe, and
make a newe ſenſe for the forſaied wordes, or els acknowledg it to be trewe
that the ſigne of the croſſe may be adored and woorſhipped , or at the leſt let
them confeſſe that *Conuerſi ſunt in vani-* 1.Timot. 1.
loquium , volentes eſſe legis doctores non in-
R *telligen-*

telligentes neq; quæ loquuntur , nequè de qui-
bus affirmant : They are turned into a
vayne bablynge talke, defirous to be te-
achers of the lawe , not vnderftanding
nether what they faye , nether of what
matters they affirme.

  Thus good readers youe fee howe the
holy fathers off the primitiue church
worfhipped and adored the figne of the
croffe.not attributing vnto it any diuine honour dewe only to god , but as it
hath bene right wel declared before off
others,an inferiour kinde of reuerence,
fuch as hath and may be geué to creatu-
res.And the examples of thes aūcient fa
thers for their holyneffe,vertue,and ler
ning, may be an inftructiõ,and fufficiét
warrant for vs to adore and worfhip the
croffe:and that without fcruple of con-
fcience.For if there had bene any idolatrie,or feare off idolatrie , in woorfhipping the croffe,nether wold thofe good
fathers haue done it them felues,nether
wold they haue commaunded their people to haue done the lieke. Such was
                       their

their zele to the honour off god. Such was their loue to the saluation off mans soule.

Nowe it remaineth that I declare, that there can be no mistruft nor feare of idolatrie in Chriften men worship-ping and adoring the croffe. And here good readers I befeke youe afke my ne-we mafter minifters, this queftion, whe ther they thinke al the fubiectes of the reaulme off England to be Chriftians? Yf they faie al be Chriftians, then muft they confeffe that al are baptized, and haue receaued the faith off Chrift, and beleue in one god father almighty, and fo forth: and haue lerned that comma-undement of his. Thowe fhalt haue no other godes but me. Yf then by bap-tifme they haue receaued the faith off Chrift, and beleue in one god father al-mighty &c. and haue lerned that com-maundement of his, that they fhal haue no other godes but him, then beleue they in no other god but in him, then ferue they no other god but him, then

make

There is no feare of idola-trie in Chriften mē vvorf hipping the croffe make they to them selues no other god but him : but whensoeuer they pray, wheresoeuer they knele, whatsoeuer gestures they vse, they geue al honour and praise to god:they haue their hartes and mindes fixed vppon him. Nor we may iudg the contrary:for they are Chriftians,and so are we also, expereffely forbed to iudg of other mens cōsciences, or to be curious or suspicious of other mens doinges.

Againe idolatrie is a sinne lurking and lying secret in the harte,which only god searching mans harte doth knowe. And what is in man no man knoweeh but the spirite of man which is in man, wherfor vnleffe thes croffe crucifiers wil make a mounte of pride and clime vp to heauen, and take god his office from him, and deriue it with out cōmiffion to thē felues, whenfoeuer they fee a Chriften man praying humbly before the crucifixe, knocking his breaft, holding vp his handes, (which geftures the old auncient fathers haue vfed) they

can

1.cor.2.

can not saye ne think (if they be Christen men them selues)that,that man cō-mitteth idolatrie. For iff as Christ saieth.The houre is come,and nowe it is, *Ioan.4.* that trewe worshippers shal worship the father in spirite and treuthe, then must it nedes be,that nowe Christen men do woorship god in spirite and treuth. For god is a spirite, and they that woorship him must woorship him in spirite and treuth.And in my poore iudgment whē yowe see men praying, it is a good consequent to saye,they be Christen men, therefore they serue god in spirite and treuth.

But perhapes to excuse their proude præsumptuous iudgment of other mens consciences, they wil say it is euident: therefor we my iudg of it: and many are so simple,that by false guides they are quickly deceued, and by the subtilty off the officiers seduced,and made put their trust in this or that image, and so for better speding of their purpose pray vn to it,For answer I say,yf it be euident,it

The heretikes objection answered.

R 3 must

muſt be euident, *aut per confeſsionem* , *aut per probationem* , *aut per faſti euidentiam*: ether by confeſsion, ether by prouffe, ether by euidence of the faſte. Yf it be euident by confeſsion, then ſome man muſt haue confeſſed it : and that is not credible. For idolatrie being an abhominable ſinne, that makeht man infamous to the worlde, and odious in the ſight of god, *Nemo præſumitur confiteri velle contra ſe*. No man is preſuppoſed to be willing to confeſſe it ageinſt him ſelff: in ſuch ſorte that it ſhalbe notorious, and bring hym into perpetual ignominie. For *defenſio eſt naturalis*, defenſe is natural, that is to ſay, euery man naturally defendeth him ſelff: and to præſume ageinſt this, is to preſume ageinſt nature. But yff any man of zeale, to furder the wicked purpoſe of ſuch as deſtroy the croſſe, haue confeſſed this abhominable ſinne of him ſelf, it is to be thought that he hath confeſſed it in no other wiſe, nor vppon any other perſuaſió, then the Iewes that wacched the ſepulchre

confeſ-

confessed that Christes disciples came
in the night whiles they were a slepe,
and stole away their masters body.

Yf it be euident by probation, then
haue they some euident and manifest
prouff of it:and that can they not haue:
for the lawe saieth, that *Probatio de ijs quæ
in animo latent haberi non potest, nisi ex sig-
nis exterioribus: sed signa exteriora inducunt
tantum præsumptionem, & presumptio nun-
quám inducit manifestam & euidentem probationem, ergo, &c.* Prouffe off those thin
ges which lye priuy in the minde cã not
be had but by external signes:but external signes bring in only a præsumption,
and a præsumption neuer bringeth in a-
ny manifest and euident proufe. Therefor of this they cã haue no euident nor
manifest prouffe. Agayne, *Præsumptio e-
lidit præsumptionem.* One præsumption ta
keth away another præsumption:there-
fore seing euery Christen mã is præsupposed to lyue licke a Christé man, *Quia
quisque præsumitur viuere secundum leges,*
because euery man is præsupposed to ly

R 4   ue

ue according to the lawe, the other præ-
fumptiõ which præfuppofeth idolatrie,
is cut of, and wyped away with theo-
ther that præfuppofeth euery Chriften
man to liue lieke a Chriften mã. And in
this cafe to iudge vppon a præfumption
it is nothinge elles, but to breke the cõ-

Mat. 7. maundemét of god, who faieth, *Nolite iu-*
dicare et non iudicabimini : Iudge not and
yowe fhal not be iudged. And who arte
thowe that iudgeft another mans fer-
Rom. 14. uaunt, he ftandeth or faulleth to his lor
de and mafter.

Nowe cõcerning the euidence of the
facte, youe muft vnderftand, that *factũ*
confiftit in externo & corporali actu, animus
in tacito & incorporali intellectu: vnde in a-
nimi effectus non poteft cadere facti euiden-
tia. A facte confifteth in an external and
corporal acte, and the mynde in a fecret
and incorporal vnderftanding (which
can not be feene) therefor the euidence
of a facte can not faulle into the effectes
of the minde, where the abhomination
of idolatrie lieth, which no man can fee,
                                              nifi

niſi qui illuminabit , abſcondita tenebrarum, Math. 16.
but he who ſhal bring to light the ſecre
tes of darkeneſſe.

Touching the other obiection, that
is the ſimplicitie of men , and deceit off
officers, nether of them hath any appa-
raunce of treuth. For firſt it is not to be
thought, that any Chriſten mã is ſo ſim
ple and ignoraunt that he can not diſcerne, and knowe a dead image from a
liue man, a ſtil picture from a quick creature. For if a hounde coming in to a
chamber where hares, hartes, and other
wild beaſtes be painted in the waul, or
cloth of arras, knoweth by the inſtincte of nature, that they be no hartes,
nor hares, nor beaſtes in dede, and iff
birdes haunting to a churche, and ſeing
this or that image, diſcerne by the inſtincte of nature that they be not men
but ſtockes and ſtones, and therefor are
bold to build their neaſtes behinde thē
and nowe and then to mute in their faces, much more muſt a Chriſten man ha
uing beſides the inſtincte of nature, reason,

No man
ſo ſimple
but that
he kno-
weth an
image frõ
a man.

son, cōmon sense, and some kinde of in
struction, be hable to discerne betwene,
stockes and stones, images and mē, lyue
creatures and dead pictures, vnlesse these profounde lerned clerkes wil make
men more brutish thē beastes, more sim
ple then byrdes, and folisher thē dawes:
and with al declare thē selues more spi-
teful then the Sarracenes, who as *Euthi*

Tit. 24.
Panopliæ
aduerf. Sa
race.

mius writeth, slaūdred the Christiās, and
caulled thē idolatours because they adored the crosse, which they thē selues de
tested. As for the other parte of the obie
ction, that any mā being their guide, or
officer in the churche shuld be so wicked, so far destitute of godes grace, that
he wold enterprise to plāt any such opi-
niō in mēs mindes, and persuade thē to
cōmit idolatrie and dishonour god, and
so for worldely gaines daūger his owne
soule, and brīg other into perpetual thra
uldome with the deuil, no Christē man
can thinke it credible in one that profes-

In orat.
funebri in
Athanaf.

seth Christ. For as S. Gregory saieth: *Vt
optimus quisq; est, Ita difficillimè aliū impro*
bum

*bũ eſſe ſuſpicatur.*As euery mã is good him
ſelf,So very hardely he ſuſpecteth another to be euil.Wherefor thes hotte ſprites entring ſo ſone into iudgemēt with
other mens cõſciences, and cõceuing ſo
euil opiniõ of other mens doinges,muſt
nedes condemne thē ſelues to be wicked
and naught:and bẽig wicked and naught
thē ſelues no maruel if they iudge ſini- Eccleſi.10
ſtrouſly of other.For *In via ſtultus ambu*
lans,quũ ipſe ſit ſtultus, omnes ſtultos eſtimat.
A foole walking in the way,whereas he
is a ſole him ſelf,thinketh al other to be
fooles: And as *Suetonius* writeth *Nero*
being the moſt lecherous lorde that liued,culd not perſuade him ſelf that any
man culd be continēt.Wherefor the pre
miſſes conſidred,I cõclude that Chriſtē
men may worſhip and adore theſigne of
the croſſe,and that no Chriſten mã ſeing another praying before the croſſe,
and image of Chriſt,and reuerētly worſ
hipping the ſame, can iuſtely cõceue of
that his external acte any feare or miſtruſt of idolatrie and ſo conſequently
take

take occasion of such external reuerence and adoration made before the crosse
to throwe it downe, and in most despi-
teful manner abuse it . And so for this
matter to auoyde tœdiousnes here I ende.

THE

THE CON-
CLVSION·

Owe good readers feing I haue declared vnto yowe the fignifications off the croſſe, and ſhewed yowe howe it was præfigured by the figures of the lawe of nature, Moyſes, and the prophetes, and ſhewed diuerſe times from heauen in the time of grace, and furder proued by ſufficient authoritie out of the auncient fathers that the ſigne of the croſſe ſhuld be in euery churche, chappel, and oratorie erected to the honour and ſeruice of god, and al other conuenient places, and vſed in al ſacramétes, impreſſed and made in mens for heades, adored and worſhipped of Chriſten men, without feare of idolatrie, and fulfilled my promeſſe in al the other articles mentioned in the preface,

I truſt,

Ecclef. 8. I truſt yowe wil not contemne the de=
claration of the aūciēt fathers, nor paſſe
ouer the doctrine of youre elders who
lerned of their forefathers , but according to the cōmaundemēt of god by his
6. prophete Ieremy aſke *De ſemitii antiquis
quæ ſit via bona*, Of the old pathes whiche is the good away , and walke in the
ſame, and reſt in that whiche ſo many
auncient, holy , and lerned fathers haue
taught yowe touching the vſe off the
croſſe in Chriſtes churche , as in a ſure,
and ſounde doctryne, and thinke that
who ſoeuer teacheth otherwiſe, and yel
deth not to the wordes of oure ſauiour
Chriſte , ſpeaking by the mouth of ſu-
che holy, and lerned prælates of his chur
che, and to that doctrine which is ioy-
1.Timo. 6 ned with pietie, is as S , Paule ſaieth, A
proude man , of no knowledge at al, but
cold and faint about queſtions and ſtrif
of woordes, of which there riſeth enuie,
contention, blaſphemie, euil ſuſpicions,
ſtriffe and debate of men corrupte in
minde, and bereathed of treuth , thinking

king pietie and godlines to be but a mar
ket matter . Whome euery good Chri-
ſté man muſt ſhunne,ſaieth S. Cyprian, *Lib.1.Epi-*
and take heede of the woulfes that ſeuer *ſtola.8.*
the ſheepe from the ſheparde, and neuer
credit their venemous voyce , nor flat
tering woordes, leſt he take darknes for
light,night for day , hunger for meate,
thurſt for drinke, poyſon for medicine,
death for liff . For looke as the wicked
old men wét aboute to defloure the cha
ſte and vertuous Lady *Suſanna*: So thés
heretikes endeuour al that they can to
corrupt by their counterfaite doctrine,
the chaſtitie of the churche, and treuth
of the ghoſpel, from whence the light,
meate, drinke, ſalue, health and life off
mans ſoule is to he had . And they take,
as S Hierome ſaieth , the teſtimonies of
ſcriptures out of the olde and newe te-
ſtament,and ſteale the wordes off oure
lorde, euery one off his neighbour the *In cap.13 .*
prophetes,Apoſtles, and Euangeliſtes, *Ieremie.*
and vſe their owne tounges ,that they
may thruſte out the venemous infe-
ction

&tion of their owne hartes.Andas S.Am

In cap.3.
ad Titum brose saieth . *Per verba legis , legem impug-
nant*.By the wordes off the lawe they
impugne the lawe. For they put vnto
the wordes of the lawe their owne in‑
terpretation ,and meaning, that by the
authoritie of the lawe they maye com‑
mend to the people the wicked deuises
of their owne heades.

Wherefor in the name of god that
Math.7. saieth vnto al his , Beware of false pro‑
phetes whiche come vnto yowe in lam
bes skinnes and within are raueninge
wolfes,and desireth the Romans by his
Rom. 19. Apostle S.Paule in moste milde and gen
tle wordes to flee from those that make
dissensions and offences contrary to the
doctrine which they had ierned , I re‑
quire yow to beware of false prophetes,
Hierem. 9 *Qui docuerunt linguam suam loqui menda‑
cium.*Who haue taught their tounges to
speake lies , and preache the visions off
their owne hartes, and vanities of their
heades, sowe cushins vnder mens elbo‑
wes,and pillowes vnder their heades,to
deceaue

deceaue their foules, and haue diſſeue-
red thē ſelues from the vnitie of Chriſt
his churche, and made diſſenſions, diuiſions,and offenſiues contrary to the
doctrine which they receaued of their
forefathers, theſe heretikes I meane,
who as S. Hierom ſaieth, *Euangelicam*
*veritatem praua intelligentia corrumpunt, & Iu.1.cap.
ſunt caupones peſſimi facientes de vino aquam.* Eſaiæ.
Corrupt the treuthe of the ghoſpel with
their naughty vnderſtanding off it, and
be very bad tauerners making water off
wine,and geue them ſelues to the wan-
ton pleaſures of the bely,eate fleaſhe,re-
ſorte ofté to the bathes, ſmel of muſke,
and being perfumed with ſwete balmes
and pleaſaunt oyntmentes,deſire to ha-
ne their bodiesfayre, propre, cleane,and
neate,and thinke nothing what is to co
me,nor beleue in the reſurrectiō,which
although they open not in woordes,yet
the ſhewe it in their workes, For if they
did beleue their ſhulde be any reſurre-
ction, they wold not enterpriſe thoſe
thinges which they doo,of thes I ſaye I
                    S   require

require yowe to beware, and as children
of light and treuth flee diuifion of vnitie, and the deuilifh doctrine of heretic
kes, from whome abhominatiõ is crept
in to al countries, *Vbi paftor eft, illuc ficut*
*oues fequimini.*Where the fheparde, is thither folloe youe liek good fheepe.

Ignat. Epi
ftola.ad
Trallia.

Amongeft heretickes youe fhal fynde
nothing that may delight yow. They ha
ue no profoũde learning as S.Hiere-
me faieth, *In hæreticis nihil aliud eft quàm*
fulgor eloquentiæ, & fenfus dialectica arte cõ-
ftructus, & fermo mortuus. In hereticke
there is nothing but a glittering glimpfe
of eloquence, and a fenfe builded by the
arte of logick, and dead talke. They ha
ue no treuth, for as S.Cyprian faieth in
effecte, *Apud prophanos & extra ecclefiam*
pofitos effe aliud non poteft nifi mens praua, &
fallax lingua, odia venenata & facrilega men-
*dacia.*Amongeft fuch as are faullen, and
become prophane men and excommu-
nicated out of the churche, there can be
nothinge elles but a wicked mynde, a
deceythfull tounge, poyfoned malice,
and

In 2.Ifaie

Lib.4. E-
pift.9.

and abhominable lyes. They haue no fi
delitie towardes the prince. And therefor Conftantine the greate would ne- *Lib.1.c.f.*
uer admit thofe that had forfake their *Trip.*
religion into his præfence, moft certely
affuring him felf, that they woulde neuer be faithful aboute their prince, who
had forfaken and betrayed their lord
and god. And the rebellions ftirred vp
by frier Luther and his companions in
Germany ageinft the emperour, in Fraunce ageinft the Kinge, in Scottland a-
geinft the Queene, and in England as
yowe knowe, be euident prouffes off
this.

They obferue no iuftice: for where
there is no founde faith, there cã be no
trew iuftice, for the iuft man liueth off
faith. Agayne where there is a fchifme,
ther can be no charitie, and where is no
charitie, there can be no iuftice. *Staphilus*
a lerned man of oure time, and coũfeler
to the late emperour, who liued fome
times familiarly with Luther, and knewe the fecrete diuifes of al the Lutherãs

S 2 tou-

touching poinctes of religion, faieth in
his Apologie that where this newe religion florisheth in Germanie, *Nulla legi-*
tima iuris disceptatio locum habet . No ordinary debating of matters by lawe hath
place, but al is done fearcely, rashly, and
seditiously, with much corruption and
parcialitie: lawes receued with general
consent, are of no force, the authoritie
of common courtes is nothing este-
med, the ordinaunce of the forefathers
set at naught, and al lawe taken awaye
in Germanie. And with vs in England
is it not almost euen so? May not we
saye?

Leges lege carent? iusque ipsum iura tenoris
Amisere sui? sic sic inuertitur ordo,
Sic rerum scœna & facies, ita vt Anglia non
* sit*
Anglia, quæ quondam priscis habitata Bry-
* tannis?*

Be not lordes heastes, na scribes fantasies, parasites pleasures, Macheuelia-
nes policies holden and folloed for law
es? Are not many matters hudled vp in
cor-

corners? examined in chambres? and determined without ordinary proceſſe of the lawe ? haue not ſome bene borne with al becauſe they were proteſtantes? ſome ouerborne becauſe they were papiſtes? ſome of late put to open pænaunce, pryſon, and furder trouble for ſpeaking of a ſprite walking vnder a nutte tree in W parke. And he that broke downe the pale, hunted without his Ladies warrant, imboſſed the white doe, and made the Cockrel crack, neuer touched? but by his holy brother adiudged innocent? I appeale here to the publick fame, and their conſciences who beare the ſway (if they haue any côſciences at al) and complainctes of them who haue felt the ſmarte of it, the more is the pitie. And for al this we may thanke hæreſie: who to cloke her deare dearlinges trechery, and help her frendes and promoters at a pynche, hath no reuerence to publick ordinaunces, and common lawes.

Wel go furder: yowe ſhall fynde no

S 3   chaſte-

chaftetie or very litle amongeft them:
For they holde this as a certé fure pofi-
tion, that a man can no more lyue without the company of a woman, then he
can abftayne from fpetting . And that
if the wiffe be ficke and impotent for
the acte of matrymonie, *Veniat ancilla,*
the hufbond may ioyne iffue with the
mayde. And that euery mã may haue as
many wiffes as he lifte. And diuerfe for
cõfirmation of this holy doctrine, haue
practifed the fame, as euery man may fee
that hathe or wil reade the ftories and
bookes written fence frier Luther begã
ne his ghofpel:who to geue al his fchol
lers example ranne out of his cloyfter,
brooke his vowe of chaftetie, maried a
nonne, after fhe had bene two yeares at
feue fa queue with the fchollers of Wyt
téberg:and by his example made almoft
euery mounke, frier, chanone, and prieft
that came to that newe Chriftianitie, to
get hym a paramour, and amaroufe or
doxie, and for a fayerer name caul her
wife, and peraduenture not contét hym
felff

Staphilus in Apolo.

Bernardi- nus Ochy- nus.

self with her nether, yff she were blacke,
browne, barren, or common to mo, as
Meretrix is a common name to them al.
And to be shorte yow shal fynde no gift
nor grace of the holy ghoste amongest
thē. For as S. Cyprian sayeth, heretickes *Lib.1.Epi*
and schismatickes haue not the holy *stola 6.*
ghost, which resteth only with the hū-
ble, resisteth the proude, and fleeth frō *Sapient.1.*
the dissembler. And such be al heretic-
kes and schismaticks. But yow wil say
it can not be chosen, but they must haue some holy inspirations, they talke so
much of the sprite. Certes what inspira
tions they haue I will not aduenture to
iudge, nor of the sprite they talke and
vaunte so muche of, but leue it to god,
yet this wil I say, yf they haue any sprite at al, it appeareth right wel by their
doinges, that it is the very selff same spri
te that sayed. *Egrediar & ero spiritus men-* *Reg.3. cap*
dax in ore omniū prophetarum eius. I wil goe *22.*
forth, and I wil be a lyinge sprite, in the
mouth of al his prophetes, or that
which holy *Ignatius* describeth, sayin-
S 4	ge,

Epift.ad
Ephef.

ge, I knowe fome who runne vp and
downe amongeſt yowe, hauing an e-
uil doctrine, of a ſtraunge and frow arde
ſprite. That ſprite is a deceauer of the pe
ople, he ſpek:th his owne fantaſies, not
thoſe thinges which be Chriſtes, it is a
falſe ſprite, an erroneous ſprite, he boſ-
teth him ſelf, he preacheth his owne va
nities, he pleaſeth him ſelf, he glorifieth
him ſelf, it is a proude ſprite, a deceyth-
ful ſprite, a flattringe ſprite, and a durtie
ſprite, a triflinge ſprite, a bablinge ſpirte,
a ſeditious ſprite, a fylthye ſprite, and a
tymorous ſprite.

Now then yf yowe can finde no gift
nor grace of the holy ghoſt amongeſt
them, what ſhal yowe finde in them?
For ſooth as S. Cyprian founde that *No
uatus* was: *Deſertor eccleſiæ, miſericordiæ ho-*
ſtis, interfector pænitentiæ, doctor ſuperbiæ, ve-
ritatis corruptor, proditor charitatis &c. A
forſaker of the churche, an enemie off
mercye, a deſtroyer of pænaunce, a teacher of pride, a corrupter of trewth, a be-
trayer of charitie, deſirous of newes, in

*Lib.*1.
*Epiſt.*1.

aua-

auarice infatiable , in fpoylinge other mens goodes raginge madde, pufte vp with pryde, alwayes curious to lerne, that he might betray,alwayes flattringe that he might deceaue , neuer faithful that he might loue,a fyer brande to en-kendle the flame of diffenfion, an hurle winde and tepeftuous ftorme to drow ne faith , and aduerfarie of quietneffe, and enemie of peace, So fhal youe finde al thofe that haue forfake the churche, thes later yeares , and openly profeffed herefie , if ye trye their doinges at the touch fhone. Againe where they præfume to faye that they teache the trewe ghofpel of Chrifte , doctrine of the A-poftells ,and fathers of the primatiue churche , examine them wel and yowe fhal finde them ftarke liers.

Chriftes Apoftles and the auncient fathers of the primitiue churche (as yo-we haue harde it fufficiently proued be fore) willed vs to make the figne of the croffe and fet it vp in churches , chap-pelles,oratories , high wayes ond other places.

places. Thes men wil haue it set vp in
no place, but hurle it owt of church,
chappel, oratorie, and other places where they beare the swaye. Christes Apo-
postles and aunciet fathers willed vs,
to make the signe of the crosse in oure
forheades, breastes, and other partes off
the body. Thes men wil haue vs make it
no where, but saye it is superstitio, so to
do. They worshipped the holy crosse,
and exhorted al Christen men to doe
the lieke. Thes men wil haue no reuerence nor honour done to the crosse.
They caulled the crosse (as yow may see
in diuerse places of this treatise) *Signum
Dei, Signum filij hominis, signum cœlestis imperatoris, Symbolum multæ benedictionis, pignus æternæ salutis, Venerabile monumentum,
viuificum signum, victoriale trophœũ,* [a] *Virtutis signum, venerabile lignum, cœlestem no-
tã, immortale signũ.* The signe of god, the

a *Ambros.
lio.6.cap.
4.de sacra
mentis.*

signe of the sonne off man, the signe of
the emperour of heauen, the token off
much blesing, the pledge of æternal sal
uatio, an honorable monument, a signe
that

that maketh lif, a triūphant banner off
victorie, a signe of vertue, an honorable
wood, an heauenly marke, an immortal signe. Thes men resemble it to the
Aegiptians *Apis*, and caulle it the catholikes māmot, and papistes idol. They ga
ue the crosse many goodly Epithethōs
and titles of honour: and saied that the
crosse is *Sancta, preciosa, venerabilis beata,
adoranda & vere honoranda*. Holy, præci-
ous, reuerend, blessed, worthy to be adored, and trewly honored. Thes men ge
ue it the vileſt woordes off reproche
that they cā deuise, and vse it as though
it were a prophane, vile, cōtemptile, and
odious thing, worthy to be maligned
and hated. Howe agreeth this with
Chriſtes Apoſtles and auncient fathers
of the primitiue churche?

Furder more when there rose a contention amōgeſt the Apoſtles which of
them ſhuld be greater, and haue the præ
eminence ouer other, Chriſt saied *Qui* Luce. 22.
*maior eſt in vobis, fiat ſicut iunior, et qui præ-
teſſor eſt, ſicut miniſtrator.* He that is grea-
                                        ter

ter amongeſt yowe, let him be as a youn
ger or vnderlinge, and he that is chiefeſt,
as a feruant : by which woordes as he
taught them al humilitie, ſo he geueth
vs to vnderſtand that then there was
one greater then another amongeſt
them. For he ſaieth. *Qui eſt maior*, He that
is greater, which woordes do of necef-
ſitie importe a maioritie. Therefore to
ende this cõtrouerſie, he appointed, the
præeminence to S. Peter ſayinge : *Tu es*
Petrus, & ſuper hanc petram ædificabo eccle-
ſiam meam. Ego rogaui pro te Petre vt non
deficiat fides tua: & tu aliquando conuerſus
confirma fratres tuos. Petre amas me, paſce o-
ues meas. Thow arte Peter, and vppon
this rocke I wil builde my church. I haue prayed for the Peter that thy faith
ſhal not fayle, and thowe beinge ones
conuerted, cõfirme thy bretherne. O Pe
ter doeſt thow loue me, feade my ſhe-
pe. And ſo al the fathers of the churche
with one vniforme conſent, interpret
thoſe wordes of Chriſte. S. Cypriã ſayeth. *Petrus ſuper quem ædificata fuit a Do-*
mino,

Math. 16.
Lucæ. 22.

Ioan. 21.

Lib. 1. Epi
ſtola. 3.

mino ecclesia, dicit, Domine ad quem ibimus? *Ser.de ha-*
Petrus, cui oues suas Dominus pascendas tu- *bitu vir,*
endasque commendat, super quem posuit &
fundauit ecclesiam, aurum sibi & argentum *Lib. 4. E-*
esse negat, Petrus loquitur super quem ad fi- *pistola. 9.*
canda fuerat ecclesia, loquitur ad Petrum Do
minus. Ego dico tibi quia tu es Petus &c. Su- *Tract. 3. de*
per vnum edificat ecclesiam. Peter vppon *simp. præl.*
whome the church was builded by oure
lorde, saieth. Lorde to whome shal whe
goe?Peter to whome Christe commen-
deth his sheape to be fead and defended,
vppon whom he layed and founded his
churche, saieth he hath no golde nor sil
uer. Peter vppon whome the churche
was to be builded speaketh. Oure lorde
speaketh to Peter, I saie vnto the thowe
arte Peter, and vppō this rocke, I wil buil
de my churche. *Super vnum ædificat.* He
buildeth it vppō one. Leo the first saieth *Epist. 7 9.*
Peter receaued the principalitie or chea-
fe præeminence of oure lorde. S. Ambro *Ad 5. Lu-*
fe saieth Peter is the suer piller of the *cæ.*
churche-S.Hierome saieth. Peter is the *In catal. ec-*
prince of the Apostels. S. Augustine sa- *clesiast.*
  scrip.
                              yeth

ieth in many places, Peter is the chea-
fest amongest the Apostels. S. Chrisostome saith: *Petrus est* a *antesignanus di-*
scipulorum, Apostolorum coriphæus b *aliorũ*
princeps, c *omnium vertex.* d *Christus Pe-*
tro per orbem tarrarum e *præsidentiam tra-*
didit. Christus illum authoritate esse prædi-
tum voluit, & reliquos f *præcellere. Christus*
Petro & successoribus g *Petri, curam ouium*
suarum committebat. Peter is the grande
capitayne of the disciples, the head off
the Apostles, the prince of al other, the
top of al. Christ committed to Peter the
rule and chiefe gouernemét of his churche through owt the worlde. Christe
woulde him to be indued with authoritie and excel the rest. Christ cómitted to
Peter, and the successours of Peter, the
cure and charge of al his sheape. And the
se newe men saie, al the Apostels were
æqual, and that Peter had no præeminé-
ec, nor prerogatiue more then the rest.
How agreeth this with Christ and the
auncient fathers off the primitiue churche?

Agay-

a Ho.1. in Epist ad Rom.
b Ho.29 in Epist.
c Ho.4 in 1.Corin.
d ho.55.in 16.Mat.
e Ho.80. Antio.
f Lib.2.de sacer.
g lib.2.de sacer.

Agayne *Ignatius* caulleth, the chur-*Epist.ad Romanos.* che of Rome where Peter had his cha-yer and seate, a churche sanctified, and lightned, by the wil of god, which also is præsident and chiefe, in the place, off the nation of the Romans, worthy off god for faith, præeminence, blessednesse and peace, founded in the loue and faith of Christe, and bearinge the holy gho-*Lib.3.E-* ste.S. Cyprian saieth it is the principal *pist.3.* churche from whence the priestely vni tie is sprounge.S. Ambrose caulleth the churche which *Damasus* in those dayes *In ca.3.ad* ruled (that was the churche of Rome) *Timoth.* the house of god. Leo the first saieth. *Roma est discipula veritatis, gens sancta, po-* *Ser.de pe-* *pulus electus, ciuitas sacerdotalis & regia, per* *tro & Paя* *sacrā B.Petri sedem caput totius orbis effecta,* *lo.* *latius præsidens religione diuina, quàm do-* *minatione terrena.* Rome is a scholler off treuth, an holy nation, an elect people, a priestely and princely citie, made by the holy sea te of blessed Peter, the head of al the worlde, furder extending her soueraintie by holy religion, then euer

it

it coulde by earthly power. *Theodoritus*
biſhop of *Cyrus* in his epiſtle ſet before
his commentaries vppon S. Paules epi-
ſtles, ſaieth the church of Rome is *Max*
ima, præclariſſima, & quæ præſt orbi terra-
rum, the greateſt churche, the moſt nobleſt churche, and the curche that hath
the præeminence and præſidéceſhip ouer

Actione
prima Con
cil Chalce-
do.

al the worlde. The good emperour Mar
tianus in his oration made to the fathers
of the coũcel of Chalcedõ, caulleth the
churche of Rome. *Thronum Apoſtolicum.*
The Apoſtolical throne.

Aut. tit. 4.

Iuſtinian the Emperour ſaieth. Rome is the countrie of lawes, the fountay

C. de ſum
ma Trinit.
& fide ca-
tho.

ne of prieſthode, the heade of al holy
churches. And theſe newe men caulle it
the hoore of Babilon, the ſeate of Anti-
chriſt, the ſincke of ſinne, the corruption of the worlde, the mother of al abhomination. Howe wel agreeth this
with the holy fathers?

Lib. 1. E-
piſt. 3.

Agayne S. Cyprian ſaieth. The churche of Rome, hath bene, and is the only
churche to which infidelitie, and vn-
faith-

faithfulnes could neuer haue accesse. S.
Hierome saieth the holy churche of Ro *Epist. ad Damas.*
me hath alwayes remained immaculate,
and shal always continue firme, stead-
fast, and immoueable. At Rome the au- *Ibidem.*
thoritie of the auncient fathers remayneth vncorrupte, there the grounde with
her fertil soyle brigeth foorth, the trew
seade of oure lorde, with an hunderfol-
de increase. *Ireneus* saieth, that in the *Lib.3.c.3.*
church of Rome that tradition which
came from the Apostles, hath always
bene kept. S. Ambrose and the fathers
off Telens writing to *Syricius* Bisshop
of Rome, saye, *Ecclesia Romana symbolum
Apostolorum intemeratum semper custodit
& seruat.* The church of Rome doth obserue and kepe the faith or Crede of the
Apostels vndefiled, and without ble-
mish. And these newe men say there is
nothing in the church of Rome but errour and heresie, nothing but vayne superstition and mans inuention. Howe
wel agreeth this with the holy fathers?

Agayne S. Cyprian saieth: *Cum Corne* *Lib.4.Epi stola 2.*

T *lio*

THE CONCLVSION.

lio esse, idem est quod cum ecclesia catholica cō municare. Et probare & firmiter tenere communicationem ecclesiæ Romanæ, est catholicæ ecclesiæ vnitatem pariter ac charitatem probare & firmiter tenere. To be with *Cornelius,* (who was then bifshop of Rome) is the very felf fame thing, that it is to cōmuni cate with the Catholicke church. And to allowe and firmely holde the focietie and communitie of the church off Rome, is to allowe and firmely holde both the vnitie, and charitie of the Catholicke churche. S. Ambrofe faieth, *De Catholicis episcopis esse, est cū ecclesia Romana cōuenire.* Tho be one of the Catholike bifshops, is to agre with the church of Rome. S. Hierome writinge to *Damafus* pope of Rome faieth. I folloinge none, but Chrift, ame made a felloe together in cōmunitie with youer holinefle, that is with the chaier of Peter: vppon that I knowe the church to haue bene builded, whofoeuer eateth the lambe with out this houfe, is a prophane and vngod ly man, whofoeuer gathreth not with the,

Lib. 4.
Epist. 8.

In oratio
funeb. de
obitu fratris.

the fcattreth abrode . He that is not
Chrift his feruant, is Antichriftes.Befi-
des he faieth *Romana fides,eft Apoftolica fi-* Lib.3.con-
*des.*The faith of the church of Rome, is tra Ruffi.
the Apoftolicke faith . *Romana fides , eft* Lib.1.con-
*Catholica fides.*The faith of the church of tra Ruff.
Rome is the Catolick faith.And by the
fe authorities of S . Cyprian, Ambrofe,
and Hierome , we fee that no man can
be a member of the Catholicke church
vnleffe he be with the Bifhop of Rome.
No mã can keepe the vnitie, and charitie of the Catholicke church,vnleffe he
kepe the focietie and communiõ of the
church of Rome . No man can eate the
lambe *Iefus* Chrifte without the vnitie
of the church of Rome. No man can ha
ue the Apoftolicke and Catholicke
faith , vnleffe he hath the faith of the
church of Rome.No man can be any of
the Catholicke Biffhoppes , vnleffe he
agreeth with the church of Rome. And
no man gathreth with Chrift,that fepa
reth him felf from the church of Rome . And thefe newe mẽ haue feparated

T 2　　them

thē selues from the vnitie of the church
of Rome, and abandoned al the authoritie of the same, and yet accompte thē
selues Catholickes. How agreeth this,
with the holy and auncient fathers?

Lib.3. c.3.   Agayne *Ireneus* saieth: It is necessa-
rie that euery church, that is to saye, al
faithful men disperfed in the worlde a-
brode, come to the church of Rome, for
the mightier principalitie, and præeminence? And so haue al churches in al a-
ges done, and when any controuersie
touching pointes of religion and matters of faith rose, the prælates assembled
them selues together, and confulted and
conferred with the sea of Rome, for de-
cision of it : as al that wil reade the stories of the church, may see. And so they
thought it their dewtie to do, lieke as
other gaue them example in the Apostels tyme. Who when the controuersie
of circumcision and obseruation of the
lawes of *Moyses* rose vp amōgest them,
agreed that Paule and Barnabe, and certen other shuld goe vp to *Hierusalem,*

to

to the Apoſtels concerning that que-
ſtion . And lieke as S. Paule him ſelf
taught them , who when he had preached the ghoſpel a longe tyme,went to
Hieruſalem, and that by reuelation,and *Galath.2.*
conferred the ghoſpel which he prea-
ched to the gentils,with them , and pri-
uatly with thoſe, who ſemed to be ſo-
mewhat,to be in eſtimation and chieffe ἰοῖς δο-
amongeſt them , leſt peraduenture he κοῦσι.
had,or ſhuld runne in vayne.And theſe
new men hauing diuerſe ſectes , opinions,controuerſies,and queſtions amon
geſt them,contrarie to the Catholicke
church, being caulled to a goodly côfe-
rence,where the beſt learned men of al
Chriſtendome were aſſembled , hauing an aſſuraunce ,and ſaulf conducte
promeſed them,to come thither, to tarry there,to ſay what they could,to pro-
pounde what they would,to returne at
their pleaſure,with al kinde of ſecuritie The pro-
that one man could promiſe another, teſtantes
would not vouchſaffe to come to that vvonld
aſſemble of lerned men,and confer the not come
to the ge-
neral coũ
cel.

T 3 do-

doctrine and ghofpel which they preached, but thought it better for them to
runne to Luther at Witteberg, to Swin
glius at Zurich, to Caluin at *Geneua*, to
Beza and his cõpanions in Fraunce,and
others in other corners, then confer as
S.Paule did with τοῖς δοκοῦσι,the chiefeſt,
the beſt lerned, the pillers of the churche. Howe agreeth this with the Apoſtels and fathers of the primitiue church?

Furder, oure fauiour Chriſt infti-
tuting the holy facrament off his body and bloud to be a perpetual comforte and foode of mans foule, faied in
moſt playne wordes. This is my body
which ſhal be geuen for yowe. This is
my bloud which ſhal be ſhed for yowe.
And ſo haue the fathers of the primitiue church taken it to be the very body
of Chriſt that was borne of the virgin,
betrayed of *Iudas*, and crucified of the
iewes, the fame bloud that flowed and
iſſued out of his ſide : and openly pro-
noũced that there is no bare figure,tro-
pe, norfigne, but that the bread and
wine,

wine by the operatiō of the holy ghoſt,
and omnipotency of god his worde, be
chaunged, not in outward ſhewe, but in
nature, into the ſubſtaunce of Chriſtes
body and bloud, as al their writinges te-
ſtifie. And thes newe men teach the peo
ple that there is nothing but bread and
wyne, nothing but a naked ſigne, nothing but a bare figure, and ſimple remē-
braunce. Howe agreeth this with the
doctrine of Chriſt and fathers of the
primitiue churche?

Agayne Chriſt toke bread in his han
des and bleſt it, and brake it. They al ty
me of their communion neuer take it
vp in their handes, but let it ſtande ſtil
vppon the table, vntil they geue it the
communicantes, and then they cut it,
vnleſſe the ſextin, or butler with his
chipping kniff haue eaſed them of that
payne. Agayne in the primitiue church,
in the ſacrifice of the body and bloud of
Chriſt, the holy fathers mingled water *Lib.8.cap.*
with wyne, as it appeareth by S. Clemēt *17.Conſt.*
and Iuſtine martir: and that as Chriſte *Apoſt.* *Apol.2.*
T 4 him

him felf ordayned. For Chriſt ſaieth S,

Lib.2.Epi
ſtola 3. Cyprian ordayning this ſacramēt , mingled water with wyne whē he conſecra
ted the cup of his moſt precious bloud,
In the ſacramétes of the body and bloud
let nothing more be offred then oure
lorde him ſelf deliured, that is bread and
wyne mingled with water ſaye the fathers of the fourthe councell kept at
Can.24. Carthage. Bread is ſet vppon the aulter,
and a chalice . Into the chalice wyne it
Lib.5.cap. put , and what els ? water ſaieth S . Am-
1.de ſacra- broſe, Becauſe water and bloud iſſued
Lib.4.
Cap.5. out of the ſide of oure lorde when it was
pearced with the ſouldiers ſpeare. Agai-
Lib.4 .ca.
4 .de ſa-
crament. ne he ſaieth wyne mingled with water
in the chalice , is made by the cōſecratiō
of the heauenly worde , the bloud off
Lib.4. ca.
14. Chriſt. Chriſt ſaieth Damaſcene taking
the cup of wyne and water, deliured it
to his diſciples ſaying drinke ye al off
this. The fathers of the ſixt general councel kept at Conſtantinople , made a
Can.32. decre that in the ſacrifice wyne mixed
with water ſhuld be offred, and they ſaye

ye that in al churches where they holy e
fathers were this order geuen from god
aboue, was obſerued,and that S. Iames,
oure ſauiour Chriſtes brother, and S.
Baſile B. of *Cæſaræa*taught this in the
liturgie or maſſe which they left vs in
writing. The fathers of the councel off
Antiſiodorum ſaye, It is not lawful to *cap.1.*
offer vp at the aulter any cup, but that
which is myngled with water: and the
prieſtes that do otherwiſe incurre greate daunger,and deadly ſinne, for which
they are not to be borne with al. For as
S. Cypriã ſaieth:We who are inſtructed *Lib.2.Epi*
of oure lord god to offer vp the cup of *ſtola.3.*
Chriſt mixed with wyne, euen as oure
lorde offred it,can not be pardoned and
borne with al,iff we do not obſerue and
kepe this tradition. And therefor writing to *Cæcilius* he ſaieth *Religioni noſtræ*
conuenit & timori, & loco & officio ſacerdo-
tij noſtri frater chariſſime in Dominico calice
miſcendo, & offerendo, cuſtodire Dominicæ
traditionis veritatem. O derely beloued
brother, it is agreable to oure religion,
and

and feare, and to the very place and office of oure priefthode to kepe the
treuth of oure lordes tradition in mix-
ing, and offring the cup off oure lorde.
By thes authorities, I meane S. Clemét
Iuftine martyr, S. Cyprian. Ambrofe,
Damafcene, and the fathers of the councel of Carthage, Cóftantinople, and
Antifiodorum, yowe fee that in the facrifice of the body and bloud of Chrift,
water was alwayes mingled with wine,
and that it is not mans deuife, but Chrifte ordinaunce, not the popes inuention, but oure lordes tradition. And yet
thes newe men vtterly contemne and
irride this tradition, and neuer mingle
water with wyne in their communion,
Howe agreeth this with the doctryne
off Chrift and the holy fathers? *

Agayne the bleffed Apoftel S. Iames, S. Bafile, and Chrifoftome in their
liturgies, or maffes which they vfed,
and left to vs in writing, made inuocation to the bleffed virgin Mary mother
of god, and other fainctes. Thes men in
their

Yf youe faye vve haue no fcripture for this, vve anfvvere yo ue vvith the fcrip- ture: Sunt & a- lia multa quæ fecit Iefus quæ fi fcribátur per fin- gula, nec i- pfum arbi- tror mun- dum capere poffe, qui fcribendi funt, libros cap.20. & 21. Ioan.

their communion vſe none. S. Cyprian *Lib.1.Epi-* deſired *Cornelius* iffhe died before him *ſtola 1.* to praye vnto god for him , and al their Chriſtē bretherne. Gregory Naziāzene *In Mono-* *dia.* praied to S. Baſile in this ſorte. Looke I beſeke the out of heauen vppon vs, and ether commaunde the weakneſſe of the raynes of my back , and payne of my iointes to go from me, or help me to ta-ke it patiently, that when I departe hen-ce, thowe maieſt receue me into euer-laſting tabernacles. Ephrem S. Baſiles ſcholler in a ſermon made De *Laudibus* *Martyrum*, praieth thus . O moſt glori-ous Martirs help me miſerable man *De laud.* with youre prayers, that in the terrible *Paulæ.* day when al ſecrettes ſhalbe opened, I *Hymno in* may obtayne mercy . *Prudentius* prayed *honorē D.* *Laurentij.* to S. Laurence. S. Hierome to *Paula*. S. *Cap.23.* Auguſtine to al ſainctes . And thes men *Meditat.* wil haue vs praye to none. Ho we wel agreeth this with the holy fathers?

S. Cyprian ſaieth that holy Martirs, *De ſtella* *& Magis.* *Clementiam Dei pro noſtris exorant labori-* *bus.* Do intreate the merciful clemency
of god

of god for oure trauelles and paines,S.
Bafile faieth he that is trobled goeth to
the forthy Martirs, he that is mery run-
neth to them: the one to haue comforte
in his miferie,and the other cōtinuaun-
ce in profperitie.And in the fame place
Ser.de. he caulleth thofe forthy Martirs . *Com-*
4 0. Mar. *munes humani generis cuſtodes : curarum ſo-*
cios , Orationis cooperatores . Common
wauffters of mankinde,companions of
oure cares , and workers with vs in pra-
yer.S.Chrifoftome faieth . Oftentimes
Ho.41. when there is no iuft man founde in
in ge. this liff,god taketh mercy vppon the li-
Ser. de pœ
niten.& uing for the vertue of the dead.And the-
conf.to. 5. refor he faieth by his prophete Efai *Pro*
Cap.37. *tegam ciuitatem hanc propter me & propter*
*Dauid puerum meum.*I wil defend this citie for my owne fake , and for my feruaunte Dauid his fake . In another pla-
Ho.27 . in ce the fame father faieth,*Dauid* after his
Math. woundes did fo fhyne, and wafht him
felf fo cleane from fpottes , that beinge
dead he could help with his prayer,
fuch as fucceded him . And in another
place

place hesaieth. *Dauid mortuus est & Eze-* *In pfal.* 50 *Ho.*2.
chiæ viuo patrocinatur: Dauid is dead, and
defendeth *Ezechias* whois a liue, S.Au- *Lib.*2.*quæ stio.exe.*
guftine fayieth God pardoneth the fin-
nes of his people thorough the prayers *cap.* 108.
of holy Martirs, and that god doth ma- *Lib.*22.*cæ.*
ny miracles, or by the prayers, or by the 10.*de ciui-*
meanes of Martirs. Leo the firft faieth. *tate Dei.*
Let vs vfe to oure amendemét the mer-
cy and gentilneffe of god fauouring vs
that bleffed Peter and al the faindtes
who haue aided vs in al oure trobles *S er in oĉa*
may vouchfaffe to helpe oure prayers *Petri & Pauli.*
before oure merciful god, for Iefus
Chrifte his fake. And thes newe men
fay that faindtes can not helpe vs, nor
heare vs when are pray vnto thé: which
is contrary to the doĉtrine of the auncient farhers, yea and the fcriptures thé
felues. For the angels and faindtes here
what we faye, and vnderftand what
we do. The Angel knewe that Daniel
was *Vir defideriorum.* A man of defires, in *Da.*10.
fauour with god for his denout praiers,
and therefor he came vnto him. The
                                    angel

angel Raphael faied to Tobie:whē thowe dideſt pray with teares,and bury the
dead,I offred vp thy praier to god. Yf the
angel offred vp Tobie his praier to god,
thē he harde his prayer , if he harde his
praier he vnderſtode his praier,and knewe that he prayed,wept, and buried the
dead . Againe Chriſt faieth in S.Luke,
there ſhal be greate ioy in heauen before
the āgels vppō a ſinner doing pænaūce.
Yf the bleſſed angels in heauē reioyſe at
the cōuerſiō of ſinners,thē they vnder-
ſtād whē ſinners do pænaūce,and cōuer
te frō their wickedneſſe , and turne to
god. Beſides Chriſt faieth to his Apoſt
les,whē the ſonne of mā ſhal ſit in the ſe
ate of maieſtie youe ſhal alſo ſit vppō the
xij.ſeates,iudging the.xij.tribes of Iſrael.
If the Apoſtels ſhal ſit in iudgemēt , and
iudge euery man according to his deme
rites , thē muſt they nedes knowe what
euery mā hath done,and what euery mā
hath deſerued, otherwyſe they can geue
no right iudgement.And yet thes newe
mē ſaie that nether angel, Apoſtel, mar
tir,

Tob.12.
Cap.15.
Mat.19.

tir,nor any other sainǎe in heaué cã hea
re vs whé we pray vnto thé, nor vnder-
ſtãd what we praye. Howe wel agreeth
this with the doǎrine of Chriſt and aũ
cient fathers off the primitiue church?

Beſides al this, *Dioniſius Areopagita*
telleth vs, that in his tyme the biſſhop *Cap.7.*
praied ouer the dead,and deſired the mer *Eccleſiaſt.*
cy off god to the pardon al his offenſes *Hierar.*
committed by humane frailtie, and pla-
ce him in the boſome of *Abraham, Iſaac*
and *Iacob*. Tertullian ſaieth in his tyme *Lib. de co-*
they made oblations for the dead.S.Cy *ro. militis.*
prian teſtifieth the ſame for his.And A- *ſtola 9.* *Lib.1. Epi*
thanaſius for his, ſaying . *Peccatorũ animæ* *De varijs*
participant aliqua beneficentia ab exangui im *quæſt.*
molatione et gratificatione pro ipſis facta:ſicut *quæſt.34.*
ſolus ordinat & præcipit qui viuorum & mor
*tuorum poteſtatem gerit deus.*The ſoules of
ſinners receaue ſome benefit of the vn-
blouddy ſacrifice and almes done for
them, as god only who beareth rule o-
uer the liue and dead doth ordayne and
cémaunde.S.Chriſoſtome ſaieth .It is *Ho.69.*
not without canſe ordained off the A- *pop.Antio*

poſtels

postels that in the dreadful mysteries

Sozo.li 9. cap. 48. *Trip.* remembraunce be had of the dead. *Epi-phanius* bisshop of Cypres hearing as he went on his iourny, that one was dead, *Lib.* 20. *de ciui.dei. cap.* 9. praied that he might rest in peace: S.Augustine saieth . The soules of good men that are dead , are not separated from the churche, which euen nowe is the kingdome of Christ , otherwise there shuld be no memory made of them at the aulter of of god in the communion of the body of Christ. Againe in his bo ke De *cura pro mortuis agenda* he saieth: Albeit it were not reade in the old scripture, yet the authoritie of the vniuersal churche is not smal , which in this custome is euident: where in the praier of the priestes which are offred to oure lor de god at his aulter, the commendation of the dead had his place. *Paulinus* wri- *Epist.*1. ting to *Amandus* desireth him to praye for one of his frendes that was dead . *Vt Deus refrigeret animam eius stillicidijs miseri cordiæ*. That god would coole his soule with the droppes of his mercy. Of this

praying

praying for the dead, the fourth coūcel
kept at Carthage maketh mentiō alfo, *Ca.79.*
and the coūcel kept at Vafe in Fraunce,
and fo hath the church alwaies vfed to *Ca. 4.*
pray for the dead, and kepe their com- *To.1.con.*
memoration at the aulter in the dreadful myfteries, as an ordinaunce of god,
and tradition of the Apoftels, as *Athana*
fius and Chrifoftome recorde vnto vs
in the places alleaged before. And thes
newe men in their communion wil haue no prayer for the dead, but preache
tothe and nayle ageinft it, as a fuperfti-
tious rite, and fuperfluous cofte. Howe
agreeth this with the doctrine of Chrift
and his Apoftles, and auncient fathers
of the primitiue church?

Agayne, God faieth to euery man by
his prophete, *Dic tu iniquitates tuas vt iu-* *Efaie. 43.*
ftificeris. Confeffe and tel thy iniquities
that thoue maieft be iuftified. And by
the wife mā he teacheth vs, that he that *Prouerb.28*
hideth his faultes fhal not be directed,
but he that wil confeffe them, and for
fake thē, fhal obtaine mercy. By his A-
V   poftel

poſtel S.Iames, he biddeth vs côfeſſe ou
re ſelues one to another: that is to ſay,
as ſome expounde it, we muſt not only
confeſſe oure ſelues to god , but amongeſt oure ſelues, one to another, men to
men, the ſheape to the ſheapard, the ſubiectes to the prælates, they that haue ſin
ne, to ſuch as haue authoritie and pouer
to forgeue ſinne: that is the biſſhoppes,
and prieſtes , to whome it was ſaied in
the perſon of the Apoſtles , Receue ye
the holy goſt, whoſe ſinnes ye forgeue,
are forgeue them . And ſo haue the fathers of the primitiue churche alwayes
taught. Tertulliâ ſaieth, he that wil treu
ly repent, muſt nourriſh his praiers with
faſting, he muſt lament, and weape , *Et
presbyteris aduolui*, and faul downe at the
prieſtes feete. And when he is at the pri
eſtes feete, what muſt he do? Origen ſaieth, he muſt open his deſeaſe, and do as
the man doth whoſe ſtomake is conte
red with fleume, and euil humours : He
muſt caſt vp al, and ſhewe his phiſition
the grounde of his deſeaſe, and follo his
coun

Cap.5.

Ioan.20.

*Lib. de pœ-
nitentia.*

*Ho.2.in
pſalm. 37.*

counsel in healing of it . He must confesse as S. Cyprian saieth, his faultes whi
les he is in this worlde, whiles his con-
fesion m ay be admitted, whiles satisfaction and remission geuen by the prieste,
is acceptable before god. S. Basile saieth,
it semeth necssary that we confesse oure sinnes to thole, to whome the dispen
sation of the mysteries of god is geuen:
for so in old tyme they that did repent,
are founde to haue confessed their syn-
nes before holy mē. *Sozomenus* declareth
in the Tripartite historie , that the old
bisshops vnderstanding , that because
men did refuse to confesse their sinnes,
they got a greater burdē of sinne, apointed a priest of good cōuersatiō, politick,
and wise, and such a one as could con-
ceale matters of secret, committed vnto
him , to heare confessions . And men
that had offended , coming vnto him
confessed their sinnes, and he according
to euery mans faulte , did inioyne them
pænaunce.

    Let vs persuade oure selues saieth

Tract. 5. de
lapsis.

In Reg.
Monach. c.
21. & cap.
99.

Lib. 9.
cap. 32.

V 2   Chri-

Homil. 41 *ad pop. Antioch.* Chrifoſtome, that we haue ſinned, and let vs not ſay it with oure tounges, but alſo with oure hartes, let vs not only caul oure ſelues ſinners, but alſo let vs counte and number oure ſinnes parti-

Epiſt. 5. *ad Theod.lap-ſum.* cularly. For in very deede ſaieth he, for a man to condemne and profeſſe him ſelf a ſinner, it is commō with infidels. Many as wel men, as women coming from the pleying of a comedie, when they conſider their owne filthineſſe, are ſory for it, and pittie their owne caſe, but they eyme not at the right maike, and therfor in no wiſe I wil caul that a confeſsion, becauſe it is not done with compuction of harte, bitterneſſe of tea-res, and putting away off ſinne, and that becauſe they vtter their ſinnes after ſuch ſorte ſaieth Chriſoſtome.

Ho. 48. *de pænitentia.* S. Auguſtine crieth to his people, and biddeth them do pænaunce, ſuch as is done in the church, that the church may pray for thē. Let no man ſay, I do it ſecretly. I do it before god, who can par-dō me, who knoweth what I do in my

har-

harte. *Ergo sine causa dictum est quæ solue-*   Math. 16.
ris in terra,erunt soluta & in cælo: ergo sine
causa datæ sunt claues ecclesiæ dei . Frustra-
mus euangeliū dei,frustramus verbum Chri-
sti. Yff it be sufficient to do pænaunce
secretly in harte,and make oure confession only to god , then was it saied to
no purpose,whatsoeuer thowe losest in
earth,shalbe losed in heauen.Then were the keyes geuen to to the church off
god in vayne , we frustrate the ghospel
of god,we make the woorde of Christ
voyd and of no effect . And in deede
yf euery man might reconcile hym selff
without the help of a prieste , to what
purpose did god the father geue the A-
postles,and in the Apostles , bisshopes
and priestes , *Ministerium reconciliationis,*   2. Corinth.
the ministery or office of reconciliation?   5.
Wel for furder prouffe of this in another,place he saieth.A man must not on   Homil. 41
ly refrayne from sinne after he hath do   To. 10.
ne pænaunce,but also before,whiles he
is whole and in good health. Fot yff he
contynewe in sinne vntil his later da-

         V 3   ye,he

ye, he knoweth not whether he ſhal be
hable to receaue any pænaunce, and cō-
feſſe his ſinnes, *Deo & ſacerdoti*, to god
and the prieſte. S.Ambroſe in his boke
De Cain & Abel, Leo in his epiſtle to *Theo*
dorus Rabanus in his boke *De pænitentia*,
S.Hierome vppon the tenth of *Eccleſia-*
ſticus teach vs the ſame, touching confeſ
ſion. By which authorities youe ſe good
readers, that mē agreued with the burdē
off ſinne, muſt faul downe at the prieſtes feete, and confeſſe their ſinnes. Youe ſee here mention made of cōfeſsion
made to the prieſte, remiſsion of ſinnes geuen by the prieſte, pænaunce in-
ioyned by the prieſte, and their opinion
condemned by S.Auguſtine who ſay it
is ſufficient to do pænaunce ſecretly in
harte before god. And the publick confeſsion vſed at the communion impro-
ued by S.Chriſoſtome. And why? he
geueth a reaſon hym ſelff, and ſayeth
becauſe they vtter their ſinnes in ſuch
ſorte, generally, and not as they ſhuld,
and he commaundeth *Per ſpecies*, par-
ticularly

cap.4.
Epiſt.91.

ticularly, euery one in his kinde. Youe see by S. Basile, that it is necessary
and nedeful to confesse youre sinnes
to them, who haue the dispensation of
Christes mysteries geuen vnto them,
that is the priestes. And thes newe men
wil haue no such secret confession, but
vtterly abandone it, and caulle it the
tormenting of mens consciences. Howe agreeth this with the doctrine off
Christ, and the Apostels, and fathers of
the primitiue church?

Besides Christ biddeth vs wacche and *Marci.14.*
pray, that we enter not into temptation.
S. Iames that we may be saued. S. Paule *Iacob.5.*
that we may be deliured from troblesо *2.Thessa.3*
me personnes and wicked mē, and that
not one houre, or two, but *Sine inter-* *1.Thess. 5.*
missione. without intermission, and *In o-*
mni loco, In euery place, lifting vp pure *1.Timot.2*
and cleane handes. So do the holy aun-
cient fathers in their homilies, epistles,
and sermons. And thes newe men forbed the people to pray in the churche,
(Which is the house of prayer. This is a *Mat.21.*

V 4   straunge

ftraunge thing yowe wil faie, and harde
to be proued. Certes it is fo ftraunge that
it was neuer hard of amongeft Chrifté
men, and yet trewe it is. Yf yowe require of me howe I proue it, I refer youe to
an iniunctió of theirs fet out amongeft
other thinges in the name of oure fo-
ueraine lady the Queenes maieftie: whe
re they geue this chardge, that no man
fhal praye whiles the minifter or prieft
is reading the feruice in the churche, but
harken to that which is founge or faied.
And I pray yowe what other thing is
this? then to faie they fhal not praye in
the churche at al. For charitie and deuotion in thes later daies waxing colde,
there is fcarce one amongeft an hundred that wil ether tarry longer in the
church, then whiles the feruice is a finging or faying, or come one quarter of
an houre before the beginning. Yf thé,
men come not to the churche, much be
fore the beginning of feruice, nor tarry there long after al is done, and whiles
they are there, are by iniunction forbed

Mé cóma
unded by
the nevve
minifters
not to pra
ye in the
churche.

                                        to

to praye , What remayneth,but that by
thes holy fathers newe cõmaundemēt,
men muſt not pray in the churche at al.

Againe Chriſt faſted forthy dayes,
to teache vs to faſte.S.Paule commaun
deth vs not to pamper vp the fleaſh,but
in al pointes behaue and ſhewe oure
ſelues as the ſeruantes of god , in wac-
ching and faſting . The holy fathers in
lieke manner commaunde vs to faſt,and
eſpecially the forthy dayes . *Ignatius* ſaieth . *Quadrageſimã ne pro nihilo habeatis:*
imitationem enim continet,Domini conuer-
ſationis . Eſteme not lent for a thing
of naught.For it doth contayne an imi-
tation and folloing of oure lordes con-
uerſation.S. Ambroſe deſireth his people to kepe this holy time of lent very
carefully,and to let no daye paſſe without faſting.For ſaieth he,*Sicut reliquo an*
ni tēpore ieiunare præmiũ eſt,ita in quadrage
ſima non ieiunare peccatum eſt.Illa enim vo-
luntaria ſunt ieiunia , iſta neceſſaria , illa de
arbitrio,iſta de lege, ad illa inuitamur, ad iſta
compellimur. As it is meritorious to faſt
other

Roma.13.

2.Corinth.
6.

Epiſt.ad
Philippenſ.

Sermo.34

other times of the yere, So not to faſte
in the lent it is ſinne. For that faſt is vo-
luntarie, this is neceſſary, that cometh
of free wil, this of order of lawe, to that
we are allured, to this we are forced.
And therefor ſaieth he, what ſoeuer
Chriſten man doth not obſerue this
holy faſt, *Præuaricationis & pœnæ reus eſt,*
quód legem diuinitus pro ſalute ſua datam.
*prædendo ipſe reſcindit.*He is gilty of a grea
te offence and puniſhement, becauſe he
breaketh by eating out off dewe ſeaſon,
the lawe geuen of god for his ſaluation
and health. S. Aguſtine talking of lent,
telleth his people, that, *In quadrageſima*
non ieiunare peccatum eſt . Not to faſt in
lent it is ſinne. Therefor he ſaieth vnto
thē, *Celebremus hos dies, cum omni alacritate*
mentis , & eos omnibus epulis , & carnalibus
delitijs præferamus . Let vs faſt thes dayes
with al cherefulnes of hart, and mir th:
and let vs præfer them before al denty
meates, and delicates of the body . And
why? *Quia quadrageſima ſpiritualis eſt vin-*
*demia.*Becauſe lent is a ſpiritual vintena-
ge or

Lent is a
lavve ge-
uen from
hcauen.

Ser.62.de
tempore.

Ser.64.
de tempore

ge or harueft. And euery man muft ga-
ther in to his barne faieth he , fpiritual *Ser. 5 5. de*
wheate, and heauely wine, *Ieiunãdo, orã- tempore.*
do, legendo. With fafting, praying, and reading. And that we may do that the
better, he geueth vs counfel to abandõ-
ne al the pleafures of the body. For he
faieth . *Iftis paucis diebus recedant impedi- Ser. 5 5. de*
menta mundi, recedat carnalis lætitia, recedãt tempore.
mundi blandimenta venenis plena, carnis gau-
dium minuatur, vt animæ lucra fpiritualia
præparentur , Let al worldely impedi-
mentes paffe away for thes fewe dayes:
Let the delightes of the fleafh paffe awa
ye . Let the venemous allurementes of
the worlde paffe awaye, let the pleafure
and paftaunce of the body be diminif-
hed, that fpiritual increafe and gaine ma
ye be præpared for the foule . And this
can not be, vnleffe we both faft from vi
ce , and pampring vp the body with fleafh, and delicate meates, the fourcees and
nources of al fenfualitie , and vice. For
Quomodo faieth *Origen , Caftitas apud eos*
incorrupta feruatur, nifi continentioribus fuf-
fulta

Homil. 11. *fuper Leui.* *fulta fubfidijis? Quo modo fcripturis operam dabunt? Quo modo fcientiæ,& fapientiæ ftudent? Nonne per continentiam ventris & gutturis? Quo modo fe quis caftrat propter regnũ cælorum nſi ciborum affluentiam refecet,niſi abſtinentia vtatur miniſtra?* Howe is chaſtetie mayntayned, vnleſſe it be held vp with very continent and ſtrayte helpes? howe ſhal men applie their paines to the reading of fcripture? howe do they ſtudie philoſphie and other ſciences? do they not al this by abſtinence and keaping the belly and throte to a thynne ordinary, and ſlender diet? Howe doth a man cut him ſelff for the kingdome of heauen, vnleſſe he cut of the adundance and ſuperfluitie of meate? vnleſſe he vſe abſtinéce for a feruitour, and helpe in this caſe? As much to ſaye no man is hable to do it. Therefor he that wil faſt, and pleaſe god with his faſting, and come to Chriſt, muſt not imbrue his fingers with brueſſe ſoppes, nor feede fat of the fleaſh pot, but cut of the fleaſhly feeding of that rotten car-
kas

kas and fack of woormes of his. For *Hec*
faieth Origen *Chriftianis ieiunandi ratio*
eft. This is the manner of fafting amongeft the Chriftians. And fo S. Auguftine for him felff, and the Chriftians
vnder him, faieth: In lent, *Abftinemus a*
carnibus quibus alijs diebus vti licet. We abftayne from fleafh which vppon other
daies it is lauful for vs to eate. Wherefor
yff we wil keape the Lenten faft, and
faft as other Chriftians do, we muft
bothe fafte from finne (which is required of vs not only at that tyme, but at
al other times, dayes, houres, and mo-
mentes of oure lifl) and alfo from pam-
perig vp the fleafh with fuch nutritiue,
and delicate meates, as the fleafhly appetite doth defire. So fhal we be fure to faft
trewly. For Chrifoftome talking of
lent faieth. *Hæ funt veræ feriæ vbi ani-*
marum falus, vbi pax & concordia eft, vbi
omnis vitæ huius apparatus abigitur, vbi cla-
mor, & tumultus, & coquorum difcurfus, &
pecudum mactationes e medio tolluntur.
Thes are the trewe holy dayes, or fa-
                              fting

Homil. 11.
fup. Leuit.

Homil. 1.
in Gene.

sting daies, where the health of the soule is regarded, where there is peace, and côcorde, where al superfluous prouision for this lif is, set a syde where there be no clamours, nor tumultes, where there is no running vp and downe of cookes, no slaughter of beastes, no bouchery open for newe bisshoppes wiffes. Whereby yowe perceue and see I doute not, good readers, that euery Christen man, shuld not only fast from synne, but also from al fleash, and delicate meates: and that this time of lent, was commended vnto vs by the example of Christ, and geuen as a lawe from god. Which S. Ambrose in other wordes also most plainly expresseth, saying. This number of *Ser.36.* forthy dayes, and fast in lent, *Non ab hominibus constitutum, sed diuinitus consecratum. Non terrena cogitatione inuentum, sed cælesti maiestate præceptum*. was not ordayned of men, but halloed by god from heauen. Not inuented by humaine fantasie, but commaunded by heauenly maiesty. And whosoeuer contemneth

this

this faſt, contemneth not the prieſtes
that exhorteth men to faſt, but Chriſt
that ſpeaketh in his prieſtes. For ſaieth
S. Ambroſe, in the place alleaged before,
Hæc non tam ſacerdotum præcepta, quàm Ibidem.
Dei ſunt. Thes are not ſo much the com
maundementes of prieſtes, as they are
the commaundementes of god. Nowe
in theſe oure dayes, thes newe men
feede the bely with fleaſh, moſt parte
off al the lent, to the greate offen-
ſe of their Chriſten brothers, and that
contrary to the doctrine of S. Paule,
who ſaieth, *Bonum eſt non manducare car* Roma. 14.
nem, & non bibere vinum, neque in quo frater
tuus offenditur, aut ſcandalizatur, aut infir- ˟ It is
matur. ˟ And therefore deſired vs to fol- good not
                                            to eate
lo thoſe thinges that mayntayne peace fleaſh, nor
and concorde, and kepe that which æ- to drincke
                                       vvine, nor
difieth one another, and not by eating any other
                                         thing in
fleaſh, to diſtroye the worke off god, vvich thy
                                         brother is
and oure weake brother, for whome diſplea-
Chriſt died. And caul thoſe that wil ſed, or of-
                                       fended, or
not beare them cōpany in their fleaſhly vveakned.
feaſtes, papiſtes and ſuperſtitious hipo-
                              crites,

crites, and besides make lent but a mans
tradition , some popes deuise , and humane policie. Howe agreeth this with,
the doctrine of Christ, and the Apostles, and fathers of the primitiue churche?

Math.20.   To conclude Christ hyring vs as
woorkemen in to his vineard, prome-
sed vs a peny (which is euerlasting liff)
for oure rewarde , yff we worke wel.
Christe willed vs to geue almes pri
uely , and saieth god shal rewarde vs o-
Math.6. penly . Christe saieth , he that recea-
ueth a prophete, in the name off a pro-
Math,10. phete, shal haue *Mercedem prophetæ,* The
rewarde of a prophete. And he that ge-
ueth a cup of cold water to the left off
Christes disciples , *Non perdet mercedem*
Ibidem.   *suam.* Shal not leese his rewarde. Christ
biddeth vs loue oure enemies: and do
good, and lend oure mony withu hoto-
Lucæ.6. pe of gaines . *Et erit merces vestra multa.*
And youre rewarde shal be greate. S. Pau
1.Corin.3. le saieth . *Vnusquisque propriam mercedem*
accipiet secundum laborem suum. Euery man
shal

ſhal receue a peculiar and propre rewar
de, according to his labour. Furder he
deſireth the Colloſſenſians, to do that
which they do, with as good a wil, as
they woulde do it before god, and not be
fore men. *Scientes quòd a Domino accipietis* *Colloſſ. 4.*
retributionem. Knowing that yowe ſhal
receue a rewarde of god. And to the He-
brues he ſaieth. *Non eſt iniuſtus Deus, vt* *Heb. 6.*
obliuiſcatur operis veſtri, & dilectionis quam
oſtendiſtis in nomine ipſius. God is not vn-
iuſt, that he can forget youre woorke,
loue, and frindſhip that yowe haue
ſhewed in his name. S. Chriſoſtome ſa-
ieth. *Dimitte res tuas apud deum, & tibi* *Homil. 15.*
multiplicem mercedem reddet. Leue thy ear- *in 1. ad Co-*
thly thinges with god, and he wil geue *rinth.*
the a manyfolde rewarde. S. Auguſtine *Lib. 1. de*
ſaieth. *Deus meus vbique præſens eſt. Ille* *Cap. 29.*
quum me aduerſis rebus exagitat, aut merita
examinat, aut peccata caſtigat, mercedemquè
mihi æternam, pro toleratis piè malis tempo-
ralibus ſeruat. My lorde and god is præ
ſent euery where. He, when he trobleth
me with aduerſitie, ether examineth my
X doinges.

doinges, ether punisheth my sinnes, and
keapeth me an euerlasting rewarde, for
my temporal aduersitie suffre'd patiently. And so do al the auncient fathers
teache, that for wel doing we shal ha
ue a rewarde of god . Thes newe men
tel vs, that oure woorkes merite nothíg
before god , nor make vs acceptable in
his sight, nor purchasse vs any rewarde
at his hande. Howe agreeth this with
the doctrine of Christe, and the Apostles, and auncient fathers of the primitiue churche? Iudge youe good people:
and tel me, who deserueth more credit,
Leo or Luther, Cyprian or Caluin, Basile or *Brentius* , Austine or *Swinglius*,
Ambrose or Amsdorf, Chrisostome or
Crammer, *Paulinus* or Parkar, Hierome
or Iuel , trewe Apostels, or false Apo-
statates , auncient fathers, or newe brothers, vertuous prælates, or vitious preachers, sounde catholickes, or fonde heretickes. In good faith as youe finde
thes newe ghospellers, contrary to the
Apostels, and fathers of the primitiue
church

church in thes pointes, So fhal youe
finde thē in al that they preach, of only faith , lack of free wil, Mariadge of
prieftes; and fuch moftrous opinions,
as they daily preach:as by good record it
may be proued,and hath bene by diuerfe lerned men alredy fet foorth at large,
and fhal yf nede require , be brought
foorth in open fhewe, to euery mans
fight, that they may fee howe groffely
they haue bene taught , and lurdely deceued,vnder pretence,and colour of the
worde of the lorde. But for this præ-
fent to auoyde tediouineffe, Iomit it,
putting youe good readers eftfone in
remembraunce, that feing al heretickes
haue the qualities aboue mentioned,
and teach contrary doctrine, to the A-
poftels, and fathers of the primitiue
church,and breake the bonde of vnitie,
yowe muft (as S. Ciprian faieth) flee
far from the contagion of fuch men, *Lib.1,epift*
and be as ware of their talke, as yowe ⁹·
wold be of a venemous cancker, or in-
fectious plage. *Sagitta vulnerans lingua* *Iere.9:*

X 2   *eorum*

eorum. Their tounge is a wounding ar-
ro. They intermingle fometimes , good
leſſons with their euil doctrine , that
they may crepe into credit, and infin-
uate them felues into the fauour of the
people , but al tendeth to no other end,
then to infect,and poyſonne their ſoules . They vſe the ſcriptures , as Origen

*Ho.*31.*in*
Luc.

faieth the deuil doth , that by the ſimplicitie,and outward ſhewe of the letter,
they may corrupt ſuch as harken vnto
them. They caul them ſelues Catholickes,and their doctrine,the treuth of godes worde, as *Arrius* and other heretickes haue done before . They ſowe cockel,darnel, and ſtincking herbes vppon
the trewe feade , that Chriſte and his
Apoſtells, Martirs, and confeſſours haue ſowed . And wil youe haue al at a
woorde ? They lye impudently , and yf
they haue reade the auncient fathers,
they knowe that they do lye , and as
longe as they liue,they wil neuer be aſhamed to lye , yf they be not let to lye,
and as their forefathers acquainted with
the

the maſter of lies,haue done before thē,
ſo they chardge the Catholickes with
lyes,as perhaps they wil do me,for diſ-
couering ſome of their falſitie, in this
litte treatiſe . But yf they do,then may I
trewly vſe that Rhetorical exclamation,
which their raging Rhetour ſometi-
mes arrogātly abuſed,and ſay, O Gregorie , O Hilary, O Auſtine , O Hierome,
O Ambroſe, O Chriſoſtome, O Ephrē,
O Baſile , O Origen , O Cyprian , O
Tertullian , O *Ignatius*, O Deniſe , O
Clement, O Paule , O Peter , O Chriſtes . Yf we are deceaued , we haue
bene deceaued , by that which was cō-
mēded vnto vs frō youe. Yf thes thīges
which are here ſet foorth,be lies, then
haue youe farced the bokes and monu-
mentes,which youe committed tó the
vewe, and ſight of al youre poſteritie,
with lies . But that can not be ſo (good
people) yf Chriſt did euer ſend the holy ghoſt , teacher of al treuth , amongeſt the Chriſtians,before frier Luther,
and his offpring, beganne to blaſe this

*Ioan.14.
15.16.*

X 3 blaſphe-

Ioan.14.
15.16.

blafphemous doctrine , that rangeth nowe ouer the worlde , as moſt certenly he did.

Wherefor once agayne I fay, be ware of them . And thinke al that they affeuere, and boldely preach ageinſt the doctrine off Chriſtes Catholick churche, ſealed with the bloud of ſo many holy Martirs, and auouched with the teſtimonies, of ſo many auncient fathers, is nothing els but mere vanities, and vayne lies. And yf they ceaſſe not to allure youe, with faire coloured wordes, from this treuth , that Chriſt , and the holy ghoſt haue taught , by the prælates off his church, to their newe inuented doctrine, and late founde faith , ſay vnto them, as S. Auguſtine, ſaied to the Manichees. *Vos & tam pauci, & tam turbulenti, & tam noui, nihil dignum authoritate præferatis.* Yowe, both ſo fewe , and ſo trobleſome, and ſo newe, can pretend nothing worthy of authoritie. And euē as that holy father ſaied of faith , So ſay youe of this doctrine that youe haue

De vtilitate credendi cap.14.

ler-

lerned here. *Hoc est iussum diuinitus: hoc a beatis maioribus traditum: hoc ad nos vsque seruatum: hoc perturbare atquè peruertere velle, nihil aliud est quàm ad veram religionem sacrilegam viam quærere.* This is commaunded from heauen. This is deliured of oure blessed forefathers. This hath bene kept vnto oure dayes. To wil to disturbe, and peruert this, is nothing els, but to seeke a mischeuous, and naughty way to treue religion. And say vnto them, that the same that kept S. Augustine, shal kepe youe in the swete bosome, and comfortable lap off the church: that is to saie, Authoritie begonne with miracles, nourrished with hope, augmented with charitie, established with antiquitie. The succession of bishopes from the sea off Peter, vntil this præsent bishop. The name of the Catholick churche, that hath only so præuayled amongest al heresies, that whereas al heretickes wold be caulled catholickes, yet for al that, when a straunger aske them, where or whether

De vtilita te credendi Cap. 10.

Contra Epi sto. Manich Cap. 4.

X 4   he

he shal go to the catholicke church, none of al the heretickes is hable to shewe
any one churche, or house. So shal yowe be sure to auoyde the perilous path,
that leadeth to damnation, and come to
euerlasting blisse, with the holy fathers
whose doctrine yowe kepe, and whose
steppes youe follo, in the knot of vnitie
and bonde of charitie. Which god off
his infinitie mercy, graūte vs al, and ce-
asse this boysterous storme of heresy,
that we may be of one harte, and one
minde, and in vnitie of spirite, serue god
in *Iesus* Christ oure lorde. Amen.

And yowe my masters, authours off
this newe religion, who haue separated
youre selues from others, staye by the
grace of god, in the vnitie of the Catho
licke churche, and haue made schismes
and diuisions, contrary to the doctrine,
wich yowe receaued off youre forefa-
2. Timot. 3 thers, *Errantes & in errorem mittentes,* Er-
ring youre selues, and bringing other
men into errour, considre for Christes
sake, what a horrible thing it is, to make a

ke a diuision, and schisme in his church,
and lerne by the diuision of the tribes of ³·*Reg.* 12.
Israel, as S. Cyprian saieth, *Quàm sine spe* *Lib.* 1. *E-*
sunt, & perditionem sibi magnam de indigna- *pist.* 6.
tione Dei *acquirunt , qui schismata faciunt,*
& relicto episcopo, alium sibi pseudo-episcopum
constituunt. Howe they are without hope, and get vnto them selues greate dam
nation, of the displeasure and indignation of almighty god, who make diuisions, and forsaking their owne bisshop,
apointe them selues some Apostatical
patriarke, or false superintendent . Ley
before youre eies the terrible punishe-
mēt, of Core, Dathā, and Abyron, who *Num.*16.
were swalloed vp into the earth a liue.
Haue in remembraunce the lamentable
end of the Mōtanistes, who as E*usebius* *Lib.* 5. *cap.*
reporteth , *Finem vitæ suæ, exemplo Iudæ* 16. *ecclesi-*
proditoris accœperunt. Ended their liffes, e- *ast. hist.*
uen as *Iudas* the traytour did . And the
sodayne death of *Arrius*, who for diuiding him self from the churche, and *ibidem lib*
rayfing a blasphæmous heresie ageinst 10. *14.* 13.
Christ, lost al his entralles in a iakes.
                                          Thinke

Think it not fufficient for youe, that yo
we knowe, and acknowledge one god
the father, one god the fonne, one god
the holy ghoft. So did faieth S. Cyprian, Core, Dathan, and Abyron acknowledge one god, feruc one god . Yet becaufe they trangreffed their appointed
dewtie, *Et coutra Aaron facrificandi fibi li-*
centiam vendicauerunt, diuinitus percufsi pœ
nas ftatim pro illicitis. conatibus pendebant.
And callenged licéce to facrifiçe, ageinft
Aaron, they were punifhed for their vn-
lauful attemptes. Nor think it ynough,
that yowe can alleage fcripture, for maintenaunce of youre doinges. The Mon
taniftes had fcripture . *Arrius* had fcripture, and al other heretikes that euer
wrote, had fcripture: and yet they were
punifhed by the mighty hand of god, becaufe they did præfumptuoufly interpre
te the fcripture, to the maintenaunce of
their owne herefie, and woulde not
with humilitie feeke the trewe meaning of it, there as they fhuld. Take heede, left by this diuifion which yowe ma
ke

Lib.1. Epi.
6.

ke vnder prætence, of reſtoring the ſin-
cere meaning of ſcripture,and trewe religion of Chriſt, yowe be founde in ef-
fect to deny Chriſt . For, *Quo modo non* Tract.in t.
negas Chriſtū in carne veniſſe , qui diſrumpis Epi. Ioan.
eccleſiam ? After what ſorte doeſt not
thowe deny Chriſt, to be come in fleaſh
who breakeſt and diſpoileſt the church,
ſaieth S.Auguſtine?and aſking the que-
ſtion,what it is to deny Chriſt , he ſay-
ieth . *Negare Chriſtū factis, eſt ſuperbire &* Ser.33. de
ſchiſmata facere . To deny Chriſt in dea- verbis Apo
de,is to be proude, and make ſchiſmes ſtoli .
and diuiſions . Beware,leſt by diuiding
youre ſelues from the churche,and brin
ging in a newe faith,yowe driue awaye,
the olde charitie,which is the bonde of Coloſſ.3.
perfection : and deny Chriſt , god and
man,who is charitie it ſelf . For, *Quam* De ſimpli-
vnitatem ſeruat , quam dilectionem cuſtodit, citate prę-
aut cogitat, qui diſcordiæ furore veſanus, ec-
cleſiam ſcindit,fidem deſtruit , pacem turbat,
charitatem diſſipat,ſacramentum prophanat?
What vnitie doth he obſerue, what loue doth he keape,or thinke vppon,who
                         lieke

lieke a made man, with raging difcorde,
diuideth the church, deftroyeth faith,
trobleth peace, difperfeth charitie, pro-
phaneth the facrament? faieth S. Cypri
an. As much to faie he hath none at al.
Tracta. 6. For fo faieth S. Auguftine. *Tu non habes*
in Epift. *charitatem, quia pro honore tuo diuidis vni-*
Ioan.cap. *tatem. Videte fi ibi eft charitas.Tollis te ab v-*
4. *nitate orbis terrarū,diuidis ecclefiam per fchif*
mata,dilanias corpus Chrifti. Thowe haft
no charitie, becaufe for thy owne aduauncement and honour, thowe diuideft
vnitie. See if there be any charitie there.
Thowe takeft thy felf away from the
vnitie of al the whole worlde, thowe di-
nideft the churche by fchifmes, thowe
doeft rent, and teare the body of Chrift.
He came in fleafh, that he might gather
together, thowe crieft, that thowe maieft difperfe, and fcatter abrode. Howe
then doeft not thowe deny Chrift, who
breakeft and difperfeft the curch which
he gathred together?

Furder whereas yowe vaunte youre
felues trewe Chriftians, and folloers of
Chrift,

Chriſt, beware leſt by this ſeparation, yowe be founde to haue litle trewe Chriſtianitie in yowe, And to follo Chriſt neuer a deale. For *Non ſequitur* *Chriſtum*, ſaieth S.Auguſtine, *qui non ſe-* *cundum ueram fidem & catholicam diſcipli-* *nam Chriſtianus vocatur.* He folloeth not Chriſt, who is not caulled a Chriſten man, after the trewe faith, and catholicke diſcipline and order. And ſo can not not yowe be caulled. For the faith which yowe teache, is nether the trewe faith (becauſe it lacketh the trewe effectes of faith, required in a Chriſten man, (as it ſhalbe proued hereafter, if yowe deny it) nether is the diſcipline and order, which yowe haue in youre congregations, the catholicke diſcipline, that is to ſaye the diſcipline receued vni uerſally in al Chriſtédome, where Chriſtes name, and religion is in dewe reuerence and honour : and neuer harde off, before frier Luther beganne to pley the Apoſtata, and ſet this freaſh faith, and ne we diſcipline abrode, Or if it were harde

*Lib.*1.*de* *ſer. domini* *in monte* *cap.*9.

off

of, in any place before his tyme, ſhewe
the churches were it beganne, the manner howe it came thither, the ſucceſsion
howe it continued, and youre credit mã
ye the better increaſe. But yowe can
not: nor euer yet coulde any heretike
before youe as S. Auguſtine ſaieth.

Contra e-
piſt Ma.
nich.cap.4

Agayne remember howe Ioram, Ioſa-
phates ſonne, for making Iuda, and the
inhabitantes of Hieruſalem, commit for

2 Paralip.2

nication, and killing his brothers, far bet
ter men, then he was him ſelf, was pla-
ged of god in his people, in his childrē,
in his wifes, in his ſubſtance, and in his
owne body. And howe Ieroboam *Qui*

3. Reg. 14.

peccauit & peccare fæcit Iſraël, Who tranſ-
greſſed the lawe of god him ſelf, and ma
de the children of Iſrael tranſgreſſe it al
ſo, was ſcourged by the mighty hande
of god, and his people ſo afflicted, that
there was not, one left, piſsing ageinſt a
waulle. And thinke that the lieke maye
happen to yowe.

Beſides, conſider that the bloud of al
thoſe, whome yowe haue deceaued, ſhal

be

be required at youre handes , at the terrible daye,and youre punifhement mul-
tiplied, both by their crying of vengeaunce vppon yowe, for deceauing their
filly foules with youre fubtil woordes,
and alfo by the fight of the Apoftles,E-
uangeliftes , Martirs , and holy fathers,
bearing witneffe ageinft yowe,for corrupting the worde of god,and wrefting
the fcriptures to a wronge fenfe, nor
ment of them , nor euer harde,or allowed by the auncient fathers ,who had
the handling of it before youre tyme.
And with al remembre that as Chrifo- *Homil. 5.*
ftome faieth.*Illud iudicium terrificum,hor* *ad Roma.*
rendum tribunal,timoris plenæ eiufdem quæ-
*ftiones & difquifitiones.*That iudgement is
terrible,that barre is dreadful, the quefti
ons and inquires of the fame,ful off terrour and feare·Then as S.Auguftine fa-
ieth, *Ordinabũtur āte infælicē animā peccata* *Ser.181.de*
fua,vt eam & cōuincat probatio,& cōfundat *temp. 4.8.*
*agnitio.*Before the miferable foule fhal be
leyed al his finnes , that the prouffe off
them may conuince him,and the ackno *Iere. 46.*
      wledging

wledging of them, confounde him. Thē
wil god take vengeaunce vppon his ene
mies. Thē shal theswordedeuoure, and
Iere. 46. be imbrued with their bloud. Wherefor
yf yowe thincke there is any god to pu-
nishe iniquitie, and rewarde vertue, Yff
youe thincke yowe haue soules to saue,
and a streight accōpte to make in another worlde, consider this aduisedly,
and thinke with youre selues, *Quám hor*
rēdū est incidere in manus dei viuētis. What
Hebre. 10. a horrible thinge it is, to faulle into the
handes of the liuing god. And neuer be
ashamed to returne to the vnitie off the
churche, from which yowe haue separated, and diuided youre selues. Let not
worldely policie, nor desire of riches, and
vaine estimation amongest men, staye
yowe from reentringe into fauour
with god. For one howers pleasure in
earthe, lose not the euerlasting threasu
re in heauen. Yf with the losse of youre
soules, yowe might gaine al the worlde,
what a fayre marte had howe made?
Wherefore for his sake that so dearely
bought

bought youe, keape youre foules from
that horrible pit of damnation. And as
by pride , yowe feparated youre felues
from Chriftes myftical body the church : So by humilitie returne to the vnitie off it againe. Yf youe continewe in
this diuifion,and fchifme , liue as com-
mendablye, as youe can , beleue al that
the fcripture teftifieth of oure fauiour
Chrift , as ftedfaftely asyowe may, yet
fhal youe neuer be membres off his myftical body , but haue his indignation
and wrath euer hanging ouer youre heades, yf S.Auguftine be of any credit ,
who crieth . *Væ illis qui oderunt vnitatem* Tracta.12:
ecclefiæ , & partes fibi faciunt in hominibus. in Ioan.
O be to them, who hate the vnitie of
the church , and make themfelues partes in men , as youe haue done with
Luther at Wittemberg , *Swinglius,*
at Zurich , Caluin at *Geneua* and o-
thers in other corners . Therefor har-
ké to the gentil requeft of S.Paule, de-
firing youe ,and al fuch as youe are,by
the name of oure fauiour *Iefus* Chrift,
Z   *Vi*

THE CONCLVSION.

Vt idipsum dicatis, & non sint in vobis schis- 1. Corinth.1 *mata,* that youe saie al one thīg and that there be no schismes amongeſt yowe. But be perfect, *in eodem sensu & in eadē sententia,* in one sense, and one opinion and sentence. And yf there be any con- Philip.2. solation in Chriſt Ieſu, iff there be any comforte of charitie, if there be any so- cietie of ſpirite, if there be any bowelles of mercy, pittie, or compaſsion in youe, fulfil his ioye, *Vt idem sapiatis, eandem charitatem habentes, vnamines, idipsum sen- tientes,* that ye drawe one way, hauing one charitie, being of one accorde, and of one minde. Be hoful in al humilitie and meekneſſe, *Seruare vnitatem spiritus,* Ephes. 4. *in vinculo pacis,* to kepe the vnitie of ſpi- rite, in the bonde of peace. Nether take it diſdainfully, that youe are put in re- membraunce of this, by so meane a man as I am. Remembre that Naaman the Si- 4. Reg. c. 5 rian by folloing the counsel of a silly gyrle, and certē seruing men, was cleane purged of his foule filthy lepre, and brought to the acknowledging, and
con-

confeſsion of the trewe god of Iſrael,
as I truſt youe may be of hereſie, and
brought to the acknowledging , and
côfeſsion of the treuth, and ioyne with
vs in the vnitie of his church, and as the
re is one ſheaparde, ſo make, *vnum ouile,*
one folde, ageinſt the coming of oure
lorde Ieſus Chriſt, to whome be al honour and glory, worlde without end
Amen.

F I N I S.

Hactenus hec lector : quod noſti rectius iſtis,
    Candidus imperti : ſi nil, hijs vtere mecũ.

  Quandoquidem Liber iſte a Domino Io-
hanne Martiale Anglo côpoſitus de Cruce, &
eius myſterijs, a viris doctis, probis, & Anglicæ
linguæ peritis , apud me fide digniſsimis, dili-
genter eſt examinatus, probatus, & vtilis iudi-
catus, qui impreſſus euulgaretur, luben-
ter eorum ſententiæ ſubſcriben-
dum eſſe iudico.
  Cunerus Petri, paſtor S. Petri Louanij,
quarto calendas octobris.

           Z 2   The

THE TABLE.

A TABLE OF
THE SPECIAL MAT·
TERS TOVCHED IN THE
EPISTLE, PRAEFACE, AR-
ticles, and conclusion, or-
derly as they be
placed.

The Præface.

Z 4   *must*

Chriſt

THE TABLE.

The

THE TABLE.

A uxen-

THE TABLE.

The

The seuenth Article.

The eight Article.

A gentil

THE TABLE.

THE TABLE.

The

THE TABLE.

A a 3

THE TABLE.

A a 4 *the*

Faultes escaped in printing.

Fo.Pag. li.

8. 1. 13. Reade, same for **fame.**
12. 1. 18. thought for though.
12. 1. 19. Aristo tel for Aristotel.
14. 1. 20. *Contrariarum* for *contrarium*
15. 2. 22. perfection for perfection.
22. 2. 16. to lye for tu lye.
28. 2. 2. letting for lesting.
33. 2. 13. *splendens* for *splendeus.*
34. 2.   in the margen, man for men.
44.1. 23. that he did for that did.
49. 2. 24. *sine* for *siue.*
64. 2.   in the margēt *panopliæ* for *pă- pliæ.*
68. 2. 12. saieth for faieth.
70. 2. 4. in case of mortalitie, for in case mortalitie.
75, 2. 18. *Paula* a noble vvoman, for P *au la* noble a vvoman.
88. 1. 5. inclosed them in gold, for inclo sed them gold.
109.1. 4. prætensed for præsented.
110.2. 8. of the crosse, for of crosse.
136.1. 21. they for the.
148.1. 1. the for they.
163.2. 17. staied, for staie.
165.2. 22. church for curch.

Fault es efcapedin printing.

Fo.Pag.li.

77. 1. 15.   the place alleaged out of **Ter-**
              tulliá, feeke in his boke *de coro*
              na militis

Cuilibet Christiano crucem Christi
intuenti.

In cruce pendentem Christum, Dominumq;
Deumqué
Quū videas, subeant quæ tibi morte dedit.
Et quia per mortem, peperit de morte trium-
phum
In cruce, corde agites & venerare crucem.
Et crucis insigni, quia sacramenta salutis
Perficit, huic grates pro cruce lætus agas.
Et crucis insigni, quia pellitur impetus hostis,
Ne

Ne pigeat tenera pingere fronte crucem.
Et crucis insigni, quia tot miracula facit,
  Vis quãta, & virtus sit, meditare crucis.
Hancque vide, sed mente colas, quod cernis in
  ipsa.
  Sic placido disces pectore ferre crucem.

Ex Hymno Prudentij.

Cultor Dei memento,
  Te fontis, & lauacri
  Rorem subisse sanctum,
  Te chrismate innouatum.
Fac cùm vocante somno
  Castum petis cubile,
  Frontem, locúmq́; cordis
  Crucis figura signet.
Crux pellit omne crimen,
  Fugiunt crucem tenebræ.
  Tali dicata signo,
  Mens fluctuare nescit.
Procul ô procul vagantum
  Portenta somniorum,
  Procul esto peruicaci
  Prestigiator astu.
O tortuose serpens,

Qui

Qui mille per meandros,
Fraudesque flexuosas
Agitas quieta corda,
Discede, Christus hic est,
Hic Christus est, liquesce.
Signum, quod ipse nosti,
Damnat tuam cateruam.

Typis Ioannis Latij.

MARTIN DE PADILLA
Y MANRIQUE
Consideringe the Obligation . . .
[1597?]

MARTIN DE PADILLA
Y MANRIQUE

Consideringe the Obligation . . .
[1597?]